THE TROUBLE WITH
CHRISTMAS

TOM FLYNN

"The destroyer of weeds, thistles and thorns is a benefactor whether he soweth grain or not."

—Robert Green Ingersoll

THE TROUBLE WITH CHRISTMAS

TOM FLYNN

Prometheus Books

59 John Glenn Drive
Buffalo, New York 14228-2197

To Susan, who survived the writing process.

Published 1993 by Prometheus Books

97 96 95 94 93   5 4 3 2 1

Library of Congress Cataloging-in-Publication Data

Flynn, Tom. 1955–
    The trouble with Christmas / Tom Flynn.
        p.   cm.
    ISBN 0-87975-848-1 (acid-free paper)
    1. Christmas—United States.
GT4986.A1F49   1993
394.2′663′0973—dc20   93-11491
                                                              CIP

Printed in the United States of America on acid-free paper.

Contents

Part Two: The Trouble with Christmas Present and Yet to Come

Preface

Humbug Indeed!

In 1633 English lawyer William Prynne published a book critical of Christmas. King Charles I had Prynne thrown in the Tower of London, tried before the Star Chamber, pilloried, fined the breathtaking sum of five thousand pounds, ejected from Oxford, and disbarred. Oh, yes, his book was also burned. I'm hoping for a friendlier reception.

In a society that prides itself on its willingness to call almost anything into question, Christmas is the last taboo. If we fully understood the origins of our holiday customs, are there some we might judge no longer worthy of us? What is the impact of the American majority's way of celebrating Christmas on groups who do not share its enthusiasm for the holiday? How has the contemporary Christmas observance oppressed the religious minorities that have been here the longest: Jews and infidels? How will it oppress the new and growing non-Christian minorities: Muslims, Hindus, Buddhists, and a worldful of other faiths? Perhaps most important, what social dislocation might result if these more newly established minorities, confident of their rights and jealous of their own traditions, refuse to be oppressed? What if the majority keeps on trying?

Trouble with Christmas is on the horizon. Before we begin, a few prefatory remarks are in order.

This is not a scholarly work. The "Christmas taboo" I mentioned seems to extend to the domain of scholarship. Considering the scope and importance of Christmas in our culture, it is amazing to behold the broad vistas of holiday lore that have never been studied—or on which studies have never been published—whose depth of analysis would support a scholarly attempt at synthesis. For this reason, too, far too many of the better histories of the holiday (and there are some very good ones) do not reveal their sources.

9

When the subject is Christmas, this problem is not as critical as one might think, for there is some reliable information about the holiday that is available from popular sources. If challenged, most Americans know that many of their favorite holiday customs have pagan roots, that the man we know as Saint Nicholas probably never existed, that the most beloved details of the Nativity story are mentioned in only one of the four gospels and contradicted in another, and more. Each December news syndicates dust off their features on the origins of holiday customs and most newspapers give them prominent play, so the information is abroad in the culture. The problem is that people put it toward the back of their minds. They listen, they read, they nod, and they go on with their celebration as though there isn't a reason in the world to think that Jesus Christ might not have been born in a literal manger in Bethlehem on the evening of December 25 in the year zero. Or was that the year one?

It was neither. But we'll get to that.

On nomenclature: As a matter of convention, I use the word "society" to refer to contemporary social structures at the broadest scale as in contemporary Western society or, where appropriate, contemporary global society. I use the word "culture" to denote the beliefs, characteristic behaviors, world view, folkways, and customs of a particular religious or ethnic group. Society, then, consists of constituent cultures, so, for example, one can speak of the British and American cultures giving rise to Christmas traditions that spread throughout society.

For dates I use the accepted nomenclature "C.E." and "B.C.E." These stand for "Common Era" and "Before Common Era" and replace the traditional, Christocentric "A.D. and B.C."

I use the term "infidels" to denote religious nonbelievers in all their countless flavors: atheists, agnostics, freethinkers, rationalists, naturalists, secular humanists, and so on.

I allow the authorities I quote to speak in their own voices. Sometimes we forget how radically feminism has revamped our language. Quotations from fifteen years ago can look dated with their inadvertent sexism. Period quotes are left intact in all their smug assumptions that the masculine pronoun covers everyone.

Finally, I cannot proceed without expressing my thanks to the people who made this book possible. First I want to thank my co-workers at *Free Inquiry* magazine, who put up with me during the assembly process and field the phone calls each holiday season: Tim Madigan, Steve Karr, Norm Allen, and Georgeia Locurcio. Special thanks are due Paul Kurtz, editor and founder of *Free Inquiry,* for his support.

Thanks also to Judith Boss, who showed how it could be done; to Dr. Gordon Stein, who put her up to it; and to all my correspondents. By mail and computer bulletin board some of them shared their Christmas experiences. Others told me I was crazy. Each informed me, challenged me, and led me to critical insights. Thanks also to secular humanists Ralph Nielsen, Greg Erwin, Joe Levee, Tom Franczyk, and Ron Lindsay, and to John Hassenfratz.

Further thanks to Jacqueline Peters, Director of Communications for the Williamsville (New York) Central School District; to Margaret Mendrykowski, Chair of the Williamsville Ad Hoc Committee on Religion in the Schools; and to Isha Francis, Paul Nogaro, and Khalid Qazi, members of the committee. I wish to stress that though they provided indispensable information, my conclusions are entirely my own. Thanks also to Karen Wood of the National Council of Christians and Jews and to Buffalo librarian Lucy Lerczak.

I owe special gratitude to my tireless researcher, Sarah Gavin Kinney, who found more material from scholarly and popular sources than I ever dreamed existed. If it's out there, she found it—three cheers!

Finally, thanks go to my editor Mary Read, and to Mark Hall, Steven Mitchell, and Linda Puzio-Hays of Prometheus Books. When I knew not what I wrought, I took comfort in assuming that one of them did.

It's traditional to say that in spite of the many fabulous folks to whom I am indebted, responsibility for errors is mine and mine alone. Let the record show I never said that.

Part One

The Trouble with Christmas
Past and Present

1

A Feast of Trouble

Contemporary Christmas, the universal winter holiday, needs to be rethought. In the hothouse of American culture, it has metastasized into a holiday of obligation that consumes an estimated one million person-years per season in the United States alone.[1] The bloated feast demands the sacrifice of thirty-six million trees, and causes almost eighty thousand tons of discarded wrapping paper to be interred in the nation's landfills.[2] Then there are the ecological and human costs of producing, wrapping, and transporting two hundred and twenty million letters and more than six million parcels a day at the height of the Christmas rush.[3]

If the holiday is expansive, it is also expensive. It fuels more than half of the average year's fur, diamond, and luxury watch sales. Hard liquor sells 30 percent faster in December than September. So eager are Americans to express their season's greetings in material form that approximately one-fourth of all Christmas purchases are billed to store charge accounts and bank credit cards. So frequently are consumers unable to pay that January leads all the other months of the year in credit card delinquencies.[4]

In return for all that spending, one might at least expect to have some fun. But holiday cheer eludes millions, according to statistics on depression, suicide, traffic deaths, and violent crime. One-third of respondents to a recent Gallup poll reported feeling depressed at holiday time.[5] All too often contemporary Christmas intensifies "sadness and loneliness," according to psychiatrist Lester Grinspoon.[6]

"It is ironic," admits even feel-good psychologist Wayne Dyer of the holidays, "that people become more anxious and depressed now than during the rest of the year, which is supposedly full of dull routine and maddening sameness."[7] We've all known the frustration of getting cut off just as we're about to squeeze into the last convenient parking space at the mall; the stress of waiting in a long, sweaty line to be told that the unaccountably popular toy we *have* to purchase has just sold out; the pressure of wedging open another space on the schedule to accommodate one more shopping trip, ascent to the rooftop with lights, or a Christmas party thrown by people no one remembers. Goodwill might come more easily if the holiday season brought more of us peace instead of anxiety. No wonder a mere 28 percent of Gallup poll respondents claimed to enjoy Christmas shopping a great deal.[8]

Criminals want a nice Christmas too. That's why police are resigned to sharp increases in purse snatching, car theft, mugging, and robbery as the season gathers momentum.[9] Because family and office parties can turn nasty when disappointment and alcohol combine, emergency personnel gear up each December for a surge in fistfight-related injuries, assorted overdoses, and the predictable tragedies of drunken highway carnage. Some of the holiday's dangers are more innocent, if not more benign. A U.S. Consumer Product Safety Commission study of holiday-related emergency-room admissions bristles with crisply understated sketches of Yuletide gone wrong:

- Patient was beaten by her mother because she dropped a Christmas ornament; sprained right thumb.

- Patient was putting up Christmas lights and fell off roof; fractured humerus.

- Cast-iron blunt object (Christmas decoration) fell off a ledge, causing laceration to forehead.[10]

Cast-iron blunt objects were certainly an indispensible part of Christmas decor in my home when I was growing up. How about yours?

For those of us who make it through the holiday intact, the post-holiday blues await. "People tend to have enormous expectations for what the holiday season will bring," said George Washington University psychiatrist Jerry M. Wiener. "Then, in January, they realize that it wasn't the answer."[11]

No wonder wags from George Bernard Shaw to Andy Rooney have shared the sentiments of a recent pundit who half-seriously concluded that "Christmas has become a net loss as a socio-economic institution."[12]

One lapsed Catholic described his abandonment of the Christmas celebration and his later return to a sharply-curtailed observance in these words:

Growing up, Christmas was traditionally a large celebration in our family. Then, it meant a chance to get together with relatives of both sides of my family for a day, relax, and enjoy their company. When I became older, Christmas became more hectic. There were obligations to spend money I didn't have on everyone I knew, and the large traditional celebration in our family decentralized into smaller gatherings at the homes of several relatives— which most often meant a day of running around, trying to squeeze everyone in. There have been hurt feelings on a few occasions when it just wasn't possible to keep this, yet another, obligation.

This was what led to an eventual examination of the Christmas holiday. Not that I ever sat down and . . . came to a conscious decision about my feelings on Christmas. I just realized that the day no longer had anything to do with the birth of Christ. . . . The old "commercialized Christmas" cliché wasn't funny anymore, it truly had become a season of social and financial obligation. . . .

I've spent the last couple Christmases at my parents' home with my brothers. It's a day I look forward to again—I don't need excuses, I don't run in and out of homes all day, and I'm not financially crippled. . . . I know absolutely that Christmas will never be what it was, but I can enjoy it again.[13]

"The trouble with Christmas," wrote two recent chroniclers of the holiday, "is that we expect so much from it."[14] That is true, of course, in a trivial sense. It is also true in a trivial sense that if you push something hard enough, it will fall over. But the trouble with Christmas goes deeper than that. It cuts to the root of what English-speaking society has been through history, and of what Western culture—in particular, American culture—is becoming. That is where the trouble lies, and with it the reasons why contemporary Christmas faces inevitable reform.

The trouble with Christmas is that American society is outgrowing it. A nation that used to be the favorite destination of immigrants from Europe has become the destination of choice for peoples from all over the world. Words like *diversity* and *multiculturalism* reflect society's painful efforts to adjust to a new reality. For the first time, American society is not simply multidenominational or even, to use a grossly misleading term, "Judaeo-Christian." Ours is truly becoming a multifaith society.

Christmas is amazingly adaptable. The holiday has met, and profited from, countless evolutionary challenges in the past century and a half. But it is also a holiday deeply rooted in Christian tradition and in the varied legacies of European paganism, from which most of our established myths and fairy tales draw their power. For the first time, Christmas must face the challenge of newcomers whose traditions have no deep connections to Christianity, to Judaism, or to the paganism underlying the folk cultures of Europe. Even for Christmas, that might be too long a stretch.

Muslims, Hindus, Buddhists, Baha'is, and other adherents of non-Western religions have always dwelt in this country. But today they are here in significant numbers, commanding greater wealth, prestige, and influence than before. Like members of other minority groups, they have learned to expect greater sensitivity and respect from the majority culture than was common before the middle years of the twentieth century. They have learned that they can use the machinery of justice to force ethnocentric majorities to let them be themselves.

At the same time, Jews and the nonreligious, America's original non-Christian minority groups, are observing the newcomers' progress. They are reflecting on the enormous gains made by other out-groups including African Americans, women, gays and lesbians, and Native Americans. They are realizing that assertiveness, not accommodation, seems to be the best way for minorities to defend their rights and expand their options in American society. As a result, many Jews and unbelievers are reevaluating the historic compromises their communities have made with the majority culture. Christmas, specifically the Christian majority's insistence that *everybody* join in observing its pet holiday, is a central bone of contention.

One of the things most Americans have forgotten is that Christmas has been controversial before. In the 1600s contention between Puritans eager to curtail the holiday and Anglicans, who were just as eager to preserve it, led to violence in both Britain and the colonies. In 1644 thousands rioted in Ealing, Canterbury, and other English towns when Cromwell's Roundheads tried to outlaw Christmas.[15] As late as 1706 a Puritan mob surrounded and stoned an Anglican church in Boston where a Christmas service was in progress.[16]

Though conflict over Christmas seems inevitable again, we can certainly hope to negotiate the difficult transitions without violence. To prepare for the changes that may lie ahead, we might begin by striving to understand this ubiquitous holiday more accurately and in greater depth.

> Most of us, if we think about it at all, have a vague idea that the celebration of Christmas began on December 25, the year Zero, when a Star rose in the East and a Saviour was born.[17]

So notes a distinguished folklorist regarding the average person's understanding of the holiday. "Of course," Tristram Potter Coffin goes on, "such was hardly the case." There is very little about Christmas that actually is as the naive f lk conception of the holiday suggests—and most Americans know it. If pressed, most Americans would remember having heard that December 25 was an arbitrary date, chosen by fourth-century church leaders for reasons that had nothing to do with the chronological date of the birth of Jesus. They would recall knowing that the Nativity could not have occurred in the year zero by modern reckoning, meaning our present calendar is wrong at its root. They would dredge up some memory of having known that the Star in the East is a legendary object, perhaps to be explained as a planetary conjunction or some quirk on an astrologer's chart. But Christmas grinds on regardless, grandly oblivious to the fact that most Americans already possess enough information about the holiday to debunk it thoroughly—if only they would put their minds to it.

Most of the information I will share in this book is readily available. Educated Americans know most of it. The role of this book is simply to bring it all together in a way that makes it easy not only to survey the facts, but to reflect on what they imply. Here are some of the surprising facts we will survey in the chapters to come. Did you know (or had you forgotten?) that:

- The odds of December 25 being the actual birth date of Jesus are no better than one in three hundred sixty-five. And that's being kind. If we take the Nativity story in the Gospel of Luke at face value, the reference to shepherds watching their flocks by night all but rules out a December birth date.

- Centuries before Christianity, ancient religions worshipped savior figures said to have been born of virgins. According to legend, their births were announced in the skies; kings and commoners passed before their cribs to pay homage. In ancient scriptures we read that the baby demigods were hidden or spirited to faraway lands to protect them from evil rulers who tried to kill them. The scriptures of long-dead faiths even claim that most of these savior-heroes were sacrificially killed, and later rose from the dead.

- An enormous number of traditions we now associate with Christmas have their roots in pre-Christian pagan religious traditions. Some of these have social, sexual, or cosmological connotations that might lead educated, culturally sensitive moderns to discard the traditions once they have understood their roots more clearly.

- The legend that St. Francis of Assisi invented the crèche, or manger scene, is patently untrue.

- So is the legend that Martin Luther invented the Christmas tree, inspired when he marveled one snowy evening at starlight shining through the boughs of an evergreen.

- Nor did Luther write the lullaby poem that we know today as "Away in a Manger."

- Clement C. Moore very likely did not write *A Visit From St. Nicholas,* the poem that bears his name and has charmed millions as *The Night Before Christmas.* Scholarship suggests he attached his name to the poem only after its success seemed assured.

- Contemporary Christmas does not come down to us from days of old. While parts of the tradition resemble medieval customs, the authentic ancient Christmas almost died by the late 1700s. The holiday we celebrate was a revival—in some ways an accidental one—that began more than 150 years ago. Writers such as Washington Irving and Charles Dickens made the holiday they were helping to invent *feel* older by injecting their writings with artificial nostalgia. It is much as if Sony had introduced the compact disc with phoney TV "newsreel" commercials in which flappers pop a CD on the old Victrola and Charleston up a storm.

- Nor is contemporary Christmas a "universal" or an "international" festival. The holiday owes its renewal to an amazingly small number of Britons and Americans. Its popularity exploded because it appealed to the hopes, fears, and illusions of English-speaking Victorians, those peerless colonialists who went on to impose their newfangled holiday on most of the rest of the world. Far from being a global feast of peace and brotherhood, today's Christmas is simply the crowning success story of Anglophone cultural imperialism.

- The Santa Claus myth is not the endearing centerpiece of childhood that most Americans think. Literal belief in Santa Claus may harm children psychologically. And contrary to adult protests that the figure of Santa Claus is just a metaphor for the "spirit of giving," most young American children believe in Santa in a most literal—and all too often, dysfunctional—way.

- Far from bringing Americans together at the winter holiday season, Christmas often alienates Jews, the nonreligious, and members of newer, fast-growing non-Christian religious minorities. People who belong to these groups take justifiable offense at being expected to join in a festival that they perceive as the sectarian feast of a religion not their own.

- When public schools, city governments, and other public bodies overstress the celebration of Christmas in either its sacred or its "secular" aspects, they run the risk of making members of non-

Christian minorities feel unwelcome in a nation that is supposed to be open to all. Non-Christians increasingly bring costly lawsuits or mount divisive protests in response to perceived abuses. Given trends in the nation's cultural and legal climates, such retaliatory actions are likely to meet with broader success and to impose harsher costs on the public bodies involved in years to come.

• Contrary to popular belief, the Christmas season seldom brings literal peace on earth. Holiday ceasefires hold uneasily in the world's trouble spots, but in most cases combatants use the time to bind their wounds and oil their weapons. When the holiday ends (or a moment before; it's important to get off the first shot), battle resumes. If the respite brings anything, it is renewed energy with which to wage war even more viciously. What Christmas in uniform *does* seem to bring is incongruity. United States Marines in Mogadishu, Somalia, on Christmas Day 1992 took breaks in shifts. Protestant troops attended a Protestant service. Catholic troops attended a Catholic service. Then the Jewish troops got their time off, for the purpose of attending a Jewish service.[18] My source does not record what text the chaplain used to perform a Jewish Christmas service, nor does it indicate what arrangements were made for nonreligious troops who wanted to spend their time feeding the hungry so they could get home sooner.

Where do you stand on Christmas? According to Gallup, 93 percent of Americans consider Christmas their favorite holiday.[19] But that still leaves 7 percent, about eighteen million people, who don't.

On the subject of Christmas, Americans tend to fall into three main camps. The vast majority, active or nominal Christians, observe the holiday in all its aspects. Included in this group are also millions of the religiously indifferent who nonetheless keep a full-fledged Christmas. Since about 40 percent of Americans are unaffiliated with any church, it follows that many of those who avidly celebrate Christmas do not identify in any strong sense with organized Christianity. Next comes the group that I call the "Old Outsiders": observant or ethnic Jews and religious nonbelievers. Depending upon how you slice your statistics, Old Outsiders may comprise as much as 13 percent of the population. They are the nation's oldest religious minorities; most have been in this country for three or four generations or longer. Their subcultures developed at a time when American society made harsher demands on newcomers than it does today. As a result, Old Outsiders have accommodated to the Christmas holiday in countless ways. A surprising number of Jews put up Christmas trees; some celebrate the holiday in its entirety. Most have expanded Chanukah far beyond its original significance. An equally surprising number of atheists, agnostics, and secular humanists keep Christmas. A growing minority celebrate the winter solstice in thinly disguised surrender to the mainstream holiday's might. Finally, there are the "New Outsiders": more recent immigrants who adhere to non-Christian religions including Islam, Hinduism, Buddhism, and dozens of minority creeds. New Outsiders may be the Americans least likely to celebrate the holiday and least predisposed to absorb Christmas traditions. They comprise at least 2 percent, and perhaps as much as 8 percent, of the national population.

Today, growing minorities in the Jewish and nonreligious communities are adopting a harder line. Over the last 25 years or so, there has been heightened consciousness among Reform, Conservative, and nonpracticing Jews that their forebears may have given away too much in order to penetrate the American mainstream. A powerful "back to the roots" movement has arrested a decades-long decline in the Orthodox population. Even outside Orthodoxy, the perception seems to be growing that full-blown Christmas celebrations are less appropriate—and more worth resisting—than American Jews generally supposed as recently as the late sixties. As for nonbelievers, since the early sixties atheists and secular humanists have been increasingly visible. Not only have they begun to show themselves more openly in society, they have been frequent litigants in important legal cases touching on the separation of church and state, and nonbelievers' rights. As a secular humanist, one of my motives in writing this book is to encourage my fellow infidels to consider reversing some of their past accommodations to Christmas in their own lives and family traditions.

Another constellation of religious minorities disdains contemporary Christmas and must not be overlooked. Several Christian sects reject all or part of the holiday observance on a variety of doctrinal grounds. Among these are the Jehovah's Witnesses, with about 750,000 members; the Worldwide Church of God, which claims 95,000 members; the Christian Science Church, which does not report its membership; and others.[20]

The trouble with Christmas is that it seduces members of America's still-dominant Christian majority culture into ignoring everything they know about equality, fairness, and cultural sensitivity for four to six weeks out of every year.

There's a feast of trouble on the horizon. Controversies over Christmas are likely to increase sharply in the years ahead. We have grown accustomed to legal battles over the crèche or menorah on the city hall steps. Wrangles over Christmas observance in the public schools are less familiar, but growing fast. Across the country, educators are confronting questions of whether to permit the religious symbols of one faith, of all, or of none in classrooms and hallways; whether to have a tree in the lobby with or without a menorah, or whether to have a tree at all; whether to include Jewish and Christian songs or program only secular music in holiday events; even whether to hold the traditional holiday pageant at all. Few questions a school district can tackle are more divisive. Few have greater potential to stall debate on other, objectively more important issues. But they cannot be ignored. Trampling on the rights and sensitivities of minorities is not only wrong, it is unconstitutional. In the next few years, I predict we will see controversies of this sort spill out of the public sector and overwhelm the private sector too. The next hot issue may concern imposed holiday observances in the workplace, which non-Christian employees will be increasingly unwilling to accept.

Despite the pain it necessarily involves, this process is healthy. It forces us to move closer to the ideal of the truly open and tolerant society envisioned in the First Amendment. Along the way, there will be growing trouble with Christmas. The trouble comes down to this:

> This period's compulsory merriment, hyper-commercialism, heavy drinking, and undue media emphasis on the idealized, two-child, two-parent, orthodox Christian family makes those who don't share such lifestyles or religious sentiments feel left out, lonely, and even somewhat un-American.[21]

In a society that is growing in diversity as rapidly as ours in the United States, there is little room for ethnic and religious chauvinism. If we cannot squeeze the insensitivity out of Christmas, it is contemporary Christmas that will feel the squeeze.

Notes

1. James S. Henry, "Why I Hate Christmas," *New Republic* (December 31, 1990): 21.

2. Marianne Wait, "Season's Greenings," *Ladies' Home Journal* (December 1990): 102.

3. U.S. Postal Service figures.

4. Robert Bezilla, ed., *Religion in America* (Princeton, N.J.: Princeton Religion Research Center, 1993), p. 46.

5. Henry, pp. 22–23.

6. Bradley Hitchings, "How to Shake Those Holiday Blues," *Business Week* (December 10, 1984): 156.

7. Wayne Dyer, *Happy Holidays!* (New York: William Morrow and Company, 1986), p. 76.

8. Bezilla, p. 46.

9. Jane Kwiatkowski, "Criminals Target Older Citizens in Eighteen Recent Cases," *Buffalo News*, December 18, 1992.

10. U.S. Consumer Product Safety Commission, July 1991. Study quoted in " 'Tis the Season to be Clumsy," *Harper's* (December 1991): 30.

11. Hitchings, p. 158.

12. Henry, p. 21.

13. Electronic correspondence, Doug from New York State, March 31, 1993.

14. J. M. Golby and A. W. Purdue, *The Making of the Modern Christmas* (Athens, Ga.: University of Georgia Press, 1986. Originally published London: B. T. Batsford Ltd., 1986), p. 141.

15. Maymie Richardson Krythe, *All About Christmas* (New York: Harper and Brothers, 1954), p. 7.

16. Golby and Purdue, p. 35.

17. Tristram Potter Coffin, *The Book of Christmas Folklore* (New York: Seabury, 1973), p. 3.

18. Associated Press, "Conflicts Mar Season Celebrations," *Rocky Mountain News,* December 25, 1992.

19. Gallup, p. 46.

20. William B. Williamson, *An Encyclopedia of Religions in the United States* (New York: Crossroad, 1992), p. 354. For teachings about Christmas in the Worldwide Church of God, see Herbert W. Armstrong, *The Plain Truth About Christmas* (Pasadena, Calif.: Ambassador College, 1970).

21. Henry, p. 23.

2

Confessions of an Anti-Claus

Everybody has a secret. Here's mine: I do not celebrate Christmas.

At all.

To me Christmas is precisely just another day.

There is no Christmas tree in my living room. I do not give Christmas gifts, nor do I accept them. I decline invitations to holiday parties (unless the company or refreshments promise to be exceptional; I'm not a prig). If I do not keep Christmas, neither do I observe any "halfway holiday" like the winter solstice. We're talking maximum Scrooge here. I suppose that is why some people call me the Anti-Claus.

Since 1984, Christmas morning has found me at my desk. When I started, I did not have keys to the office where I worked, so I did my nine-to-five at home. Today I have keys, so I spend Christmas at the office. I get up early, commute to work, put in a full day, and commute home: the whole career routine. Of course, now that I work for *Free Inquiry,* the nation's largest secular humanist magazine, when I come into the office on Christmas day I seldom find myself completely alone. Even so, it is sometimes disheartening how few of my co-workers slog in. They live without religion but nonetheless celebrate the holiday.

I enjoy working on Christmas day. There's no traffic to fight. The phone hardly rings. I get a lot done. But there are drawbacks. Try to find a restaurant that's open for lunch!

The woman I live with is a nominal Lutheran. She keeps Christmas in the usual way. She has a private study that she decorates lavishly, though we leave the rest of our apartment bare. The alarm that sounds on Christmas morning is meant to wake us both. She has to get up too, to go and spend the holiday with her family.

For several years now, we've shared a special Christmas morning greeting. We roll over and I tell her, "Merry Christmas." She tells me, "Happy just another day."

And that is how I treat the holiday. When Christmas falls on a weekend, I do not go into work just to prove a point. December 25, 1993, is a Saturday, so I'll probably spend the day puttering around the apartment and catching up on freelance work as I would on any other Saturday.

Christmas 1994 falls on Sunday. I expect I'll start my day as I have begun my Sundays since I left the Roman Catholic church in the late 1970s. I'll sleep late.

People who do celebrate Christmas have a terrible time understanding people who don't. It is part of the unconscious arrogance that this ubiquitous festival breeds. So I spend more of my time than sometimes seems productive explaining why I have chosen to sit Christmas out.

I am often asked insightful, sensitive questions about elements of my early biography that might have influenced my decision to live Yule-free, questions like "What the hell went wrong during your childhood?"

With that in mind, I will leave off developing my argument to indulge in a little autobiography. It is not that I love to talk about myself; I know from experience that some readers will not listen to anything I have to say about the holiday as long as an absence of data gives them license to fantasize about explanatory pathologies rooted deep in my past.

I was born in 1955 in Erie, Pennsylvania. Though both my parents came from Roman Catholic backgrounds and kept a fairly strict Catholic household, I was the only child of two only children. The downside of this is that neither of my parents had the opportunity to learn from siblings who preceded them into parenthood. Thanks to various accidents of demography, they also had few close friends who had started families at the same time they did. So when I began reading fourth-grade-level texts and spelling out complex sentences with building blocks at age three, years before *Sesame Street* made such stunts routine, they did not realize that anything unusual was going on.

Their first clue came when the parish Catholic school administered some kind of prekindergarten entrance exam. I scored so high that the school did not want to take me. In those days Roman Catholics were strongly discouraged from sending their children to public schools. The parish school made an exception.

So it came to pass that I entered kindergarten in the Erie public school system. I was one of two children in my whole kindergarten class who walked in knowing how to read. More important, in a large, urban K–6 public elementary school I was one of fewer than two dozen Catholics. This was in 1960, when compulsory prayer and Bible readings were the norm in public schools in the Northeast. From kindergarten through second grade, I listened to readings from the King James version of the Bible. At that age I didn't understand that Catholics used a different and less accurate translation of the Bible, the so-called Douay-Rheims version. But from time to time I heard passages that I had earlier heard in church, or in the tiny Sunday school classes then provided for Catholic children attending public school. I knew the readings at school differed from the versions I had heard at my church. And I knew that the Roman Catholic faith was the one true faith, from which it obviously followed that other denominations were passports to hell (this was also before Vatican II). So I feared for my soul.

From kindergarten through second grade, I listened to prayers led by the teacher at the beginning of the school day. I listened to the Lord's Prayer, which Catholic tots knew only as the "Our Father," and something was wrong with it. My teachers were adding a sentence just before the end: "For Thine is the power and the glory, forever and ever." Jesus never said that! At the time I did not know that Protestants traditionally used this sentence, which Catholics preferred to omit. All I knew was that my teachers were trying to improve on the only prayer personally dictated by the son of God. So I feared more deeply for my soul.

From kindergarten through second grade, I attended compulsory Christmas assemblies at which religious music was performed. I had no problem with the idea of a Christmas assembly; at that age my life was essentially a year-long Christmas cult whose scriptures were Saturday-morning TV toy commercials. What did bother me was that when they sang "Away in a Manger," they sang it to the wrong tune. Now I know they were using the popular melody composed in 1877 by James R. Murray. Catholics preferred the James E. Spillman melody, to which the English song "Flow Gently, Sweet Afton" is also sung. In this case I *did* know that the relevant distinction between the melodies had to do with whether one was Catholic or Protestant. I knew that because I had once heard the Murray melody played at home, from a recording. My maternal grandmother was in the room. An otherwise mild-mannered woman, she had once told me with approval that in her day the nuns taught that Protestants who collapsed with heart attacks on the sidewalk could properly be stepped over and ignored since they were going to hell anyway. Hearing "Away in a Manger" set to that alien tune, she hissed, "That's how Protestants sing it!" and made a great show of tuning out until the song ended. So when I sat in those grade-school Christmas assemblies and heard the lullaby performed to Murray's melody, I knew I was in the presence of profound evil. And I feared, if possible, even more deeply for my soul.

I used to walk home all but quaking with fear. The Sunday-school nuns loved to ask us children where we would spend eternity if we were unexpectedly run over by a truck. I was convinced that if I were hit by a truck on the way home from school, I would die without an opportunity to be shriven of the Protestant corruption I had been forced to absorb that day. As a result, I may have been the only Catholic seven-year-old in the country who secretly cheered for Madalyn Murray O'Hair as her highly-publicized litigation wound through the courts.

In 1962 and 1963 the bombshell Supreme Court decisions ending compulsory prayer and Bible readings in public schools became the law of the land. (I would later learn that Madalyn's case was actually the least important of the three lawsuits involved.) I vividly remember my relief that the King James Bible and the "expanded" Lord's Prayer no longer darkened my school days. My contentment intensified at the third-grade Christmas assembly. For the first time the program stuck to secular songs like "Santa Claus is Coming to Town," or to hymns like "O Come, All Ye Faithful" that seemed uncontroversial. At least, Catholics and Protestants sang them to the same tune.

It never occurred to me then to ask what Jewish or atheist children thought of all this. It was enough for me that observances that empha-sized differences between Protestant and Catholic practice—and made it clear that the Protestant agenda was the agenda of the school, and hence of the community—had been suppressed.

I remained a moralistic, superior little Catholic twit well into high school. I used to lecture female classmates for wearing their skirts too short. In a sizable suburban junior high school I knew only one frank atheist, and I baited him mercilessly. Wherever you are, Mark English, I'm sorry. You were right.

In time my relentless Catholicism began to waver. As an adolescent, I did not feel that I was inching away from my faith. I felt that the church was inching away from me. It was a sensation I shared with millions of Catholics at that difficult time. The reforms of the Second Vatican Council were percolating down to the parish level. The nuns had taught (or at least implied; I *was* very young back then) that every detail of church practice had been personally dictated by Jesus Christ to Saint Peter, in triplicate. I imagined that the records kept by the stenographer present must have been interred in a vault somewhere beneath the Lateran Basilica. And now the winds of reform were stirring the deepest foundations of the church! The altar was rotated so the priest faced the congregation. To this preteen Catholic, it seemed that the sublime miracle of the Holy Eucharist—which I then understood as the literal, physical transformation of bread and wine into the body and blood of Christ—had been reduced to a theatrical exhibition. Wrenched out of its mysterious, uplifting Latin mother tongue, the exalted mystery of the Mass croaked forth in a workaday English that made its profundities seem crass.

I learned to question. I started out by asking how the Roman Catholic church differed from the various Protestant denominations. I "knew" that God's hand guided Catholicism while the Protestant sects were buffeted by the mundane forces of organizational politics and practical expedience. But where was the proof? In time I came to the bitter conclusion that there was no visible difference between Catholic "truth" and Protestant "error" when one compared the worldly achievements of the respective institutions. It took a couple of years before my emotions were capable of encompassing the realization that my reason had discovered. Once that happened, I moved on to bigger questions. If Catholic and Protestant were functionally indistinguishable, could I at least see clear signs in history that God favored the Christian churches over their heathen competitors?

Just as I never found a clear, supernaturally mediated advantage of Catholic over Protestant, so I was unable to find strong evidence for the temporal superiority of Christianity over the other world religions. If one went by the criterion of worldly success and the core doctrine's ability to resist distortion by historical forces, a thinking person would convert to Islam. Could all the world religions be the same under God? Could they all be equally true—or equally false? Again I had to delay my inquiry to let my emotions catch up with what I had deduced.

If these questions sound naive, bear with me. I had never heard of philosophy. I thought I was the only person in the world haunted by these doubts, and dealt with them as deftly as one can who neither possesses the tools nor understands the nature of the work.

It was at this point in my epistemological maunderings that the time came to choose a college. Realizing that I had drawn away from the faith, my parents encouraged me to attend a Catholic university. Realizing that I was posing tough questions about my religion, they cast a special spotlight on Jesuit institutions. The priests of the Society of Jesus are famed as the intellectual Arnold Schwarzeneggers of Rome. Surely, my parents imagined, they would answer my questions and set me on the true path once again.

Things didn't quite work out that way. Still, I owe the Jesuits at Cincinnati's Xavier University a great debt. They introduced me to philosophy. For me to discover as a college freshman that towering intellects had wrestled profoundly with the issues of knowledge, truth, cosmology, and verification I was trifling with was a comfort and a revelation. After I had completed a few courses, I began my own reading in philosophy and theology. With gathering speed my adolescent presuppositions collapsed. In time, though not without pain, I came to discard my belief in God just as I had outgrown my confidence in Christianity against the other world religions—just as, even earlier, I had forsaken my exclusive faith in Catholicism.

I will always be grateful to the Jesuits at Xavier University. Without them, I might not be the atheist I am today.

And in a perverse way, I will always be grateful that I was born precocious and a Catholic. Because I grew up within a Christian tradition, I can understand the religious notions, fears, and superstitions that drive so many in this society. (Just try to explain the motives of zealous anti-abortion protestors to religious liberals who have never known conservative Christianity from the inside!) Yet though I was a Christian, I also experienced life in a religious minority. I knew the pain of feeling an unwelcome guest in my native land. I knew what it was like to be told by the reigning institutions of society, explicitly or implicitly, that my beliefs were second-rate. Looking back, I have to admit that in objective terms many of those beliefs *were* second-rate. I was trapped in the most naive and primitive sort of Catholicity: the sort that perhaps, even among Catholics, only children can take seriously. I know now how wrong I was to feel that an extra verse in the "Our Father" or the wrong tune behind "Away in a Manger" endangered my spiritual welfare. But if my misgivings seem foolish today, the pain they brought me then was real. I will never forget how it felt to be on the receiving end of religious discrimination.

Perhaps there was no other way I could have learned as vividly as I did, as young as I did, the moral necessity of a strict separation of church and state. I knew the human truth behind Jefferson's glorious abstraction, the "wall of separation." No weaker barrier will let people who hold mutually contradictory creeds coexist in a free society. Strong faith can inspire otherwise reasonable people to see in small disagreements issues important enough to die for—or kill for. It is one of humanity's less endearing qualities, and one against which democracy needs to protect itself.

Finally, I will always be grateful that I had the experience of challenging, examining, and rejecting the central doctrines of my childhood one by one. I grew up at a rare time when society encouraged individuals to try their hands at reinventing themselves. And so I did. I pondered whether I wished to remain an American and a speaker of English (I did) and a resident of my native city (I did not). I weighed whether the conventional life plan of marriage, home, and children was for me, and decided it was not. I tried on new hometowns and began calling into question all the opinions I had received, whether political, economic, historical, moral, or religious. I became as

one who tears off from himself the restraints of tradition and custom and asserts his absolute independence. He endeavors to make his mind a blank; he makes a clean slate, so to speak, and begins all over again. He says:

I will make myself as if I knew nothing, had learned nothing, had been taught nothing. I will begin to learn now, and I will meet every fact, every law, every doctrine, with denial and opposition, and will not admit one of them into my mind, will not believe one of them until I am forced to do so by a demonstration![1]

William Graham Sumner composed those words while he was still an Episcopalian minister. He intended them as a savage critique. But times have changed. Encountering this passage as an adult, I quivered to recognize the credo under which I had spent years remanufacturing my life. Imagine mentally projecting yourself outside your culture, past the debris of your experiences and past the drag of your heritage. That was the ideal toward which I strove. If I could not make of myself precisely the person I yearned to be, at least I could identify, and try to change, the effects of the early influences that had made of me someone of whom I disapproved.

What if every conviction, each opinion, all the traditions and outlooks that were physically possible for you lay at your fingertips? What would you select? Would Christmas be among your choices?

If you answered yes without thinking about it, reading this book may encourage you to change your mind.

I had been an atheist for several years before I pulled the plug on Christmas. At first I celebrated the holiday conventionally: gifts, a tree, Christmas parties, a rushed motor trip to my parents' house and back in weather that was often unfit for sled dogs, the works. Already I had the idea that Christmas was incompatible with my new belief system. Celebrating the birthday of a god I no longer believed in rankled. But I was not ready for decisive action just yet. One year I sent winter solstice cards. The solstice did not really appeal to me as a holiday, but it was something nonreligious people did. The next year I sent out the ultimate contradiction: atheist Christmas cards. I suppose half the people who got them burned them.

I moonwalked through Christmas 1983, having decided that it would be my last. In mid-1984 I told my family that I would not observe the holiday in any form: that I would not come down to Erie, that I would spend the day in front of my typewriter writing copy for the advertising agency that then employed me.

I was astonished at their shock.

My parents had been troubled but tolerant when I left the Catholic church. It was harder for them when I became an atheist, but they came to terms with that too. Once they'd ridden out that trauma, I imagined that my foregoing Christmas would be only a small pothole in the boulevard of their lives. I was wrong. Years later, I still don't altogether understand why it was so difficult for them. Once you've accepted that your son is an atheist, why should his giving up Christmas seem like anything more than a formality?

I can't answer that question. I suppose I never will.

Summer 1984 blended into fall. As the leaves fluttered from the trees and the tinsel scuttled up the lamp posts, I confronted my next surprise. I was startled by the depth of my anger at Christmas. There was no escaping its brutal ubiquity. Life swarmed with Christmas. Christmas suffused. It suffocated. It pervaded the streets, the malls, the workplace, the outdoors, the music on the radio. It left no void into which a nonparticipant could retreat.

There is a germ of truth in the stereotype of Scrooge. Scowling comes easily when all you want is peace. Pretend you're an apartment dweller. On every side noisy neighbors have conspired not to leave you a moment's asylum from the racket of their month-long party. Forget about complaining to the landlord; she bought the booze! During my first few "un-Christmas" seasons, I felt that same sour anger. Every "Merry Christmas!" was a rebuke, every store clerk's inquiry whether I wanted my purchase gift-wrapped a covert insult.

Along the way, I learned a bitter solidarity with Jews and with more experienced atheists, with Hindus and Muslims and Buddhists and every other American for whom Christmas is someone else's holiday. When I celebrated Christmas, I never truly realized how relentlessly the observant majority shoves its festival down the throats of outsiders. Having placed myself in the outermost circle of outsiders, I experienced the arrogance of Christmas with unprecedented force.

Need a new watch in December? A flashlight battery, a quart of milk? The stores thunder with holiday shoppers. The streets ossify. Traffic creeps like holiday fudge left out in the car overnight. If a simple errand means driving past a mall, add fifteen minutes to your travel time.

I found myself trying to anticipate my consumer needs early in October, stocking up on items I knew I'd require and hoping that few emergencies would force me into the consumer maelstrom. The disturbing art of buying all one's needs months in advance came easily to me.

My "angry period" lasted for about three Christmases. Since then I've mellowed. Today I look upon the holiday commotion equably, as a temptation overcome. Christmas neither appeals nor angers any more; it is something neutral, foreign, part of the furniture of someone else's life. Last time I went to a mall in December, it was fun. Benignly I observed shoppers thronging the kiosks, jostling in and out of the stores like cattle in a chute. I felt a deep, sweeping contentment because I knew that unlike them, I could have chosen to be elsewhere.

An initial rage that fades with time appears to be common when Yule users go cold turkey. British pundit James Cameron expressed it in delectably overblown language:

> The onset of Christmas and its attendant vulgarities no longer fills me with petulance and woe, alarm and despondency, sound and fury, but with a kind of awful nostalgia—nostalgia not for the days of innocence but for the days of indignation. Gone, gone are the days of exasperation and mockery. The old wheel comes round: I have passed through my Christmas tantrums and now regard the whole jigamaree as does a little child, with uncomprehending wonder. How *can* it still go on? How can it ever stop?[2]

I hate to use psychobabble, but in retrospect my decision to "just say no" to Christmas has been an empowering experience in the best sense of that word. I chose to root out of my life a complicated holiday that appeals strongly to the parts of the human psyche I least wanted to pander to. And I did it. There is life after Christmas, made more fulfilling for the knowledge that I made of my life what I yearned for. Instead of spending a tenth of each year preparing for, enduring, and then cleaning up after a holiday that no longer fulfilled me, I turned to society and said "No, thanks." There is a sublime feeling of mastery that comes from so thoroughly redirecting your life—and having things come out the way you'd hoped for.

At last I can page through the good and the bad memories Christmas holds for me and consider them with something approaching objectivity. I remember the thrill of Christmas shopping in downtown Erie, which today hardly exists. Those childhood excursions among the lumbering buildings and uniformed bell-ringers, counting out my nickels and dimes and darting between the snowflakes from one magical store to the next, imbued me with an abiding love of city life. The music, the lights, the toys, the family rituals filled me with a visceral joy that sometimes seemed likely to explode my little body from somewhere deep inside my chest. My childhood Christmases still hold a greeting-card warmth for me.

There are also disturbing memories. I was five or six when a playmate around the corner (who had given his parents a difficult year) received no presents. In his stocking he found only a lump of coal. He was devastated. Later I learned how rare it is for parents to follow through on the "lump of coal" threat; as a child, I assumed everyone knew a kid or two whom Santa had snubbed on Christmas Eve. Needless to say, after that I exerted vast efforts to be good. The runups to my next few Christmases were full of apprehension, like the week before report card day.

For one close friend in second grade, the preholiday period brought a different sort of anxiety. He had done something terrible (by the standards of a seven-year-old, at least) over the summer and gotten away with it. Mom and Dad suspected nothing, but he knew he had not fooled Santa Claus. He lived in dread of Christmas morning, when his parents would see that the living room held presents for everyone but him, and demand to know what he had done not to deserve any Christmas. Of course, Christmas morning did not bring the exposure he feared, an experience he found deeply disillusioning—like the time you find out that the magic word Grandma gave you doesn't really stop the playground bully. He had tested the world's system of justice, and it didn't work.

I also remember standing on the staircase at home in my pajamas, proudly clutching that year's letter to Santa Claus. My mother snarled at me, "You stupid farmer!" because I was ten and still writing letters to Santa. A bright child too eager to heed authority, I had constructed a dizzying tracery of nested rationalizations to preserve my belief in the figure of Santa Claus. The nuns—and my parents too, if by implication— had told me that I was supposed to believe whether it made sense or not. So that was what I did. Fourteen years later, an even grander scaffold of teetering evasions would collapse as I finally abandoned my belief in God. But that time, I would swing the hammer for myself.

Now the positive memories return. Believe it or not, after college I actually earned my living in the holiday business! I designed Halloween and Christmas promotions for nonprofit organizations, from two national health agencies to a struggling museum whose major asset was a manmade cave running parallel to the old Erie Canal. If everyone waxes nostalgic about a part of his or her youth that was deliciously misspent, this was mine. I was the low-budget impresario of Halloween "haunted house" attractions that would be torn down November first and be reborn by Thanksgiving as Yuletide paradises with names like "Santa's Workshop." I discovered by accident that one could design a Frankenstein laboratory set in such a way that all the phoney "control consoles" could be turned upside down, painted in brighter colors, and used with their electrical wiring intact as the North Pole data processing center. Children would shriek in delight as actors in toy soldier uniforms pored over their brightly flickering readouts to predict the world's weather on Christmas Eve, using the very same hardware with which an actor portraying Dr. Frankenstein had "created unnatural life" two months before. With some red and green paint and a change of superstructure, the torture tables from the Spanish Inquisition room made dandy elf workbenches. It took volunteer artists less than two hours to transform the throne of Satan into that of Santa. The large vinyl letters spelling out the occupant's name could all be recycled, of course; indeed, only three of them had to be moved. One year I even recycled a ten-foot-tall, fully operational guillotine. Reborn in Santa's workshop, it cut gift-wrapping paper to length with inarguable authority.

I look back on those years with nostalgia and a certain amazement. When I was designing all those quick-change set pieces to serve Halloween in one month and Christmas in the next, I had no idea why the trick was working so well. As we will see, Halloween and Christmas spring from common roots. Many of their traditions are distorted mirror images of one another.

Where Christmas is concerned, a mighty underground river of symbolism, tradition, and imagery flows through the foundations of society. Contemporary Americans would recognize some of it as positive, but be surprised to see that other aspects have quite negative implications today. But that seldom happens, because hardly anyone takes the trouble to understand Christmas in detail.

The trouble with Christmas will only get worse if ignorance and naiveté continue to be our guides. We will need surer signposts if we will adapt this most ubiquitous holiday to the demands of a newly multicultural society without giving rise to rancor, divisiveness, and occasional violence.

The need is urgent for someone who has seen and lived *both* sides of this holiday to take stock of what's good and what's bad about Christmas. We can no longer afford to mistake candy coatings for truth.

Notes

1. William Graham Sumner, "Individualism," in Robert C. Bannister, ed., *On Liberty, Society, and Politics: The Essential Essays of William Graham Sumner* (Indianapolis: Liberty Fund, 1992), pp. 5–6.

2. James Cameron, "Nasty Seasonal Thoughts," *New Statesman and Society* (Christmas supplement 1991): 43.

3

The Age Before Christmas

Most Americans know something about the pre-Christian roots of Christmas. We should. Annually the media bombard us with information, misinformation, and disinformation about the origins of the holiday. We read how Christmas trees came from the Druids. We see on television how our festive holiday dinner is based on the medieval wassail bowl. We hear on the radio how the traditions of gift giving and the Twelve Days of Christmas come to us unmeditated from ancient Babylon. We hear it all each year, but most of it doesn't sink in.

That may be just as well. You see, each of these "examples" of the holiday's pre-Christian past is wrong. Each is a claim I have seen made by writers who should have known better. They presented these falsehoods next to, and often inextricably entwined with, accurate information about the origins of Christmas. Maybe that is why so many Americans throw up their hands and give up on the whole idea of understanding how the modern Christmas came about. It might help to explain the durability of the comforting but groundless notion that Christmas started from scratch with the birth of Jesus.

Of all the ideas one can have about the holiday, the one that Christmas leapt full-blown into the world on the day a certain infant was laid in a manger is the most misleading conception of all. Contemporary Christmas draws its inspiration from three rich bodies of tradition:

(1) Pre-Christian traditions

(2) Christian traditions

(3) Post-Christian traditions.

Of the three, Christian traditions have contributed the least to Christmas as it is celebrated around the world today. Yet no holiday is viewed by non-Christians as more representative of Christian culture. If Christmas never became Christianity's most important religious holiday (Easter holds that honor), it has been that religion's most conspicuous ambassador to the secular world.

They say that "research is plagiarism from multiple sources." If that's true, then nothing Americans do bears the marks of more exhaustive "research" than contemporary Christmas. Even a superficial study of the holiday and its history cannot help but amaze us with how little about the modern holiday we know is authentically Christian. Few aspects of it were unknown in the days before Christianity. Scarcely a scrap of it seems to be wholly based in early Christian faith and practice. Certain elements of contemporary Christmas *were* unknown in pagan times, but most of them were spliced on recently by secular influences. Distinctive, original Christian contributions to the Christmas feast are about as common as diet books at the North Pole.

The pre-Christian elements of Christmas hail primarily from Europe. They can be divided into two broad bodies of tradition. From southern Europe come such familiar pagan traditions as feasting, fertility rituals, tree worship, and the exchange of gifts. From the harsher lands of northern Europe come the ancient conventions we identify with the term "Yule." The Yule log tradition, now almost forgotten, rose from this stream. So too are many of the details of holiday feasting, the ritual use of candles, and the earliest forerunners of Santa Claus. Winters may be gentler in southern Europe, but they still bite. So we see customs relating to the winter solstice in both the northern and southern traditions. Both traditions also single out coniferous plants because they keep their leaves during the winter. Sometimes modern-day holiday customs can be traced to items in both the northern and southern traditions, which may have shared a superficial resemblance but meant very different things when they arose.

Here is a brief review of the pre-Christian sources from which some of our best-loved holiday traditions sprang.

Evergreens symbolize immortality and the continuity of life. No doubt they first attracted attention by their obstinate vitality in the face of wintry blasts before which other living things retreated.

According to traditions so old that their origins cannot be traced, when the wind blew harsh and the hills lay cloaked in their mantle of white, evil spirits roamed the land. In that midwinter stillness, it was believed that one might read one's fortune for the coming year. From this may have come our custom of New Year's resolutions.

It was also believed that one should not labor too hard during the holiday season, lest demons trip one up or steal into the body while one's mind is on one's work. One need not be a rocket scientist to imagine how an icy season could have given rise to folk beliefs about hostile sprites who love to make people fall down. Such common experiences as dreams and encounters with the mentally ill might have been enough to ignite superstitions about demonic possession. But pre-Christian Europeans were not defenseless. The surest protection against evil spirits was thought to be the evergreens: box, yew, bay, larch, ivy, rosemary, juniper, holly, fir, spruce, and pine.[1]

The Romans, too, decorated their homes and public places with evergreens near the time of the winter solstice. Among the forerunners of today's holiday gifts were *strenae,* tree branches presented to political and military leaders as tokens of loyalty.

Aside from the Christmas tree, the most ancient traditions relating to evergreens probably revolve around the *Yule log.* Yule log traditions arose in northern Europe; Roman documents do not mention them until well into the Christian era. The Yule log cult never took firm root in the New World. Today it is largely extinct in Europe too. Commonly able-bodied boys and men would go into the woods, find an immense log, and bring it into the house with great ceremony. It might be blessed, decorated, or anointed with wine before it was set alight, usually with a fragment of the past year's Yule log that had been saved for that purpose. A proper Yule log would burn for days, and while it burned the normal routine of living would be set aside in favor of holiday rituals. A pig or other animal would be roasted over the log's flames. Wheat or seeds might be showered upon it in hopes of guaranteeing a good harvest the next year. Another tradition involved beating the burning log with a stick; it was sometimes believed that for each spark struck from the log a lamb, piglet, or calf would be born that spring.[2] When the Yule log burned out, that would also mark the end of the holiday season.

Historians of the holiday have traced the Yule log tradition back to early Norse legends of Yggdrasil, a mystical tree imagined to be as big as the universe itself. Yggdrasil was said to nestle the Norse paradise, Valhalla, in one of its roots and the underworld in a second. The third root contained Midgard, our world. According to lore, each root was being gnawed by tireless serpents; when they chewed through all three roots, the world would end.[3]

Other signs also point to an extremely early origin for the Yule log. As recent as the last century, Serbian peasants would move tables, stools, and fire irons away from the fireplace before bringing the Yule log into the house. If such implements originated too recently to have a place in the Yule log rituals, those rites must have been ancient indeed. French peasants drew a human figure on the log with chalk before it was lighted. The Cornish traditionally called their log "the Mock." The word then meant what it does today, "imitation" or "substitute." Yet tradition never specified for what the log was intended to substitute, an omission sometimes seen when a custom descended from something now considered shameful. At least one historian of the holiday has speculated that the French and Cornish practices may link the Yule log to dimly-recalled traditions of human sacrifice.[4]

The holiday's most conspicuous smaller plant is *mistletoe*. Called in olden days the "tree thief," it is a parasite that clings to the upper branches of oaks. It completes its life cycle without touching the ground. Historically, mistletoe has long been associated with both magic and fertility. Sprigs of mistletoe were once fastened over the conjugal bed on the wedding night. Our modern use of mistletoe as a social aphrodisiac is clearly related.

Nineteenth-century German immigrants to the United States were among the first to use a recognizable *Christmas tree* in this country, so it is often assumed that the Christmas tree hails from the traditions of northern Europe. In fact, it is more authentically a product of much older southern traditions. Ancient Egyptians viewed the evergreen tree as a fertility symbol. During the winter solstice they decorated their homes with palm fronds, using them as Romans would later use boughs of fir.[5]

Christians have often tried to deny that the Christmas tree has a pagan heritage. One popular story claims that Martin Luther invented the *tannenbaum*. Despite the popularity of this tale, it is untrue. Understandably, stories that attributed the tree to Luther did not impress Roman Catholics. So Catholics made a groundless origin claim of their own. The *New Catholic Encyclopedia* strains to trace the *tannenbaum* to the German *paradise tree*.[6] This tree symbolized the Genesis story's Tree of Life in the Garden of Eden. Trimmed with red apples and tiny figures of Adam, Eve, and the serpent, it was displayed on the feast of Adam and Eve, traditionally December 24. The paradise tree might make a promising ancestor of the Christmas tree if the custom were not too recent. It peaked in Germany in the eighteenth and nineteenth centuries.[7] The *New Catholic Encyclopedia* itself admits that recognizable Christmas trees appeared as early as 1605.[8]

We'll return to the development of the Christmas tree in chapter eight. In the meantime, if the origins of the *tannenbaum* are not ancient enough, consider the *twelve days of Christmas*. In what contemporary scholars might consider a breathtaking overstretch, Christmas chronicler Earl W. Count tried to trace the twelve days back to the eleven-day Babylonian New Year festival *Zaǧmukku*. Despite the shakiness of this claim, Count's 1948 book *4000 Years of Christmas* remains a favorite of reporters combing for holiday trivia.

The ancient Egyptians observed a year-end festival called *Sothis*. *Sothis* lasted five days, not twelve. It originated in the conflicts between solar and lunar calendars. The Egyptians used both, even though the two calendars would drift days apart in a single year. The problem was solved by creating a lunar calendar of twelve thirty-day months, then bringing it back into agreement with the sun by adding five days at the end of the year. That was *Sothis*: a five-day period that belonged to no month, during which routine obligations would be set aside in favor of revelry.[9]

The Babylonians were also said to observe a temporary exchange of roles between masters and slaves. This tradition is almost unknown in the United States, but it has deep roots in Europe. Called "the Lord of Misrule," it is unequivocally associated with Christmas.[10] Schoolboys used to take command of their schools. Children would parade through the towns, hear cases of law, and sometimes put their parents briefly in the stocks. Boys would don priestly robes and hold irreverent mock Masses in church. In today's British armed forces, officers still serve Christmas dinner to enlisted men. We see a faint echo of the tradition when U.S. presidents share Christmas or Thanksgiving dinner in the field with American soldiers overseas.

Agrarian symbolism also played a major role in the evolution of Christmas. Late December was a time when herding peoples would slaughter livestock for which there was not enough provender to last the winter. In southern climes, it was the time when the year's last harvest would be in and stored. Many eating and drinking traditions we associate with Christmas began in connection with agrarian feasts that resembled Thanksgiving more closely than Christmas. The lavish Christmas dinner has come through the centuries more or less intact, though its menu has changed. Hardly anyone eats boar's head anymore. Christmas drinking traditions have changed more sharply. Yet though the wassailing tradition has faded, heavy drinking remains inseparable from the holiday for better or worse.

Chapter four will focus on the elements that Christmas has in common with Thanksgiving, New Year's, and also with the mock-sinister feast of Halloween.

Gift giving is an inescapable part of Christmas. Christian legend assumes that the tradition began when the Magi presented gifts to the baby Jesus. Unfortunately for Christianity, to believe that you have to pitch centuries of history out behind the manger. Long before New Testament times, the Romans were exchanging gifts. Roman gift giving had political connotations. The previously-mentioned *strenae* were evergreen branches or sometimes fruits given by subjects to their rulers.[11] In time the tradition of cultivating those in power became more explicit. When the powerful realized that they could not only have their opponents fed to the lions but hold out for better New Year's presents too, tree branches and fruit fell out of favor. It became fashionable (or prudent) to brown-nose one's leaders with urns, jewelry, and similar art objects. In time, all pretense was abandoned and Roman authority figures came to expect simple, open gifts of gold or currency.[12]

All of this simply reflected a larger tradition of presenting gifts when meeting one whose authority or prestige exceeded one's own. The Magi are shown presenting gifts to the baby Jesus not because they wanted to launch Christmas, but because that was how any educated person would approach a king. When the head of state of some Third World country— or the mayor of a small American town—visits the White House, the visitor brings the president a gift. Why? What can lesser leaders possibly have that the president of the United States really needs? Cynical political humor to the contrary, it is not a payoff: "Okay, General, that's one porcelain horse for a billion dollars in foreign aid. Thanks for the cavalry sword, Governor, we'll break ground for the supercomputer factory in your state tomorrow." No, this curious custom preserves a tradition of tribute that has come down to us almost unchanged from the days of the Caesars.

Another Roman tradition called for presenting money to tradespeople and artisans at holiday time. It would not do for patricians just to drop coins into recipients' calloused hands, so the custom grew up of nestling the money in little clay boxes. It traveled with the Roman legions to England, where it has continued to the present. Since Christmas day itself was re-served for family and close friends and the shops might be closed, it be-came traditional to remember tradespeople on the day after Christmas. The little boxes are no longer made of clay, but they are still used, which is why British Commonwealth countries mark December 26 as Boxing Day. (Contrary to much British and Canadian humor, the day was not so named because people spend it boxing up ugly gifts to return to the stores.) Boxing Day has no exact analogue in the United States, but we see faint echoes in the American tradition of giving small gifts to letter carriers, newspaper carriers, babysitters, and others who do recurrent ser-vice work.[13]

The largest single trove of pre-Christian elements that shaped con-temporary Christmas is the ancient world's rich stock of *astrological sym-bols*. We have already touched on the importance of the winter solstice to the development of the holiday in the ancient world. As the daylight dwindled and the land grew barren, those who studied the heavens began to fear that the days might never stop getting shorter. Even though summer had returned in prior years, might *this* be the year when the pendulum never swings back, when the cold and darkness never end and all life dies off in shivering despair? When one sees the universe as the plaything of the gods, not as a place of more or less orderly natural processes governed by physical laws, such fears are understandable.

The Romans called their solstice festival the *Saturnalia*. Saturnalia was a time of ecstatic revelry, celebration, eating, and drinking. It was at once a solstice observance and a harvest festival. It was named for Saturn, the Roman god of agriculture, whose name was derived from the Latin verb *sero,* "I sow."[14]

From the Romans also came another Christmas fundamental: the date, December 25. When the Julian calendar was proclaimed in 46 C.E., it set into law a practice that was already common: dating the winter solstice as December 25. Later reforms of the calendar would cause the astronomical solstice to migrate to December 21, but the older date's irresistible resonance would remain.

The final and conclusive pagan legacy is the simplest of all: the idea of Christmas as a *birthday celebration* in the first place. To the early Christians the idea of celebrating the birthday of a religious figure would have seemed at best peculiar, at worst blasphemous. Being born into this world was nothing to celebrate. What mattered was leaving this world and entering the next in a condition pleasing to God. Further reducing the relative importance of one's sojourn in this world was the conviction of the early Christians that the apocalypse was close at hand. They took literally the promise of Matthew 24:34 that "this generation shall not pass away before all those things [the Apocalypse] take place."

When early Christians associated a feast day with a specific person, such as a bishop or martyr, it was usually the date of the person's death. Even St. Nicholas was remembered with a feast day anchored to the date of his death, traditionally December 6. No, if you wanted to search the New Testament world for peoples who attached significance to birthdays, your search would quickly narrow to pagans. The Romans celebrated the birthdays of the Caesars, and most non-Christian Mediterranean religions attached importance to the natal feasts of a pantheon of supernatural figures.

If Jesus Christ was born in Bethlehem, and his purpose in coming was anything like what is supposed, then in celebrating his birthday each year Christians do violence, not honor, to his memory. For in celebrating a birthday at all, we sustain exactly the kind of tradition his coming is thought to have been designed to cast down.

In reviewing the age before Christmas we have seen only a fraction of the pre-Christian influences that helped to shape contemporary Christmas. Other ancient legacies helped to give form to *all four* of the holidays Americans observe during the fourth quarter of the year. Still other bequests from the pre-Christian past cast disturbing new light on the idea at the very heart of Christmas: the idea of Jesus Christ as the son of God who took physical form, who walked among us at a particular time and place and would be said to die and rise again for the remission of the sins of humankind. It is to these matters that we turn next.

Notes

1. Earl W. Count, *Four Thousand Years of Christmas* (New York: Henry Schuman, 1948), p. 64.

2. Patricia Bunning Stevens, *Merry Christmas!: A History of the Holiday* (New York: Macmillan, 1979), p. 49.

3. Maymie Richardson Krythe, *All About Christmas* (New York: Harper and Brothers, 1954), p. 77.

4. Stevens, p. 49.

5. Gary Soulsman, "Christmas Tree Has Its Roots in History," *Newark* (N.J.) *Courier-News,* December 24, 1992.

6. *The New Catholic Encyclopedia* (New York: McGraw-Hill, 1967), p. 659.

7. Count, pp. 73–74.

8. *The New Catholic Encyclopedia,* p. 659.

9. Stevens, pp. 26–28.

10. Ibid.

11. Tristram Potter Coffin, *The Book of Christmas Folklore* (New York: Seabury Press, 1973), p. 37.

12. Stevens, p. 32.

13. Ibid., p. 58.

14. Alexander Murray, "Medieval Christmas," *History Today* (December 1986): 32.

4

Trick or Tree

In popular conception, Christmas is the holiday that celebrates the birth of Jesus Christ. Everybody knows its traditions come in varied forms. Nonetheless, most Americans believe that all Christmas customs relate in some essential way to a unique historical event that occurred in Bethlehem around two thousand years ago.

The sacredness believed to dwell at the heart of Christmas makes the wholesale appropriation of older traditions acceptable. It justifies lending borrowed customs new dignity, if at the price of permanently distorting their meaning. In time, it binds elements that once had quite different associations into the holiday's antiseptic symbolism. It is a strange "halo effect" that lets Christians see the purity and beneficence of their baby Jesus shining through the face of a TV special's badly animated Rudolph the Red-Nosed Reindeer. But millions of Christians manage it, Christmas after Christmas.

But what if many of our dearest holiday traditions are neither unique cultural responses to the Christmas story, *nor* pre-Christian rituals "rescued" from paganism? What if they are practices originally associated with other holidays within the Christian tradition?

Our major year-end holidays—Halloween, Thanksgiving, Christmas, and New Year's—share common roots. Consider Halloween. Aside from April 15, when taxes are due, it is the one day on which it is socially acceptable to obsess about evil and death. Today its morbid horrors are blunted with humor for the young, but there was a time when they were accepted in their original, unsanitized versions. Parents as well as children believed traditional tales of ghosts, goblins, and demanding spirits. In the centuries before All Hallows' Eve was invented, such macabre beliefs were associated squarely with another holiday: They were part of Yuletide.

If some of our most ancient traditions came to us from the pagan societies of southern Europe, some of the most visceral holiday imagery came to us from the north. Myths, symbols, and traditions bequeathed to us by ancient Nordic and Germanic peoples formed the fertile soil from which elements central to all our fourth-quarter holidays have sprung.

The pagan Germanics began their year not with the winter solstice, but in October or November, with the first breath of winter weather. They marked the start of the new year with an extravagant agrarian feast. The idea of a festival dedicated to excessive eating and drinking probably arose independent of the similar festivals that southern pagans celebrated in December.

How did this festival begin? Authorities differ. Presumably it had to do with the need to eliminate excess animals that could not be maintained through the winter. Forced slaughter would create a short-term surplus of meat just when alcoholic beverages fermented from the summer's fruit or grain crops would first be ready to drink. It would also coincide with the time when the crushing round of farm chores would be at its lightest. Time, energy, and enthusiasm would be available for roisterous celebration.[1]

When human beings understand little about the workings of their world, myth-making comes naturally. It is easy, and somehow reassuring, to imagine that the vast forces of thunder, rain, snow, and life itself are under someone's control. So much the better if the "someone" or "some-ones" are powerful cosmic personages. Better still if they have personalities and emotional responses not unlike our own. Primitive peoples could make such imaginative leaps at the drop of a hat. We moderns are scarcely superior.[2] Having gone that far, it was only expedient for our ancestors to fancy that their existing harvest festival might do double duty by propitiating the powers of the universe.

Pagan agrarian festivals are so ancient that no one knows their origins. On the other hand, we know exactly where and when Christians observed their first harvest holiday. In 601 C.E., Pope Gregory I despaired of persuading England's Anglo-Saxons to give up their centuries-old tradition of sacrificing oxen in late autumn, so he proclaimed the first Thanksgiving. That way, if the Anglo-Saxons insisted on sacrificing their cattle, they would at least be observing a Christian rite instead of worshipping demons. "From obdurate minds it is undoubtedly impossible to cut off everything at once," Gregory dourly observed.[3]

But we get ahead of our narrative. In ancient northern Europe, it was easier to ascribe dark natures to one's deities than in the balmy south. The early Germanics called their chief deity Yolnir. In time he lent his name to their new year's festival. In Old Norse it was called *Jol;* in Old English, *Geol.* The name is familiar to us as *Yule.*[4] Yule was a twelve-night festival. Likely it began as strictly a new year's festival, only later to become associated with the winter solstice.

Over the centuries, Yolnir was renamed Woden, later Odin. The old Germanics viewed him as the "all-Father," one of the creators of the world. They also credited him with the invention of their runic alphabet. Legend confided that Woden once hanged himself on a tree, pierced by a spear. He hung there suffering for nine nights. At the final moment, he took a drink of mead and cried out the runes of the Norse alphabet.[5] The story of Woden's nine days on the tree sometimes disturbs Christians. It parallels the Gospel narratives of Jesus' nine hours on the cross, complete with a spear wound, a bitter drink, and a final declaration, in ways that raise uncomfortable questions. (We will examine more ancient gods and heroes whose legends resemble the traditional story of Jesus in chapter five.)

Thanks to Norse myth and Wagner's operas, we think of Woden as a one-eyed old adventurer who welcomed to his celestial drinking hall the spirits of all brave warriors who had fallen in battle. The old Germanics gave him a darker side, conceiving him as a cosmic outlaw who rode the storms on a great white stallion. The traditional German *Schimmelreiter,* Rider of the White Horse, and *Schlapphut,* Flapping Hat, are sky-rider figures who grew out of this concept of Woden. It was a powerful image, and centuries later it would be echoed again in the popular picture of St. Nicholas. Long before Nicholas was imagined riding in a sleigh, children pictured him riding a white courser through the skies. There was another parallel to Woden: One of the earliest miracles ascribed to Nicholas involved the power to command storms. We will examine St. Nick more closely in chapter six.

Woden was not thought to ride alone. He was believed to lead the armed hordes of the heroic dead on unpredictable rampages. In time, northern pagans came to imagine Woden's troops less as the ghosts of warrior dead, and more as demons. *Wodenes her,* Woden's army, transformed into *Wütnendes heer,* an expression still common in Scandinavia that Earl Count has translated as "raging rout." Woden's hordes were not the only supernatural antagonists the Germanics thought they had to worry about. Spirits of the woods and the mountains were said to be more active during Yule. So were the shades of family dead. To the northern pagans at the time of the harvest festival the land fairly bristled with specters.[6]

There was a peculiar north-European preoccupation with the dark forces of the night during Yuletide . . . the special season was supposed to liberate ghosts and demons from their normal restrictions.[7]

It became traditional to set out food offerings for whatever might come bumping by in the night. Ancient Germanic and Celtic traditions spoke of a goddess who visited each household on the eve of the new year. Wise householders set out a meal for her. A similar tradition was reported in Scandinavia, and in England by no lesser figure than the Venerable Bede (673–735).[8] Woden was often conceived with a hag—variously named Holda, Perchta, Berchtel, or Berchta—riding the storms at his side.[9]

In time, the interval when evil spirits roamed free came to be associated more strongly with Halloween than Christmas. Halloween was originally known as All Hallows' Eve. It was the night before the religious observance of All Hallows' Day—now All Saints' Day (November 1)—which honored those who had died in a state of grace. Halloween, of course, acknowledged those for whom grace was not an option. Today this is echoed benignly by countless costumed children. In place of the propitiatory meal once left for the goddess stands the candy given to trick-or-treaters.[10]

Door-to-door begging *as a Christmas custom* faded away only recently. It survived for centuries in the English wassailing tradition. Revelers weaved from house to house. At each door they demanded a gift of fruit or strong drink:

> Wisselton, wasselton, who lives here?
> We've come to taste your Christmas beer.
> Up the kitchen and down the hall,
> Holly, ivy, and mistletoe;
> A peck of apples will serve us all,
> Give us some apples and let us go.
>
> Up with your stocking, on with your shoe,
> If you haven't any apples, money will do.
> My carol's done, and I must be gone,
> No longer can I stay here.
> God bless you all, great and small,
> And send you a happy new year.[11]

Even today, Christmas hangs onto some of its old Gothic imagery. Santa Claus courses mystically over the world much as Woden did. He leaves treats of presents or a trick of coal, and is traditionally "propitiated" with milk and cookies. On a very deep level, then, they are one: the pint-sized demon at your door Halloween night who (formally, at least) exchanges his or her forbearance from soaping your windows for a handful of candy, and the jolly old elf who is imagined to slither down the chimney and exchange a hurried snack for stockingsful of joy—or judgment.

Scandinavia has a tradition of *Julebuk,* a frightening figure said to be Woden. Julebuk visited households at holiday time wearing a fearsome horned mask. Despite his devilish appearance, he would distribute gifts to the children.[12] As for Berchta, she didn't just play Sancho Panza to Woden's Don Quixote at the head of the "raging rout." She became a precursor both of St. Nicholas/Santa Claus and of the witches of Halloween. During the twelve nights of Yule she was said to visit each house in the community, driving a wagon or riding a pale horse, accompanied by sprites and elves. Her visit was awaited with a mixture of joy and fear, for Berchta would judge hearth and home, blessing households she approved of and cursing those that displeased her. To influence her decision, a meal of fish and dumplings would be left out. There would also be a serving of oats for her horse.

In later years, after northern peoples had accepted a Roman-style calendar whose year began in January, Berchta's traditional arrival shifted to December 6, later celebrated as the feast of St. Nicholas. The newer tradition demanded that all of the household's work be completed before Berchta came. The wagon and plow were hidden. Spinning ceased and the distaff was emptied of yarn. All family members had to be abed and asleep before midnight, a demand still imposed on American children in preparation for Santa Claus. As in olden times, Berchta's judgment would determine the family's fortunes in the year ahead.

Still later, the Berchta tradition moved south, giving rise to the Italian Christmas myth of Befana. The name is a corruption of the vernacular name for the Epiphany. Befana was said to leave gifts for good children and "tricks," including coal, for those who misbehaved. But if children had been very bad, the story went, she might carry them away to the underworld.[13] Again, intimations of horror cling to the figure of the Christmas visitor who leaves the children's gifts.

Another old European tradition held that Christmas eve was a bad night to be outdoors. Among the evil spirits roaming free were said to be the shades of the family dead. These were believed to return to their old homes on Christmas eve. If no tasty snack hd been left for them, they would put a curse on their living descendants.[14] This is one of the least appealing variations of the Berchta legend: It has no upside! The dead give no gifts. They leave no blessing. The best one can hope for is to persuade them not to lay a curse.

In scattered communities across Europe and England, boys would dress up in a frightening costume crowned by a simulated horse's head. The head could be an elaborate wood carving that was worn on the shoulders. The most ornate of them featured a lighted candle deep within the eyes. Wearing such paraphernalia, youngsters would shamble from house to house during the holiday season. At each door they would demand gifts. The horse had many names. The best known is "Old Hob," a familiar bringer of mischief in English folklore.[15] Another aspect of Old Hob shaped Halloween: the carved face lighted by a flickering candle is an effect American families recapture when they carve their Halloween jack-o-lanterns.

In medieval England, France, and Ireland, boys "hunted the wren" on the day after Christmas. This charming tradition was one that moderns might try to discourage among their housecats. The children would find a wren and kill it. Then they would impale the bird's carcass on a long stick and parade it from house to house. Of course, at each door they would beg for treats.[16] Merry Christmas.

Finally, consider old Candlemas. English Candlemas, traditionally February 2, marked the very last day of the holiday season. Indoor Christmas greens that had repelled evil spirits throughout the season now were to be taken down and burned. Failure to do so was believed to release evil spirits. Poet Robert Herrick looks at this tradition winkingly, writing of a time when the belief was already held only by the naive:

> Down with the Rosemary, and so
> Down with the Bays and Mistletoe.
> Down with the Holly, Ivie, all,
> Wherewith ye dressed the Christmas Hall.
> That so the superstitious find
> No one least Branch left there behind.
> For look how many leaves there be
> Neglected there (maids trust to me)
> So many *Goblins* shall ye see.[17]

If Nordic Yule began as a new year's celebration, Old Scotland maintained that spirit for centuries. Not until the twentieth century did Christmas finally replace New Year's as Scotland's favorite winter holiday. Not surprisingly, among the Scots New Year's, not Christmas, spawned the traditions most reminiscent of Halloween. Early in the afternoon on New Year's Eve, poor Scottish children went door-to-door in well-to-do neighborhoods. Swaddled in sheets, holding the excess fabric out before them like pockets, they cried out "Hogmanay," the vernacular word for one quarter of an oat cake. The wealthy would open their doors and deposit the requested treats in the children's improvised pockets. So ancient was this custom that the Scottish new year holiday itself came to be called Hogmanay. The tradition survived until the mid-nineteenth century. One of its characteristic rhymes has been preserved. The trick-or-treat flavor comes through clearly:

> Get up, goodwife, and shake your feathers,
> And dinna think that we are beggars;
> For we are bairns come out to play,
> Get up and gie's our hogmanay![18]

Though the harvest festival is ancient, our American Thanksgiving dates back only to 1621. Not surprisingly, its identity and customs remain tightly linked to those of Christmas. The menus of the traditional Thanksgiving and Christmas dinners are almost identical. So are the roles of the two meals as focal points for ingatherings of extended families. Today, Thanksgiving seems to be evolving backwards, moving closer to Christmas. It is almost less important as a holiday in its own right than as the "official" opening of the Christmas season. Nowhere is this process clearer than in the many Thanksgiving Day parades. Sponsored by department stores, the reigning institutions of commercialized Christmas, they invariably climax with the figure of Santa Claus enthroned atop the very last float.

Thanksgiving comes to us after a long series of imperfect reflections. In the beginning was the Yuletide feast, celebrated in October or November. As southern traditions that linked Christmas with the winter solstice began to merge with northern traditions that did not, the northern Yule feast seemed to fall too early in the year. Presumably a copy of the feast was attached to the growing Christmas custom. This not only moved the agrarian festival closer to the winter solstice, but also to a time more appropriate for harvest celebrations in the warmer climates of the south. The Pilgrims of Massachusetts Bay would duplicate the feast once more. They projected it back into November, nearer its original date. This would be a simple matter for people familiar with Christmas feasting. But the Pilgrims were Puritans who did not celebrate Christmas. Thanksgiving as they created it was an imperfect duplicate of a ritual meal whose customs they neither understood nor practiced. (We will look more closely at Puritanism in England and America in chapter seven.) To bring Thanksgiving and Christmas into their current relationship, one more reflection would be needed. It took place in the nineteenth century. At this time the menu of the American-style Thanksgiving was growing in popularity. It had begun to push aside traditional foods like goose, boar's head, sausage, mince pie, and plum pudding on the Christmas table. The turkey Ebenezer Scrooge sent to Bob Cratchit's house in Charles Dickens's *Christmas Carol* was a suitable Christmas entree. But in 1843, when the story was written, turkey was only one of several possible choices. *A Christmas Carol* had an enormous influence on the later development of the holiday. One of its legacies is that Scrooge's turkey—accompanied by the stuffing, potatoes, cranberry sauce, and other accouterments of the American Thanksgiving—is the star of most Christmas dinners today. (We will turn again to Dickens in chapter eight.)

Christmas did not give up all of its magical heritage to Halloween. It clung to the image of a mystical figure abroad in the skies on a magical night. Also retained was the tradition that domestic tranquility and juvenile slumber were prerequisites for the enchanted visitor to arrive. As for the eighty-four million cookies that will be left out for Santa Claus this Christmas Eve, they are a gesture of hospitality rooted in the gifts of food left fearfully to propitiate the visiting dead.

Finally, New Year's came to absorb most Christmas traditions related to predicting one's fortune in the coming year. About the only such custom that remained attached to Christmas was that of the bayberry candle: "A bayberry candle burned to the socket / Brings joy to the house and wealth to the pocket." New Year's came to inherit yet another copy of the harvest festival, this time with an overwhelming emphasis on drinking.

Even now, our inventory of the pre-Christian antecedents of contemporary Christmas is far from complete. To Christians, the invariant center of their holiday is the figure of the Christ child. But is even the Jesus story as original—or as credible—as traditionalists assume? Or is the Nativity story itself the pre-Christian world's ultimate contribution to Christmas? To that prickly question we will turn next.

Notes

1. Earl W. Count, *Four Thousand Years of Christmas* (New York: Henry Schuman, 1948), p. 49.

2. For a thorough exploration of the idea that human nature predisposes men and women to imagine and develop religious ideas for the psychological comfort their supposed explanatory power brings, see Paul Kurtz, *The Transcendental Temptation* (Buffalo, N.Y.: Prometheus Books, 1986).

3. The Venerable Bede, *Ecclesiastical History* (I, c.20), cited in Alexander Murray, "Medieval Christmas," *History Today* (December 1986): 36.

4. Ibid., p. 32.

5. Count, p. 52.

6. Ibid., p. 53.

7. J. M. Golby and A. W. Purdue, *The Making of the Modern Christmas* (Athens, Ga.: University of Georgia Press, 1986. Originally published London: B. T. Batsford Ltd., 1986), p. 23.

8. Murray, pp. 34–35.

9. Berchta would later become the prototype for the sinister sidekick believed to accompany St. Nicholas. Named Klausauf, Knecht Ruprecht, or Black Pete,

this figure was responsible for switching bad children. The twigs carried for that purpose may echo the original Roman *strenae,* or they may have had a unique origin in Northern lore. The "sidekick" tradition never made a very solid transition to the New World, and is now almost gone in Europe as well.

10. The phrase "trick or treat" preserves in a whimsical form the veiled threat of what lies in store for those who fail to yield up the expected gift. In this connection, it is interesting to note that the last generation of American children who are likely to experience "traditional" trick-or-treating has already been born. Suburban sprawl and rising fears about criminals who prey on the young have inspired many communities to discourage door-to-door activities in favor of structured Halloween parties. Before too long, the trick-or-treat custom will require a historical explanation just as the "raging rout" does today.

11. Tristram Potter Coffin, *The Book of Christmas Folklore* (New York: Seabury Press, 1973), p. 33.

12. Golby and Purdue, p. 230.

13. Patricia Bunning Stevens, *Merry Christmas!: A History of the Holiday* (New York: Macmillan, 1979), p. 75.

14. Clement A. Miles, *Christmas in Ritual and Tradition, Christian and Pagan* (London: Fisher Unwin, 1912), pp. 181; 233–37.

15. Stevens, p. 45.

16. Ibid., p. 51.

17. Robert Herrick, "Ceremony Upon Candlemas Eve," quoted in Krythe, *All About Christmas* (New York: Harper and Brothers, 1954), p. 48.

18. Stevens, p. 119.

5

The Babe and the Bathwater

After World War II, American merchants accused of overcommercializing the holiday joined with community organizations and launched a great campaign to "Put Christ Back in Christmas." To those familiar with history, it is not a problem of putting Christ back in Christmas. The problem is establishing that he was ever there at all.

The familiar story of the birth of Jesus is anticipated in countless pre-Christian traditions. These legends present a vast crowd of redeemer man-gods. Every one of them was once believed to have come to earth under miraculous circumstances and become a savior. Understandably, the clergy are not eager to announce what they have learned from the study of ancient literature. But the shocking fact (to orthodox Christians, at any rate) is that scarcely a detail of the traditional Nativity story cannot be found in at least one pre-Christian legend.

Secular humanist propaganda? No, this is what is taught to most mainstream Protestant ministers. In the pews? That is another matter. Mainstream churchgoers might be shocked to learn how many of their basic religious beliefs their pastors do not share.

Today's pastors seldom preach what they know about Christian origins. Why such a gulf between what mainstream clergy know and what members of their congregations believe? Some pastors admit that speaking out would be bad for business. Others have so refined their views that they no longer think Christians ought to worry about whether the New Testament is true. In the late fifties, theologians like the German thinker Rudolf Bultmann embarked on an explosive effort to "demythologize" Christianity.[1] Bultmann strove to strip away the fantastic elements that had accumulated over two millennia in order to concentrate on the faith's historic core, whatever that was. Of course, Bultmann and his ilk did not peel away only the mythology of Christmas. They went after everything from the resurrection and the raising of Lazarus, to the feeding of the five thousand and the making of wine from water at Cana. They sought a lean, mean Christianity that would no longer be vulnerable to the criticism of rationalists.

In the sixties, theologians like Harvey Cox would seek to redefine Christianity from the ground up, taking as their *starting point* that "God is dead," that is, that traditional ideas about God were already too badly damaged to command belief.[2] Today's silver-haired ministers absorbed the thinking of Bultmann, Cox, and others in their seminary classes. To the degree they came away from this training still committed to a Christian ministry, they faced a dilemma. "We will spend our lives preaching the Scripture, yet we know we will never be able to demonstrate its truth," they might have worried. "What can we salvage of Christianity?" What they salvaged was often an abstracted ideal of Christ as teacher, calling men and women to lives of love, peace, justice, and goodwill, and little else. Biblical scholar R. Joseph Hoffmann captures the compromise made by this generation of Protestant clergy: "If the historical Jesus could not be known, at least the Christ of the church's preaching would survive."[3]

The average, say, Congregationalist or Presbyterian church member could probably engage his or her minister in a few minutes of private conversation and quickly induce the reverend to set forth the pre-Christian precursors of Christ in such a fashion that the poor churchgoer might think he or she was actually conversing with a secular humanist debunker!

What happened?

In the nineteenth century, scholars began to study the Bible in earnest as a work of literature. They chipped away at it with new tools of literary criticism and archaeological inquiry, and were sorely disillusioned by what they uncovered. Respected scholarly works arguing that Jesus never existed appeared frequently in the latter half of the nineteenth century and the first half of the twentieth. The claim that Jesus is wholly fictional is seldom heard today. But many—perhaps most—Christian New Testament scholars outside of the fundamentalist tradition think of Jesus primarily as a charismatic teacher. They no longer think that he performed miracles. In their eyes, he may never have thought of himself as the literal son of God. It is not necessary, they conclude, for Jesus to have done these things to explain how the *claims* that he did them could have become attached to the gospel narratives as Christianity grew. So numerous are the pre-Christian prototypes of Jesus that their legends might account completely for the more mystical aspects of the Jesus story.[4] In general, mainstream and liberal Christian scholars see eye-to-eye with their secular humanist counterparts on these issues.

Other authorities continue to argue that Jesus never lived. The most respected is British linguist G. A. Wells. Wells claims that when the books and letters of the New Testament are arranged in their true chronological order, one can literally watch mythical elements attach themselves one by one to the story of Jesus. The earliest documents are the handful of Epistles that most scholars agree Paul actually wrote. They say a lot about Christ, but surprisingly little about Jesus. It is, Wells suggests, as if Paul had not heard most of the Jesus stories familiar to modern Christians at the time he composed his epistles. The gospels were written decades later, and as everybody knows, they are devoted to narrative about Jesus. Matthew, Mark, and Luke, the "synoptic Gospels," try to provide an orderly account of the life of Jesus. Wells observes that when the synoptics are arranged in chronological order (Mark is oldest), stories told about Jesus clearly grow more fanciful with age. Accounts of the same event in two or three gospels are almost always simpler in Mark and more elaborate or unearthly in Luke or Matthew. Miracle stories, in particular, grow progressively more detailed and fantastic.[5] Wells's argument is not widely accepted, even among secular humanist Bible scholars. But one cannot observe how easily Wells finds support *in the New Testament* for his theory that Jesus never existed without realizing that the Bible is a far more ambiguous document than conservative Christians would have us believe.

At this stage in my argument you, the reader, may choose to accept or reject these claims based on your faith orientation. The point to remember is this: From secular humanists to mainstream Protestants, experts on the Bible and ancient mythology agree that putting Christ into Christmas took *work*. The hardest job might have been clearing space on an already cluttered conceptual workbench for yet one more god-man born of a virgin.

Pre-Christian God-Men

By the time people began to preach and write about the birth of Jesus, the god-man who came to earth was already an old idea. In what follows, we will review some of the best known forerunners of Jesus. None of them boasts *all* of the characteristics we ascribe to Jesus, but most of them have one, or two, or a handful of attributes that contemporary Western readers will recognize as precursors of the Christmas story.

Ancient Egyptians worshipped *Osiris,* a god-man associated with agriculture.[6] Osiris was the product of an affair between Geb, the earth god, and Nut, a sky goddess who was the wife of the sun-god Ra. Learning that Nut was pregnant by Geb, Ra decreed that she should give birth in no month and no year. Nut seemed doomed to gestate eternally, an unwelcome prospect even for a goddess. One of her other lovers, the god Thoth, won a bet with the moon. Thoth demanded one seventy-second part of every day. After a year he had accumulated five new days. This part of the legend was a "just so story" designed to explain the origin of *Sothis,* the five-day holiday season added to the end of the 360-day Egyptian calendar in order to conform solar and lunar time-keeping. Conveniently for Nut, the *Sothis* season belonged to no month and no year. Now she could give birth without violating Ra's curse, and not a moment too soon. On the first day of *Sothis,* Nut gave birth to Osiris. On the second she gave birth to Horus the elder, on the third to Set, on the fourth to Isis, and on the fifth to Nephthys. Even at the time of the ancient Egyptians, the year-end holiday was a birthday season for gods.

Osiris married his sister Isis, and the two reigned as king and queen over the Egyptians, who were then primitive cannibals. The two taught their subjects to grow grains and fruits, and to make wine. Osiris roamed the earth teaching all peoples agriculture and viticulture. Back in Egypt, jealous brother Set and seventy-two others (a number related to the Egyptian zodiac) plotted to kill Osiris. Gerald Larue believes the details of the plot were fabricated by the Roman historian Plutarch and added to the story centuries after it was believed by ancient Egyptians.[7] In any event, Osiris was killed by treachery, sealed into a wooden coffin, and set adrift on the Nile. This part of the legend sounds like a rehearsal for the story of Moses, who as an infant was supposedly set adrift on the Nile in a basket made of reeds in order to escape an *attempt* on his life. Osiris's casket reached land and a tree grew up around it. A Syrian king chose the tree entombing Osiris to be fashioned into a pillar in his palace. Some authorities consider the man-god encased in a tree a distant precursor of the Yule log. By subterfuge Isis made her way into the king's court and transfused the essence of Osiris into the body of the Syrian king's young son, an early form of resurrection.

The Osiris myth shows us several fundamentals of the Christmas story. We see a divine hero born at year's end whose resurrection is associated with the renewal of growth in spring. This pattern would be preserved unbroken to the present: Christians celebrate the birth of Jesus near the end of the year. And they celebrate his resurrection at Easter, a spring holiday whose exact date is still determined by reference to the moon! Also in this myth we see the divine hero threatened by hostile plotters, a device that would resurface with the story of Herod and the flight into Egypt. For good measure, we encounter elements that would later shape the story of Moses and, perhaps, a distant ancestor of the Yule log.

Horus the younger, whose myth is intertwined with that of Osiris, embodies other characteristics of Jesus. While Isis was searching for the body of Osiris, the legend relates, she took refuge in a papyrus swamp. There she conceived and bore Horus the younger. The conception was unnatural. Authorities differ on whether she conceived asexually or through an act of necrophilia, but in any event the younger Horus was conceived by means other than conventional sexual intercourse—if not virgin birth, a long stride in that direction. Horus stayed with his mother until he was twelve years old. No mention is made of him until age thirty, when he was baptized and received into godhead. This is strikingly similar to the Jesus of the gospel of Luke. We see Jesus briefly at age twelve, when he is accidentally left behind at the temple. The narrative leaps ahead to show us Jesus at age thirty, being baptized by John the Baptist and entering into his public ministry.

The Phrygians worshipped *Attis*, a god who was born of a virgin named Nana.[8] Attis was hanged on a tree, and in death he achieved union with the goddess Cybele. In Phrygian myth Cybele and Nana served as alter egos for one another. Looking back, we might be reminded of the Osiris myth, in which Isis was both the sister of Osiris and his wife. Looking forward, we might think of the virgin Mary, who served as a mother to Jesus but later, in her role as the Queen of Heaven, became a platonic companion to God the Father.[9]

Four thousand years ago, the worship of *Adonis* was popular in Syria. Thirteen hundred years later the cult would make its way into Greece. Adonis was adapted from the Sumerian Dumuzi and the later Semitic/Phoenician Tammuz. Like them, he was believed to die each autumn and descend to the underworld. His mother Ishtar would descend to rescue him, bringing on the rigors of winter. Near the time of the spring equinox his death would be observed for three mournful days, followed by a resurrection that symbolized the revival of plant life.

Adonis acquired his name by mistake. The Semitic peoples among whom his cult originated called him "Adonai," which meant simply "God." The word appears without translation in contemporary Bibles. As Greeks adopted the worship of Adonis they mistook "Adonai" for the god's proper name.

The stories of Adonis and Jesus are startlingly similar. Though Ishtar was simultaneously mother and consort to Adonis, she was sometimes described as a virgin. Numerous religious artworks have survived that depict Ishtar holding Adonis as a child. They possess all the elements we now associate with traditional renderings of the Madonna and child. Jerome, an early Christian scholar, reported that one of the most important groves sacred to Adonis was located in Bethlehem, long before that village was identified as the birthplace of Jesus.[10] Well into the sixth century C.E.,

Christian art depicted Jesus as a muscular, clean-shaven, blond young man with a dimple in his chin—the very image of Adonis to this day.[11] The traditional bearded Christ with long brown hair seldom appeared until the sixth century.

The Greeks also related the tale of *Dionysos,* who was said as a baby to have mounted the throne of his father, Zeus, and behaved disrespectfully. In this we may see a precursor of the European "Lord of Misrule" tradition. Of course, in his capacity as the god of wine and celebration, Dionysos would embody many of the aspects of the harvest festival, the wassail bowl, and other aspects of Christmas that involve indulgence in food and drink.[12]

Greek legend also gave us *Perseus,* whose mother Danäe was a virgin impregnated by a shower of gold sent from Zeus.[13]

The cult of the sun god *Mithras* began in Persia more than six centuries B.C.E. and spread across Asia Minor. Mithraism took root throughout the Roman Empire. It was a mystery religion, like Christianity, but it was more popular than Christianity until about 400 C.E. In 274 C.E. the Roman emperor Aurelian proclaimed the birth feast of Mithras an official holiday, *Natalis Solis Invictus,* the "Birthday of the Unconquered Sun."[14] The date of that feast was December 25.

Believers differed as to how Mithras had been conceived. One popular tradition described his mother as a mortal virgin. Another claimed he was born when lightning (the sky god's male principle) struck a broad expanse of bare rock (the earth goddess's female principle). Mithras's followers agreed on most of the rest of his biography. Mithras was said to have been born in a cave. There, shepherds and traveling wise men paid homage to the infant god, arriving on a day later celebrated as Epiphany. As an adult, Mithras healed the sick, restored sight to the blind, made the lame walk, cast out devils, and raised the dead.

Sound familiar yet?

Because of Mithraic influence, Christianity moved its sabbath from the Jewish Saturday to *Sun-day.* So freely did the early Christians borrow from Mithraism that the third-century church father Tertullian complained: "Oh, how much more faithful are the heathen to their religion, who take care to adopt no solemnity from the Christians."[15]

Another third-century patriarch, Origen, condemned the very idea of celebrating Christ's birthday. To him, it aped Mithraism and other pagan cults to observe the Nativity the same way one might celebrate the birth of a "boy Pharaoh."[16]

Non-Christians delighted in ridiculing Christianity for its debts to Mithraism. Early Christians were so badly stung by this that they claimed Satan had invented Mithraism a few centuries before the coming of Jesus for the sole purpose of confounding the future Christian church![17]

If Mithraism gave early Christians the jitters, the Hindu story of *Krishna* would have made them apoplectic had they known about it. Here was a tale of a savior god-man that anticipated almost every detail of the Christian story, yet it arose thousands of miles to the east, in a country that had little or no contact with the Bible lands! Perhaps the broad outlines of the myth harken back to Indo-Aryan days, when the peoples who would conquer the Indian subcontinent had not yet diverged from those who would populate northern Europe.

Krishna, the second person of the Hindu trinity, implanted himself in the womb of Devaki, a human virgin. While pregnant with Krishna, Devaki was visited by an angel who announced that she would be the mother of a great and godly personage. Krishna was born while Devaki and her husband were journeying to a foreign city to pay a tax. Born in a cave, Krishna was visited by traveling wise men who offered valuable presents. They had been attracted to the cave by the star that heralded his birth. Disturbed by the star, a hostile king ordered the slaughter of all male babies within his kingdom. An angel appeared to Devaki and her husband, warning them to flee with their baby to a faraway country where they could be safe. Krishna grew to adulthood. After a period spent teaching and performing miracles, he was crucified. Dying, he was wounded with an arrow. At the moment of his death, darkness fell over the earth.[18]

Parallels to the Jesus of the gospels and Christian tradition are obvious, but there's more. Early Christianity accepted as divine a number of "holy books" that were rejected for various reasons after the sixth century C.E. As a group, these purged books are known as the *Apocrypha*. The name gave rise to *apocryphal,* in popular speech a word for claims that seem credible but are almost surely untrue.

One Apocryphal gospel reports that Jesus spoke full sentences aloud while still an infant. Hindu scriptures say the same about the infant Krishna. Others added details about the birth and early life of Jesus that strengthened the parallels between Jesus and Adonis. Some Apocryphal stories verged on the ludicrous. In *The Infancy Gospel of Thomas* there is a scene worthy of Monty Python. Slighted by another youth on a village road, young Jesus strikes him dead in front of numerous witnesses. The witnesses rush to Joseph, who has heard it all before: the willful young Son of God was always damming up rivers, withering people's limbs, and slaying playmates in their tracks. Joseph punished Jesus for killing the village boy, so Jesus blinded the villagers who had turned him in. Now Joseph was mad. He "arose and took him [Jesus] upon his ear and wrung it sore."[19] This story has nothing to do with Christmas, of course. But it shows how easily absurd details could bond, even to what was supposed to be the most sacred of all narratives.

One final ancient custom stretched this whole business of virgin births and stars in the East to the breaking point. To add stature to the lives of great rulers, military leaders, philosophers, and other very mortal figures, sympathetic writers often embellished their biographies with miracle stories. Virgin births were claimed for the Caesars, for Plato, Socrates, and Aristotle, and for the mathematician Pythagoras. Many were said to have died under sacrificial circumstances and then to have risen again.

In the ancient world there was nothing unusual about having it said that you were born of a virgin, that you were worshipped by kings in your crib, or that you healed the sick, walked on water, and rose from the dead. It was harder to attract notoriety *without* having fantastic claims attached to your memory. Whatever else we might ask of a genuine son of God, actually having existed in the manner his biography describes belongs high on the list. We might next ask that the biography be *unique*. A real messiah ought to have a few miracles on his résumé that never occurred to the hack biographers of emperors. The Jesus of traditional Christmas narratives fails on both counts. If Jesus lived as an ordinary mortal—if his character was just remarkable enough to trigger the myth-making machinery of his time—the claims we hear about Jesus are just what we might expect to hear.

Contradictions in the Bible Account

Damning as it appears, the pre-Christian record is only part of the reason for taking the traditional story of Jesus with a grain of salt. Lay non-Christian sources aside and focus solely on the Christmas narrative presented in the New Testament.

What do the evangelists say about the birth of Jesus? As a group, nothing. The oldest gospel, Mark, opens when Jesus is already an adult. The strangest gospel, John, opens with Christ as an ideal and disembodied presence floating high above the earth. Only Matthew and Luke have anything to say about the Nativity. Two out of four isn't even a quorum and, more often than not, the stories told by Matthew and Luke disagree.

What most of us know as "the story of Christmas" is a masterwork of cherry-picking. This treasured quote from Matthew is spliced to that favorite moment from Luke, creating a narrative that delivers all the expected plot points and sweeps the contradictions under the rug.

Let's do something even devout Christians too seldom do. Let's read the Christmas sections of Matthew and Luke all the way through, one after the other. Let Exhibits A and B speak for themselves.

The gospel according to Matthew 1 and 2 (RSV) reads:

The book of the genealogy of Jesus Christ, the son of David, the son of Abraham. Abraham was the father of Isaac, and Isaac the father of Jacob, and Jacob the father of Judah and his brothers, and Judah the father of Perez and Zerah by Tamar, and Perez the father of Hezron, and Hezron the father of Ram, and Ram the father of Ammin'adab, and Ammin'adab the father of Nahshon, and Nahshon the father of Salmon, and Salmon the father of Bo'az by Rahab, and Bo'az the father of Obed by Ruth, and Obed the father of Jesse, and Jesse the father of David the king.

And David was the father of Solomon by the wife of Uriah, and Solomon the father of Rehobo'am, and Rehobo'am the father of Abi'jah, and Abi'jah the father of Asa, and Asa the father of Jehosh'aphat, and Jehosh'aphat the father of Joram, and Joram the father of Uzzi'ah, and Uzzi'ah the father of Jotham, and Jotham the father of Ahaz, and Ahaz the father of Hezeki'ah, and Hezeki'ah the father of Manes'seh, and Manes'seh the father of Amos, and Amos the father of Josi'ah, and Josi'ah the father of Jechoni'ah and his brothers, at the time of the deportation to Babylon.

And after the deportation to Babylon: Jeconi'ah was the father of Sheal'tiel, and Sheal'tiel the father of Zerub'babel, and Zerub'babel the father of Abi'ud, and Abi'ud the father of Eli'akim, and Eli'akim the father of Azor, and Azor the father of Zadok, and Zadok the father of Achim, and Achim the father of Eli'ud, and Eli'ud the father of Elea'zar, and Elea'zar the father of Matthan, and Matthan the father of Jacob, and Jacob the father of Joseph the husband of Mary, of whom Jesus was born, who is called Christ.

So all the generations from Abraham to David were fourteen generations, and from David to the deportation to Babylon fourteen generations, and from the deportation to Babylon to the Christ fourteen generations.

Now the birth of Jesus Christ took place in this way. When his mother Mary had been betrothed to Joseph, before they came together she was found to be with child of the Holy Spirit; and her husband Joseph, being a just man and unwilling to put her to shame, resolved to divorce her quietly. But as he considered this, behold, an angel of the Lord appeared to him in a dream, saying, "Joseph, son of David, do not fear to take Mary your wife, for that which is conceived in her is of the Holy Spirit; she will bear a son, and you shall call his name Jesus, for he will save the people from their sins." All this took place to fulfill what the Lord had spoken by the prophet:

> Behold, a virgin shall conceive and bear
> a son,
> and his name shall be called Emman'uel
> (which means, God with us).

When Joseph awoke from sleep, he did as the angel of the Lord had commanded him; he took his wife, but knew her not until she had borne a son; and he called his name Jesus.

Now when Jesus was born in Bethelehem of Judea in the days of Herod the king, behold, wise men from the East came to Jerusalem, saying, "Where is he who has been born king of the Jews? For we have seen his star in the East, and have come to worship him." When Herod the king heard this, he was troubled, and all Jerusalem with him; and assembling all the chief priests and scribes of the people, he inquired of them where the Christ was to be born. They told him, "In Bethlehem of Judea; for so it is written by the prophet:

> And you, O Bethlehem, in the land of
> Judah,
> are by no means least among the rulers of
> Judah;
> for from you shall come a ruler
> who will govern my people Israel."

Then Herod summoned the wise men secretly and ascertained from them what time the star appeared; and he sent them to Bethlehem, saying, "Go and search diligently for the child, and when you have found him bring me word, that I too may come and worship him." When they had heard the king they went their way; and lo, the star which they had seen in the East went before them, till it came to rest over the place where the child was. When they saw the star, they rejoiced exceedingly with great joy; and going into the house they saw the child with Mary his mother, and they fell down and worshiped him. Then, opening their treasures, they offered him gifts, gold and frankincense and myrrh. And being warned in a dream not to return to Herod, they departed to their own country by another way.

Now when they had departed, behold, an angel of the Lord appeared to Joseph in a dream and said, "Rise, take the child and his mother, and flee to Egypt, and remain there till I tell you; for Herod is about to search for the child, to destroy him." And he rose and took the child and his mother by night, and departed to Egypt, and remained there until the death of Herod. This was to fulfill what the Lord has spoken by the prophet, "Out of Egypt I have called my son."

Then Herod, when he saw that he had been tricked by the wise men, was in a furious rage, and he smote and killed all the male children in Bethlehem and in all that region who were two years old or under, according to the time which he had ascertained from the wise men. Then was fulfilled what was spoken by the prophet Jeremiah:

> A voice was heard in Ramah,
> wailing and loud lamentation,
> Rachel weeping for her children;
> she refused to be consoled,
> because they were no more.

But when Herod died, behold, an angel of the Lord appeared in a dream to Joseph in Egypt, saying, "Rise, take the child and his mother, and go to the land of Israel, for those who sought the child's life are dead." And he rose and took the child and his mother, and went to the land of Israel. But when he heard that Archela'us reigned over Judea in place of his father Herod, he was afraid to go there, and being warned in a dream he withdrew to the district of Galilee. And he went and dwelt in a city called Nazareth, that what was spoken by the prophets might be fulfilled, "He shall be called a Nazarene."

Luke 2:1–20, 3:23–38 (RSV) reads:

In those days a decree went out from Caesar Augustus that all the world should be enrolled. This was the first enrollment, when Quirinius was governor of Syria. And all went to be enrolled, each to his own city. And Joseph also went up from Galilee, from the city of Nazareth, to Judea, to the city of David, which is called Bethlehem, because he was of the house and lineage of David, to be enrolled with Mary his betrothed, who was with child. And while they were there, the time came for her to be delivered. And she gave birth to her first-born son and wrapped him in swaddling cloths, and laid him in a manger, because there was no place for them in the inn.

And in that region there were shepherds out in the field, keeping watch over their flock by night. And an angel of the Lord appeared to them, and the glory of the Lord shone around them, and they were filled with fear. And the angel said to them, "Be not afraid; for behold, I bring you good news of a great joy which will come to all the people; for to you is born this day in the city of David a Savior, who is Christ the Lord. And this will be a sign for you: you will find a babe wrapped in swaddling cloths and lying in a manger." And suddenly there was with the angel a multitude of the heavenly host praising God and saying, "Glory to God in the highest, and on earth peace among men with whom he is pleased!"

When the angels went away from them into heaven, the shepherds said to one another, "Let us go over to Bethlehem and see this thing that has happened, which the Lord has made known to us." And they went with haste, and found Mary and Joseph, and the babe lying in a manger. And when they saw it they made known the saying which had been told them concerning this child; and all who heard it wondered at what the shepherds told them. But Mary kept all of these things, pondering them in her heart. And the shepherds returned, glorifying and praising God for all they had heard and seen, as it had been told them. . . .

. . . Jesus, when he began his ministry, was about thirty years of age, being the son (as was supposed) of Joseph, the son of Heli, the son of Matthat, the son of Levi, the son of Melchi, the son of Jan'nai, the son of Joseph, the son of Mattathi'as, the son of Amos, the son of Nahum, the son of Esli, the son of Nag'gai, the son of Ma'ath, the son of Mattathi'as, the son of Sem'ein, the son of Josesch, the son of Joda, the son of Joan'an, the son of Rhesa, the son of Zerub'babel, the son of Sheal'tiel, the son of Neri, the son of Melchi, the son of Addi, the son of Cosam, the son of Elma'dam, the son of Er, the son of Joshua, the son of Elie'zer, the son of Jorim, the son of Matthat, the son of Levi, the son of Simeon, the son of Judah, the son of Joseph, the son of Jonam, the son of Eli'akim, the son of Me'lea, the son of Menna, the son of Mat'tatha, the son of Nathan, the son of David, the son of Jesse, the son of Obed, the son of Bo'az, the son of Sala, the son of Nahshon, the son of Ammin'adab, the son of Admin, the son of Arni, the son of Hezron, the son of Perez, the son of Judah, the son of Jacob, the son of Isaac, the son of Abraham, the son of Terah, the son of Nahor, the son of Peleg, the son of Eber, the son of Shelah, the son of Cai'nan, the son of Arpha'xad, the son of Shem, the son of Noah, the son of Lamech, the son of Methuselah, the son of Enoch, the son of Jared, the son of Maha'laleel, the son of Cai'nan, the son of Enos, the son of Seth, the son of Adam, the son of God.

Matthew 1:18–25 and 2 and Luke 2:1–20 disagree on almost every detail. The popular image of the baby Jesus worshipped by wise men *and* shepherds is nonbiblical. Matthew says wise men, Luke says shepherds. Neither says both. The star in the East? Only in Matthew. The heavenly host in the sky? Only in Luke. The slaughter of the innocents? Only in Matthew. The manger? Only in Luke. Matthew says Joseph and Mary were residents of Bethlehem; they moved to Nazareth only after the flight into Egypt, to avoid the possibility of persecution by Herod's son who still reigned over Judea, where Bethlehem was located. Luke says Joseph and Mary were residents of Nazareth all along. The only reason Jesus was born in Bethlehem was that Joseph had to travel there to enroll in the census.

Matthew's narrative strongly echoes the myth of the birth of Krishna. As for Luke, from its story of the virgin birth, to its brief anecdote about Jesus at age twelve, to its unexplained silence until it resumes the story with Jesus as a man of thirty, it follows the ancient tale of Horus the younger much too closely for comfort. Matthew and Luke are also remarkable for the things they leave unsaid. Even believing Christians are sometimes startled to learn how many familiar details of Christmas lore are missing from the gospel Nativity stories. Matthew's wise men are unnamed; their traditional names of Gaspar, Melchior, and Balthasar first appear in a sixth-century Armenian narrative.[20]

Count on your fingers while comparing the two gospels' genealogies of Jesus (Matt. 1:1–17, Luke 3:23–38) and you'll get a real surprise.[21] Matthew lists all the generations between Abraham and Jesus. Luke can top that; his account goes right back to Adam. Between Jesus and David, Matthew lists twenty-eight generations. Never one to accept the doctrine that "Less is more," Luke lists *forty-one* generations between Jesus and

David. Matthew traces the descent of Jesus through the Old Testament kings, as one might expect, and most of the names appear in the Old Testament. The logic behind Luke's path of descent is more obscure, and many of the names he mentions appear nowhere else in the Old or New Testaments. Some are repeated; the genealogy in Luke contains two Matthats, two Cain'ans, and two Josephs in addition to Joseph the husband of Mary. Even for generations whose existence both Matthew and Luke acknowledge, the names seldom match. Matthew and Luke cannot agree on the names of Joseph's father and grandfather. In fact, they give different names for every ancestor between Joseph and Zerub'babel, a Jewish leader who lived around 500 B.C.E. That's right, over the *five-hundred-year span* immediately preceding the birth of Jesus, Matthew and Luke, whom some Christians consider divinely inspired, cannot agree on the name of a single one of Joseph's ancestors!

These disparities are so obvious that they attracted comment long before nineteenth-century biblical criticism. Christian writers twisted logic like pretzels to claim that one evangelist traced Jesus' lineage through Joseph, the other through Mary, clearly contradicting each text's plain statement that it was tracing through Joseph.

Why were the genealogies necessary? Matthew and Luke were both concerned to present Jesus as the Messiah expected by the Jews. According to Jewish tradition, the Messiah was to be of the lineage of David. Though they went about it differently, each evangelist took great pains to establish that Joseph was descended from the house of David. And here we confront the ultimate contradiction of the biblical Christmas story. According to the doctrine of the Virgin Birth, Jesus was the son of God and Mary. Tracing Joseph's lineage back to David is futile. What difference can Joseph's genealogy make? Joseph is not the father!

Here two contradictory ideas about Jesus intersect. Actually, they collide like an eastbound freight train and a southbound propane truck. Either Jesus is the Jewish Messiah, and therefore descended from David through his paternal lineage, or Jesus is the son of a virgin, conceived by the Holy Spirit. The conflict recalls one of the central challenges that faced the early Christians. The baldfaced attempt to combine two contradictory traditions about Jesus' nature reflects the way that the Judaizing tradition and the Hellenizing tradition in early Christianity never really resolved their differences.

Early Christians thought of their religion as a new Jewish sect. They wanted to convert as many Jews as they could before the end of the world, which they expected soon. Gentiles were not part of the equation. Then the primitive church faced two great disappointments. First, few Jews converted. Second, the world failed to end. Some Christian missionaries began to approach non-Jews. The Pauline epistles record the soul-searching that brought on. Could Gentiles become Christians without submitting to Jewish law? On this question hinged the new religion's marketability. Gentiles hesitated to embrace Judaism's complex dietary codes. The requirement that adult male converts submit to circumcision was a real nonstarter! To attract Gentile converts, Christianity would have no choice but to relax its demand that new members first become Jews. In the same way, Christianity would have no choice but to Hellenize—to incorporate more of the qualities that Greek-influenced Gentiles looked for in a religion.

> [T]he doctrine of the Virgin Birth, without which no prophet or savior-god could be a divine incarnation, was so common among ancient cults that it was impossible for any religious founder to achieve acceptance without it. . . . [T]he Virgin Birth, interpolated early in the second century, was invented to make of Jesus a Christ whom the pagan world could accept.[22]

That the Messiah descended from Israelite royalty did not impress non-Jews. Accustomed to Mithraism and other mystery religions, Gentiles expected a hero figure that was part-god and part-human. They expected the hero to be born of a virgin, to be worshipped by strangers as an infant, to work miracles, and ultimately to die and rise again. In the process of making Christianity attractive to Hellenized Gentiles, all of these pagan characteristics were eventually added to the figure of Jesus.

Jewish Christians would never part with their Messiah, so the genealogies had to stay. Likewise, Gentile converts to Christianity would never part with virgin birth. Unable to cast off either tradition, Christianity simply held its breath and charged forward carrying them both. The amazing thing is how easily the new religion got away with it.

Placing the Christmas Story in History

When we try to reconcile the traditional Christmas story to what is known about the history of the ancient world, still further contradictions emerge. When was Jesus born? Around 550 C.E., when time was still counted from the founding of Rome, an astronomer and theologian named Dionysius Exiguus—literally, "Dennis the Short"—deduced a birth year for Jesus that would later become enshrined as the year one C.E. No one now accepts that Jesus was born in the year one, in part because Herod died four years earlier. So when did the Nativity occur? The traditional answer is that Jesus was born while Herod ruled Judea (according to Matthew) and while Quirinius was governor of Syria (according to Luke). Quirinius held office in Syria twice, from 6 to 4 B.C.E. and again from 6 to 9 C.E. His first term coincided with the reign of Herod.

Luke wrote of a vast census, yet Roman records give no indication of so huge an undertaking. The historian Josephus describes a census during Quirinius's second term as governor of Syria, but this cannot be the enrollment described by Luke. Josephus described a modest project, not the colossal exercise Luke suggests. Anyway, to conform with both Luke and Matthew the census would have to have been proclaimed in the first term of Quirinius, while Herod still lived, not in the second![23] Moreover, no known Roman census would have required Joseph to drag his pregnant fiancée halfway across Palestine in order to register at Bethlehem.

Luke is unequivocal on this point. The census was designed so that every man had to return to his ancestral home city to be counted. Joseph had to go to Bethlehem because he was of the house of David. This was not some crazy program imposed on Palestine alone; it was described as the decree of Caesar Augustus, binding on the whole Roman Empire. A moment's reflection should suffice to demonstrate how absurd this is. Did every legionnaire in Gaul desert his post and march home to be enrolled? Did every politician, merchant, artist, or philosopher who had come from the countryside and made a fortune in Rome close up his villa and head back to the hills? Where would draft animals and wagons be found to support such a migration? How could the Empire function while this great disruptive exodus boiled in all directions?

Imagine the effect a census like that would have on the United States today. Aside from some Native Americans, the entire population would have to trek to Ellis Island, or San Francisco, or New Orleans, or Cleveland, or Jamestown, or Plymouth Rock—to whichever port of entry through which one's paternal line had entered the country. Of course, the Roman Empire was not peopled almost exclusively with immigrants and the descendants of immigrants, like the United States. But it had a level of internal mobility appropriate to its broad borders and the technologies of the day. If any Roman administration had ever been crazy enough to attempt a census designed like the one in Luke, the resulting disruption could never have failed to be preserved for us in the historical record.

Improbable as it was, the "great census" was simply the plot device Luke relied on to get Mary and Joseph from Nazareth, where he knew Jesus grew up and where he assumed that Mary and Joseph had always lived, to Bethlehem, where tradition required that Jesus be born, and back.

As for the slaughter of the innocents, did it actually occur? Not unless two of the ancient world's better historians chose just that moment to look the other way. Nicholas of Damascus wrote a complete biography of Herod. Nicholas never mentions such an act. Josephus's *Antiquities of the Jews*[24] documented Jewish life under Herod. Herod was a cruel king, and Josephus reveled in documenting smaller Herodian atrocities. Had Herod committed anything remotely like the slaughter described in Matthew, Josephus would have pounced on it. But he does not mention it.

It is easy to see how the story could have made its way into the gospel without needing to be true. Like Luke, Matthew needed a plot gimmick. Unlike Luke, Matthew pictured Joseph and Mary as natives of Bethlehem, so he needed a reason to get the family out of Judea after the Nativity and into Nazareth. Contemporary writers of thrillers might chide Matthew for having chosen a disproportionate means to his end. Matthew had Herod kill off every male under the age of two in Bethlehem, with, of course, one prominent exception. If this gargantuan artifice strained the credulity of readers, it still sufficed only to get the Holy Family to Egypt! A further contrivance, Joseph's fear of Herod's son, was necessary to transplant Jesus, Mary, and Joseph to Nazareth, where the writer of Matthew meant to send them all along.

If the available evidence will not permit us to guess the year of Jesus' birth, can we do any better with the date? In fact, there is no reason even to imagine that December 25 might be the actual birth date of Jesus. The date was already established as a holiday in several traditions. No, the odds that the historic Jesus was actually born on December 25 are, at best, 365 to 1. Even those odds may be overly generous, for evidence in the gospel of Luke all but rules out a winter birth date. Recall that the shepherds were out in the fields watching their flocks by night. Palestine is warm, but not tropical. To this day, shepherding peoples in the region leave their flocks in the pastures overnight—and stay outside with them—only in the nicer weather. In some areas, the flocks are supervised by night only in the spring, during the lambing season. This is the only clue the gospels give that links the Nativity to a specific season of the year, and it argues *against* a December birth date.

Christmas Among the Early Christians

Even devout Christians must admit—as mainstream and liberal Christian clergy do—that much of what we know as the "story of Christmas" is simply the result of a process of literary accretion. Its elements are inspired by, or just appropriated from, the legends of earlier holy "personages." Even if Christianity is true, the story of Christmas is unworthy of it.

If Nativity lore accumulated over time, in a way unrelated to the life of the "historic" Jesus, then we might expect the first Christians not to have observed the feast of the Nativity. And they did not, as even conservative religion writer George W. Cornell acknowledges:

> For more than 300 years after Jesus' time, Christians didn't celebrate his birth. The observance began in fourth century Rome, timed to coincide with a mid-winter pagan festival honoring the pagan gods Mithra and Saturn. The December date was simply taken over to commemorate Jesus' birth, since its exact date isn't known. Consequently, the fusion of the sacred and the profane characterized the celebration from the start.[25]

Early Christians celebrated Christmas on a variety of dates. Almost from the start, some Christians observed December 25: the date is described as Christmas in a Roman almanac from 354 C.E.[26] Church father John Chrysostom says that Julius I, pope from 337–352 C.E., commissioned a study to determine the date of Jesus' birth. Based on its findings, Julius declared December 25 the official date in 350 C.E. In 379 or 380 C.E., a Christmas sermon was preached at Constantinople on December 25.[27]

Other dates remained popular for some time. January 6, traditionally the day the wise men visited the baby Jesus, is still the most important day of the Eastern Orthodox Christmas season. Other dates on which early Christians celebrated their redeemer's birth have passed from use or been acquired by other holidays: February 2, English Candlemas and also the American Groundhog Day; March 25, now preserved as the traditional date of Jesus' conception; and April 19, May 20, and November 17, dates that no longer carry any special meaning. But by the fourth century C.E., December 25 was well on its way to dominance.

The first recorded use of *Christmas* or *Christ's Mass* as the name of the holiday appeared shortly after the death of Julius I in 352 C.E. The first Christmas sermon recorded in a Western church dates from 383 C.E.[28] The first eyewitness account of a Nativity observance—held at Bethlehem, complete with a crib—dates from 400 C.E. So much for the legend that St. Francis of Assisi invented the crib at Greccio in 1223 C.E.![29] In 438 Emperor Theodosius proclaimed Christmas a legal holiday of the Roman Empire. In 535 C.E. the emperor Flavius Justinian (483–565) reaffirmed the status of Christmas as an official Roman holiday. In 567 C.E. the Council of Tours proclaimed the period from December 25 to January 6 as a twelve-day holy festival. Here, the cross-fertilization between Christmas and the pagan traditions of northern and southern Europe came full circle. The north's twelve-day feast of Yule had been absorbed into the holy season of Christmas.

With that, Christmas was off and running. It became popular as a coronation day. In 800 Charlemagne had himself crowned Holy Roman

Emperor on Christmas day. On Christmas 1066 William the Conqueror was crowned king of England. On December 25, 1100, Baldwin of Edessa was crowned king of the Latin Kingdom of Jerusalem, a short-lived political unit created during the First Crusade. Legend even claims that it was on a Christmas day when Arthur drew the sword Excalibur from the great stone, qualifying himself to become the mythical king of Camelot.[30]

Separating the babe of the Christian message, if such there ever was, from the bathwater of pagan traditions and historical accidents is far more difficult than most Christmas enthusiasts suspect. In my research, I found only one Christmas custom that seems to belong exclusively to Christianity. Christians appear to have invented the Midnight Mass out of whole cloth.[31] Celebrated in Rome as early as the fifth century, it alone appears not to have significant pagan antecedents.

Our search for the dividing line between pre-Christian and authentically Christian sources for the modern Christmas observance is at last at an end. Who would have expected the quest to take so long, and produce so little? It is more evidence, as if it were needed, that the trouble with Christmas cuts deep, right to the holiday's core.

Notes

1. Rudolf Bultmann, *Jesus Christ and Mythology* (New York: Charles Scribner's Sons, 1958).

2. Harvey Cox, *The Secular City: Secularization and Urbanization in Theological Perspective* (New York: Macmillan, 1965).

3. R. Joseph Hoffmann, ed., *The Origins of Christianity: A Critical Introduction* (Buffalo, N.Y.: Prometheus Books, 1985), p. 14.

4. For an overview of this approach to Jesus scholarship, see Gerald A. Larue and R. Joseph Hoffmann, eds., *Jesus in History and Myth* (Buffalo, N.Y.: Prometheus Books, 1986). See also Gerald A. Larue, *Ancient Myth and Modern Life* (Long Beach, Calif.: Centerline Press, 1988); R. Joseph Hoffmann, ed., The Origin of Christianity; Martin A. Larson, *The Story of Christian Origins* (Washington, D.C.: Joseph J. Binns/New Republic, 1977); Michael Arnheim, *Is Christianity True?* (Buffalo, N.Y.: Prometheus Books, 1984, orig. pub. London: Gerald Duckworth and Co.); R. Joseph Hoffmann, *Jesus Outside the Gospels* (Buffalo, N.Y.: Prometheus Books, 1984); Jaroslav Pelikan, *Jesus Through the Centuries: His Place in the History of Culture* (New Haven: Yale University Press, 1985); and others. Most books on the Jesus of history written by liberal Christian, Jewish, or secular scholars since about 1940 reflect a similar model of the origin of stories about Jesus related in the Gospels and early Christian literature. For a typical account of how the crucifixion could have come about if Jesus never claimed

to be the son of God, see Ellis Rivkin, *What Crucified Jesus?: The Political Execution of a Charismatic* (Nashville, Tenn.: Abingdon Press, 1984).

5. George A. Wells, *The Jesus of the Early Christians* (London: Elek/Pemberton, 1971); *Did Jesus Exist?* (London: Elek/Pemberton, 1975); *The Historical Evidence for Jesus* (Buffalo, N.Y.: Prometheus Books, 1982); *Who Was Jesus? A Critique of the New Testament Record* (LaSalle, Ill.: Open Court, 1989).

6. David Adams Leeming, *The World of Myth* (New York: Oxford University Press, 1990), pp. 148–51.

7. Larue, p. 156.

8. Leeming, p. 155.

9. Ibid.

10. Jackson, *Christianity Before Christ* (Austin, Tex.: American Atheist Press, 1984), pp. 47–65.

11. Morton Smith, *Jesus the Magician* (San Francisco: Harper and Row, 1978), and Pelikan, *Jesus Through the Centuries.*

12. Leeming, pp. 156–57.

13. Charles Guignebert, "The Birth of Jesus," anthologized in Hoffmann, ed., *The Origins of Christianity*, p. 245.

14. Patricia Bunning Stevens, *Merry Christmas: A History of the Holiday* (New York: Macmillan, 1979), p. 34.

15. Tertullian, "On Idolatry," quoted in R. J. Condon, *Our Pagan Christmas* (Austin, Tex.: American Atheist Press, undated; reprinted from London: National Secular Society, undated).

16. Maymie Richardson Krythe, *All About Christmas* (New York: Harper and Brothers, 1954), p. 2.

17. Justin Martyr, *First Apology* LXVI; Tertullian, *On Baptism* V. Cited in Larson, p. 182.

18. Leeming, pp. 225–26; Jackson, pp. 69–70.

19. Hoffmann, p. 118.

20. Stevens, p. 19.

21. For the contradictions between the genealogies of Jesus presented in Matthew and Luke, see Isaac Asimov, *Asimov's Guide to the Bible* (New York: Avenel, 1981; combined edition, orig. pub. New York: Doubleday, 2 vol., 1968–69), pp. 774–82, 937–40; Kersey Graves, *The World's Sixteen Crucified Saviors: Christianity Before Christ* (New York: Truth Seeker, 1960; revised and enlarged edition, orig. pub. 1875), pp. 79–81; Arnheim, pp. 14, 30; Guignebert, pp. 238–41; Larson, pp. 461–62.

22. Larson, pp. 154, 456.

23. Asimov, pp. 924–25.

24. Arnheim, p. 29.

25. George W. Cornell, Associated Press wire service feed, December 18, 1992. Cornell's claim is supported in J. C. J. Metford, *Dictionary of Christian Lore and Legend* (London: Thames and Hudson, 1983), p. 67; *New Catholic Encyclopedia,* p. 656; Earl W. Count, *4000 Years of Christmas* (New York: Henry Schuman, 1948), p. 33; and elsewhere.

26. Metford, p. 67.

27. *New Catholic Encyclopedia,* pp. 656–58.

28. *New Catholic Encyclopedia,* pp. 656–58.

29. For crib at Bethlehem in 400 C.E., see Alexander Murray, "Medieval Christmas," *History Today,* December 1986, p. 37. For traditional Franciscan account, see Metford, pp. 75, 166.

30. Stevens, p. 56.

31. Ibid., p. 41.

6

A Nick in Time

Still hoping to identify truly Christian influences upon the development of contemporary Christmas? You might think to look at Saint Nicholas. What do we know about the figure the Romans called *Sanctus Nicolaus,* the Germans called *Sankt Nikolaus* or *Sanct Herr 'Cholas,* and the Dutch (somewhat later) would call *Sinter Klaas*?[1]

Not that much.

Nicholas lived from the late third century to the early fourth century C.E. His life spanned the reigns of the Roman emperors Diocletian, Maximilian, and Constantine.[2] He was born circa 280 C.E. at Patara, a port city in the province of Lycia in Asia Minor. Nicholas's parents were wealthy Christians. When they died in an epidemic, Nicholas inherited their fortune. He moved to Myra, the provincial capital. There, the wealthy and capable young man pursued a career in the church. He rose quickly, and was named Bishop of Myra while still relatively young.[3]

In February 303, the pagan Roman emperor Diocletian and his commanding general Galerius launched a general persecution of Christians. An imperial edict dated February 24, 303 C.E., ordered Christian churches destroyed. To avoid being imprisoned, Christians had to hand over their sacred books to be burned. Christians holding public office were to lose their appointments, and Christians in the upper classes would be stripped of their privileges. But the February edict was designed to avoid bloodshed and the creation of martyrs. Instead, individual Christians would be welcomed back to paganism with open arms. All they had to do was renounce their Christian ways, a requirement some Christians considered excessive.

A second, harsher edict, issued in the summer of 303, ordered bishops and other leaders of the Christian communities arrested and jailed. They were to be held without possibility of release until they publicly sacrificed to the gods of Rome. Nicholas was probably seized and jailed in connection with the enforcement of this edict.[4] Two more edicts would follow, further widening the scope of the persecution.

Christians were treated harshly, especially in regions under the personal control of Galerius. Thousands were imprisoned; many died. Thousands more renounced their faith, handed over their scriptures, and sacrificed to the pagan gods. So many Christians defected during this period that when the persecution ended, the church instituted the sacrament of confession for the first time. By confessing, *traditors*—Christians who had given in to Rome—could purge their consciences in private and reingratiate themselves into the Christian communities.[5]

Thousands of others, among them Nicholas, maintained their resolve. Diocletian's determination to jail stubborn Christian bishops indefinitely strained even the resources of the Roman Empire. The historian Eusebius complained that real criminals were repeatedly set free to clear space in the jails for unyielding Christian leaders.[6]

When Diocletian and Maximian abdicated in 305, the persecution of Christians was temporarily withdrawn. The bishops, including Nicholas, who were still jailed for refusal to sacrifice, remained in custody. On July 25, 306 C.E. Constantine took the throne as one of several contending "emperors." At about the same time, Maximin, another aspirant to the imperial throne, renewed the wholesale persecution of Christians. Over the next several years, Constantine dramatically improved his position. "He faced the same alternative as Diocletian," one historian summed up, "to destroy [Christianity] or give it power."[7] If Constantine was originally unsure which alternative he preferred, his choice was clear after he converted to Christianity in 312.[8] The conversion of Constantine may be the most important single change of heart in the history of the ancient world. Even so, developments were prompting all the would-be emperors to reconsider their opposition to Christianity. By 311 Galerius had ended persecution of Christians in the territories he controlled. Not to be outdone, the embattled Maximin issued an edict of toleration in late 312. As for Constantine himself, in February 313 he forged a short-lived alliance with the emperor Licinius. Jointly they issued the Edict of Milan, the real turning point in relations between the Roman Empire and the Christian Church. This document recognized Christianity as a free religion and gave it a place superior to the traditional cult of the Roman gods.

As a result of either Maximin's edict of 312 or the Edict of Milan, Nicholas was freed from prison.[9] In time, he was elevated to the rank of archbishop.

There is substantial disagreement over the date of Nicholas's death. The dominant tradition holds that he died in 326 C.E. on December 6, the date that became established as the traditional feast of Saint Nicholas.[10] One version of the story holds that in the year he died, Nicholas attended the Council of Nicaea and helped to establish Trinitarianism, dying of a stroke after making a convincing point in a climactic council debate.[11] Yet another tradition holds that Nicholas lived into his sixties, dying in Asia Minor about 341 C.E.[12]

Take away the melodrama about Roman persecutions and there isn't very much to the historical biography of Nicholas. So sketchy is the data that in 1969 Pope Paul VI removed the feast of Saint Nicholas from the Roman Catholic calendar and made his veneration optional for Catholics.[13]

It is when we set history aside and look into Nicholas's *legendary* biography that his story begins to assume familiar proportions. The principal myths about the life of Nicholas are collected below.

Legend tells us that young Nicholas resolved to use his parents' fortune to perform good works in secret. In so doing he hoped to live up to Matthew 6:3–4, which counsels, "But when you give alms, do not let your left hand know what your right hand is doing, so that your alms may be in secret . . ." (RSV). This decision would be expressed later in the life of Nicholas through a pattern of anonymous gift giving, usually under cover of night.

Myth also tells us *how* Nicholas came to be named Bishop of Myra at such a tender age. The previous bishop had died unexpectedly, leaving deadlocked factions unable to agree on a successor. One night, an elder had a dream, receiving the peculiar instruction that the first person named Nicholas to enter the church the next morning should be named bishop! Of course, the devout Nicholas of Patara was among the first to enter the church next morning, and the unexpected honor fell to him.[14] This motif is often repeated in myths designed to explain the otherwise unlikely accession of a hero to some high office. It is certainly reminiscent of the legend of Arthur and the sword in the stone. Is it coincidence that Arthur is said to have drawn Excalibur on Christmas day?

The legends also tell us that when the pious young bishop visited the Holy Land, which the historic Nicholas may very well have done, he was so attracted to the ground Jesus supposedly walked that he resolved to move there permanently. The story says God had to command Nicholas not to resign his bishopric. Instead, he was to return to Myra and meet his destiny.

As Nicholas sailed home, that destiny began to unfold. It was on this voyage that Nicholas is said to have performed the first of his many miracles. Those miracles tend to fall into four main categories:

(1) Miracles associated with the sea

(2) Miracles involving children

(3) Miracles involving material plenty

(4) Miracles that so baldly imitate or outdo the miracles of Jesus that Christian readers may be forgiven for finding them blasphemous.

As Nicholas sailed home from Palestine, a violent storm came up. The sailors feared for their lives, but Nicholas went up on deck, calmly offered a prayer, and the storm abated.[15] Another source adds that during the storm, a sailor had been flung out of the boat and drowned. After he had calmed the waters, Nicholas stepped over the gunwale, strode across the water, pulled the drowned man out of the waves, carried him on deck, and restored him to life.[16] With this addition, the legend goes several strides beyond the Jesus story it had started out imitating. This is a pattern we will see repeatedly in the Nicholas lore.

On another voyage, Nicholas restored the life of a sailor who had suffered a fatal fall from a mast. Later, he discovered that the captain of the vessel planned to sell him into slavery instead of returning him to Myra. Nicholas called up a high wind that pushed the ship back to Asia Minor. When the vessel washed ashore, Nicholas simply stepped off and out of the evil captain's plans.

The Serbs and Bulgarians preserve an old folk song that tells of Nicholas falling asleep during a well-lubricated gathering of the saints. St. Basil, who is pouring the wine, takes offense when Nicholas passes out so early. When Nicholas awakens, St. John asks him why he drifted off. Gently upbraiding his companions, Nicholas tells them that he wasn't sleeping at all. He had to dash off to quell a storm in the Aegean Sea![17]

But the powers of Nicholas were said to control more than the sea, the weather, and the bodies of sailors. One legend spoke of a famine that ravaged Lycia. Eager to help his people, Nicholas strode to the port where grain ships paused for supplies on their way to Constantinople. Each ship's cargo had been precisely weighed and lay in the holds under imperial seal. Still, Nicholas begged each captain to hand over a fraction of his cargo to feed the starving in Lycia. Reluctantly, the captains agreed. They gave Nicholas a small store of grain and sailed on, praying that when they arrived at the imperial docks their explanations for the shortfall would be accepted. Instead, on arrival, they found their holds miraculously full. Back in Lycia, Nicholas had multiplied the small stipends of grain into a surplus that fed all of Asia Minor for two years.[18] The miracle of the loaves and fishes fades by comparison. But even this is not the most outlandish story in which Nicholas outshines Jesus.

The three sons of a rich Asian merchant had come to Lycia to complete their studies. They ran afoul of an evil innkeeper who killed the youths, stole their money, dismembered their bodies, and pickled the pieces in three wooden barrels. Visiting the inn, Nicholas obtained miraculous knowledge of the innkeeper's guilt and of the whereabouts of the pickled body parts. He pried open the barrels and out of each one pulled one of the students, restored to life, with his body *and his purse* intact![19] This story presents a miracle far more audacious than anything contained in the gospels. In addition, it establishes that unlike many Christian heroes, Nicholas did not restrict his services to the poor.

Other miracles attributed to Nicholas cemented his stature as a defender of the young. One simple story related that Nicholas was able to exorcise a possessed boy just by making the sign of the cross over him.[20] A more involved legend tells of Basilios, a youngster from Myra who was kidnapped and enslaved by Arab pirates. One night Nicholas flew through the air to the child's side, scooped him up, and whisked Basilios back to Myra, dropping him gently into his father's courtyard. Then he scurried away so that no one would know who had returned Basilios to his home and hearth.[21] Another tale concerns a woman who lived in a remote village. When Nicholas made a rare visit to her village, she was so anxious to see him that she forgot she had left her baby in a pot over the fire. (Apparently this was a common way of bathing young children, and safe enough if the pot hadn't been over the fire very long.) The woman remembered what she had done during her audience with Nicholas. Distraught, she begged the good bishop to do something. Nicholas told her to return home. When she bustled back into her kitchen, expecting the worst, she found her baby sitting unharmed in boiling water, playing delightedly with the bubbles.[22]

Of course, the best known Nicholas legend is the one that announced his qualifications to succeed Woden and Berchta as the giver of Yuletide gifts.

In Myra there lived a nobleman and widower who had three young daughters. Once wealthy, the family was almost penniless. There was no money for dowries for the three girls—in third-century Asia Minor, an intractable problem. Without dowries, the girls would be unmarriageable. Nicholas, not yet a bishop, knew of the family's crisis. He resolved to take action in his usual covert manner.

When the oldest girl approached marriageable age, Nicholas crept up to the widower's house in the middle of the night. He carried a bag containing enough gold for a respectable dowry. Taking care to ensure he was not seen, Nicholas threw the bag of gold into the oldest girl's bedroom, then melted into the shadows. Versions differ. In the simplest, Nicholas simply threw the bag through an open window. In another variant, Nicholas threw the bag so high into the air that it arched up over the housetop and dropped down a chimney. In a third, the girl had washed her stockings before retiring, and they were hanging from a hook on the mantelpiece to dry. Nicholas threw the bag of gold through a window and into a stocking. The more elaborate variants sound like "just so stories" designed to explain why Saint Nicholas comes down the chimney or leaves gifts in stockings.

The father was delighted to have a dowry for his oldest daughter, and he told everyone in town about his good fortune. But no one knew the benefactor's identity.

A few years later, the middle daughter approached marriageable age. Nicholas crept back by night and threw another bag of gold into the middle daughter's room. Again, the father exulted. But Nicholas's secret remained secure.

In time, the youngest daughter approached marriageable age. When the time was right, Nicholas filled another bag with gold and stole out into the night. Again he found the proper sleeping room and tossed in the bag of gold. But this time Nicholas was grabbed from behind and pushed to the ground. Strong hands turned him onto his back to face his assailant. It was the widower! Anticipating that the mystery donor might strike again, the poverty-stricken nobleman had lain in wait. Recognizing Nicholas, now the bishop, the widower thanked him profusely. In one version, Nicholas swore the widower to secrecy, an oath that was kept until after the death of Nicholas. In another, Nicholas could not persuade the widower to keep the secret, and the next morning all Myra learned what Nicholas had done.[23]

At least two forms of cultural fallout are traceable to the legend of the daughters and the gold. The first is that Nicholas was considered the patron saint of, among many other causes, marriageable young women. The second is somewhat stranger. Though the story had Nicholas bestowing his three bags of gold over a span of several years, it became popular to show the three bags together. The pawnbroker's symbol of three balls is directly descended from the once-familiar icon of Nicholas's three bags of gold.

Saint Nicholas became one of the most popular figures in all Christendom. Almost every European language includes one or more family names based on "Nicholas," including Nijssen, Klaassen, Clausen, Klasesz, Colijn, Nichols, Nicholson, Colson, and Collins, among others.[24]

Nicholas was particularly beloved among the Dutch, whose sailors heard the tales of Nicholas in Asia Minor. They were the first to spread his cult to western Europe. To this day, children in the Netherlands get their holiday gifts on Saint Nicholas's Day, December 6, and not on Christmas.

The country that probably devoted itself most deeply to Nicholas was Russia. Some six centuries after the death of Nicholas, Vladimir of Russia went to Constantinople to be baptized. The tales of Nicholas he brought back took Russia by storm. Saint Nicholas became the patron saint of the Russian nation.[25]

In due course, Nicholas became the patron saint of damned near everything. Both Greek and Russian sailors adopted him as their patron. Even in the landlocked Balkans, Nicholas was celebrated as a rescuer of ships. From this beginning grew the Nicholas of legend who became patron saint of merchants, travelers, and even pirates.[26] Of course, Nicholas quickly became known as the patron saint of children. In London, England, he was named the patron saint of bankers, too. Banks and pawnshops had a common origin, so it may have been the connection between Nicholas and the pawnshop symbol that endeared the bankers to him. Nicholas became the patron saint of the cities of Liege, Belgium; Lucerne, Switzerland; and Freiburg, Germany. He was also known as the patron saint of criminals because of the years he spent in Diocletian's jails. In England, thieves were sometimes called "Saint Nicholas's clerks," an intriguing twist on the image of a saint who was usually associated with giving.[27]

Some of the customs that grew up around Nicholas reached back to far older holiday traditions. European monasteries celebrated a "Nicholas festival" in which young boys traded roles with the monks. One youth would dress up as Saint Nicholas, complete with bishop's robes and miter. The other children would impersonate members of Nicholas's traditional retinue. Together, the costumed children would take over the church and hold a mock Mass.[28] In later years the Nicholas festival spilled into the streets. In Austria, men and women still live who can remember when the boy bishop and his entourage used to pour out of the church carrying switches, passing from house to house and demanding tasty tributes, another echo of the kinship between Christmas and Halloween.

Nicholas grew so popular that he even cropped up in non-Christian religions. Northern pagan peoples, including the Samoyed and the Laplanders, adopted him as the equivalent of a patron saint. Our contemporary American vision of Santa Claus as a denizen of the North Pole may stem in part from the gowing identification of Nicholas with peoples of the far north.[29]

The vigor of the Nicholas cult, and the breadth of its diffusion, can be expressed in other ways too. Across Europe, more churches were named for Saint Nicholas than for any of the apostles! England alone had four hundred churches named for Nicholas, more than the number named for the country's patron saint, George. There were three hundred in Belgium, forty in Iceland, and as many as sixty in the city of Rome alone.[30]

It is in Holland and Germany that the forerunners of contemporary Santa Claus traditions developed most fully. The children of the lower Rhineland were the first to set out small wooden objects such as toy ships, or simply their shoes, by the chimney on December 5, Saint Nicholas Eve. Echoing the Berchta tradition, the children would fill the shoes with grain for Nicholas's horse and go to bed. When they awoke on Saint Nicholas Day, they would find that the grain had been replaced by gifts.[31]

Armed with this understanding of the Saint Nicholas myth, we are in an ideal position to look back on the Nordic myths of Woden and Berchta. One by one, explicitly Christian aspects in the figure of Saint Nicholas were swapped for pagan elements familiar from the Woden/Berchta tradition, leading toward the contemporary figure of Santa Claus.

The milk and cookies Americans leave out for Santa are more reminiscent of the snack one left for Berchta. Dutch and German children leave hay for Nicholas's horse, but nothing for the saint himself. By contrast, among the Norse and Germanics, it was Woden or Berchta for whom the plate of fish and dumplings was left. Sometimes children left grain for the horse as well, but there was *always* a snack for the elfin visitor. Modern-day Americans know which side their bread is buttered on. They ply Santa with milk and cookies while the reindeer stand on the roof and fend for themselves.

Santa's snack formed the center of an unusual family tradition that an Erie, Pennsylvania, schoolmate told me about when we were in the second or third grade. Just before bedtime Christmas Eve, he and his parents would make a ceremony of setting out the milk and cookies for Santa Claus. On Christmas morning, his parents would call attention to the milk and cookies. The cookies would be half-eaten, the milk half-drunk. They would make a great show of marveling that the milk was still cold and fresh even though it had sat out all night. It had to be the magic of Santa Claus! For as long as he could remember, he had relished the chance to finish off the milk and cookies Santa had left behind. The glass would be so cold it almost hurt to hold onto. The milk would be sweet and fresh. At age seven, he was becoming more curious. If Santa's power could preserve the milk overnight, would it work longer? Could the milk sit out for days, weeks, or months, and would it still be cold and fresh? He drank all but one last swallow of the milk. Putting down the glass with a half-inch of liquid in the bottom, he announced his plan. He would take the milk to his room and let it sit until summer, until school started next year, maybe longer. He noticed his parents' discomfort, but of course failed to understand it. As Christmas morning wore on, his mother and father prompted him a few more times to finish his milk.

Eventually they realized he really meant to leave it out indefinitely. As the family was preparing to go to church, he spotted his mother pouring the milk out into the sink. "That's the Santa Claus milk! I'm saving it!" The inevitable tantrum followed. Christmas was ruined for him that year.

Looking back, it is obvious what happened. After he went to bed each Christmas Eve, his parents would stay up assembling and arranging the presents. They would drink half of the milk, or pour it back into the carton, then whisk the glass into the refrigerator. On Christmas morning they would rise first (no small sacrifice, that) and set that ice-cold half-glass of milk out by the cookies. There is something disturbing in the lengths to which parents will go to fabricate physical evidence in support of the Santa Claus myth. It is popular to call such deceptions "cute," but don't they really amount to laying traps for youngsters' emerging capacities for critical thinking? And don't they always court the risk of unintended consequences? I wonder how his parents felt about their "lovable, ingenious" little trick as they drove stiff-lipped to church on Christmas day, a spanked and sobbing seven-year-old left home alone, confined to his bedroom.

We can identify strong echoes of the Yule visitors of pagan lore in the Saint Nicholas of legend. Nicholas was said to visit all the houses in the world on Saint Nicholas Eve, riding through the wintry skies on his pale horse, clad in a bishop's robes and mitred cap. He would carry gifts for the good children, and a bundle of wooden switches with which to humble the bad ones. In some communities, a costumed Nicholas went from house to house before the holiday. He was often accompanied by a gruff sidekick, a threatening figure with a name like "Black Pete." If a switching was called for, Pete would administer it. The philosopher Herbert Spencer suggested that Saint Nicholas was an updated version of the Norse god Thor.[32] Thor flew about the world in a chariot pulled by two white goats, but he was seldom associated with domestic visits during Yule. Christmas chronicler Earl Count related Nicholas back to the figure of Woden:

> And this is how a god turns into a saint. Both Woden and Saint Nicholas are travelers of the road; they wander afoot and on horseback, inspecting the deeds of mankind, making sure that right and order prevail. They do this when the days of the year are shortest, when a new year is on its way, when the fortunes of the future are being cast. Both of them ride the storm; they can subdue it or they can rouse it. They have ended up by becoming the same person.[33]

Holiday historian Patricia Bunning Stevens saw Nicholas primarily as a successor to Berchta.[34] Both Woden and Berchta were believed to inspect and judge households. But the role as a nocturnal bringer of gifts was much more strongly associated with Berchta than with Woden. And that, of course, was the role Saint Nicholas fulfilled as none had before.

Perhaps the strangest interpretation of the Nicholas legends came from two mid-twentieth-century psychiatrists, Joost A. Meerloo and Adriaan de Groot. Meerloo and de Groot viewed Saint Nicholas as a successor not to Woden or Berchta, but to pagan fertility gods. And they interpreted the bags of gold that enabled the three young women to marry as symbolically filled with semen![35] Writing in 1987, sociologist Russell Belk gave the de Groot–Meerloo theory short shrift. "Our modern fertility figure," Belk corrected, "is the Easter bunny."[36] But *that* is a matter for another book.

The greatest remaining mystery of old Saint Nick concerns his migration across December. When and why did he cast aside his own feast day and become an appurtenance of Christmas? It happened first in Germany. After the Reformation, Protestants criticized Saint Nicholas Day as an unwelcome Catholic holdover. A great campaign was launched to establish an alternate gift bringer, in hopes of weaning children from the cult of Nicholas. The reformers knew the value of brand preference and name recognition. The figure they tapped for the task of replacing Saint Nicholas in children's hearts was none other than Jesus Christ. They encouraged a cult of the *Christkindl* or Christ child. In the Christkindl materials that survive today, the baby Jesus is portrayed rather incongruously as a pint-sized, fast-flying bringer of gifts for good little boys and girls. Being the Son of God, the Christkindl didn't have to waste time asking whether children had been bad or good. He *knew*. And as the keeper of the keys of heaven and the harrower of hell, he carried the biggest switch of all, so he had no need for a sinister sidekick on his annual rounds. Naturally, the Christkindl did not come on December 6, as Nicholas had. He came on his own feast day of Christmas. In time, the idea of Christ child as gift bringer faded. But when the Nicholas tradition returned, December 25 was immovably established as the day on which children expected their holiday gifts. And the Black Pete tradition had been struck a blow from which it would never fully recover.

We have advanced to the point in our story where the Nicholas myth had taken root across most of Europe. Finessing the transition from the traditional Saint Nicholas to our contemporary figure of Santa Claus would demand further transformations. In chapter nine we will see how recent, and how little grounded in any previous tradition, many of these modern metamorphoses really are.

As for the Saint Nicholas of tradition, the mythical figure through whose legends so much of our modern Christmas once passed, history shows us little about him that is authentically Christian. Most of the elements that define him are solidly pre-Christian. If any portion of the Nicholas myth can be said to depend on a uniquely Christian contribution, it is the body of almost blasphemous folk tales that attribute to Nicholas miracles matching or exceeding those of Christ.

The non-Christian side of contemporary Christmas has always cast a giant shadow—and not solely in relation to Saint Nicholas. In the next chapter we will see how a Christian rebellion against the pagan face of Christmas almost ended the holiday for good.

Notes

1. Maymie Richardson Krythe, *All About Christmas* (New York: Harper and Brothers, 1954), p. 24; "Sanct Herr 'Cholas" comes from a chapter heading in Tristram Potter Coffin, *The Book of Christmas Folklore* (New York: Seabury, 1973).

2. Earl W. Count, *4000 Years of Christmas* (New York: Henry Schuman, 1948), p. 57.

3. Krythe, p. 24; Count, p. 57.

4. W. H. C. Frend, *The Rise of Christianity* (Philadelphia: Fortress Press, 1984), pp. 455–60.

5. Martin A. Larson, *The Story of Christian Origins* (Washington, D.C.: Joseph J. Binns/New Republic, 1977), p. 620.

6. Frend, pp. 460–63.

7. Larson, p. 600.

8. Ramsay McMullen, *Christianizing the Roman Empire: A.D. 100–400* (New Haven, Conn.: Yale University Press, 1984), p. 102.

9. Krythe, p. 25.

10. Count, p. 57.

11. Warren O. Hagstrom, "What is the Meaning of Santa Claus?" *American Sociologist* (November 1966): 248.

12. Krythe, p. 26.

13. Coffin, p. 76.

14. Krythe, p. 24.

15. Ibid., p. 25.

16. See Sheryld Ann Karas, *The Solstice Evergreen: The History, Folklore and Origins of the Christmas Tree* (Boulder Creek, Calif.: Aslan Publishing, 1991).

17. Count, p. 58.

18. Krythe, p. 25.

19. Coffin, p. 77.

20. Ibid.

21. Patricia Bunning Stevens, *Merry Christmas! A History of the Holiday* (New York: Macmillan, 1979), p. 78.

22. Coffin, p. 77.

23. For the story of the daughters and the gold, see Count, pp. 59–60; Krythe, p. 26; Stevens, pp. 78–79; Coffin, pp. 76–77.

24. Stevens, p. 28.

25. Krythe, p. 29.

26. Count, pp. 58–59.

27. Krythe, pp. 28–29.

28. Ibid., pp. 61–62; Krythe, p. 29.

29. Count, p. 29.

30. Stevens, p. 78; Krythe, p. 29; Count, p. 58.

31. Count, p. 63.

32. James Harwood Barnett, *The American Christmas: A Study in National Culture* (New York: Macmillan, 1954), p. 26.

33. Count, pp. 62–63.

34. Stevens, p. 79.

35. Joost A. Meerloo, "Santa Claus and the Psychology of Giving," *American Practitioner and Digest of Treatment* (December 1960): 50–53; Adriaan de Groot, *Saint Nicholas: A Psychoanalytic Study of His History and Myth* (New York: Basic Books, 1965).

36. Russell Belk, "A Child's Christmas in America: Santa Claus as Deity, Consumption as Religion," *Journal of American Culture* (Spring 1987): 89.

7

Christians versus Christmas

Can it be? Was there really a time when Christians came within a hair's breadth of pulling Christmas down from the marquee of our culture, like the title of a movie people have stopped coming to see? Yes, it can be—and there was. If history had dealt the cards differently, December 25 might be "just another day" for us all.

Christians versus Christmas in England

In England, where so many of our Christmas traditions arose, fervid Christians dealt Christmas a blow from which it *almost* never recovered. The story begins in the seventeenth century, so let's see how the prospects looked for Christmas in the British Isles as the century opened in 1600 C.E.

Christmas seemed secure in England itself. The Anglican church was dominant. It was doctrinally moderate, politically conservative, and inordinately fond of Christmas. At that point, little separated the Church of England from the Church of Rome, except their views on the marital escapades of Henry VIII. The Church of England had made common cause with the Cavaliers, Royalist conservatives who favored the Crown in its growing squabbles with Parliament. Aligning with Parliament and against the Cavaliers was a group of strict and fiery Protestants who became known as the Puritans. They were so named because they wanted to "purify" the church of all vestiges of what they saw as idolatry, popery, and superstition.

The Puritans disapproved of Christmas. They chose not to celebrate it and they didn't want others enjoying it. Inevitably, Christmas became a political litmus test. One's stance on Christmas came to symbolize one's position in the increasingly volatile conflict between Anglican conservatives and Puritan reformers.

To the north dwelt another religious minority that had little use for Christmas. Scotland's Presbyterians found the holiday unbiblical. For a diversion at winter solstice time, they preferred Hogmanay, their traditional New Year's feast. In Scotland, too, Christmas had become a focus of religio-political controversy. The Presbyterian church had suppressed its observance in Scotland as early as 1583. In 1618 the English king, James I, felt compelled to reinstitute Christmas by force of arms. But a scant two decades later, in 1638, the General Assembly of the Church of Scotland had banned Christmas again.

Across the British Isles, there was trouble with Christmas. Though the holiday had been a familiar bone of contention for decades, it was holding its own. What changed? A leader arose in the Puritan ranks who would worry that bone like a mastiff launching into an old slipper. His name was Oliver Cromwell. Before his emergence, the Royalists won almost every skirmish between the two sides; ill-organized Parliamentary troops were no match for the seasoned, disciplined standing army. Cromwell's inspiration was to forge a regiment drawn from all social classes whose members shared a single characteristic. All were "godly" men; in Cromwellspeak, that meant they were fiercely committed to the harsh and ascetic Christianity of the Puritans. The idea worked. Egalitarianism and fanaticism combined to give the regiment a discipline and fighting spirit that made it the equal of Royalist forces. Cromwell's experimental regiment earned the nickname "Ironsides" and became the model along which Parliamentary forces were reorganized under his command.[1]

At last civil war broke out in 1642. Puritan forces gained control of the country quickly, though Charles I would not be beheaded until 1649. Cromwell's forces set out at once to remake England in the image of their ideals. Churches were cleared of statuary. Cults of the saints were viciously suppressed. Forms of worship that struck Puritan reformers as "popish" were stamped out.

Also on the Puritans' list of targets was Christmas. Because Cromwell understood the popular fondness for the holiday, he intended to delay efforts to stamp it out until the Puritan control over the country was more firmly established. But within two years, reformist zeal against the holiday would outrun even Cromwell's capacity to control.

In 1644 zealots forced an ordinance through Parliament that declared Christmas a day of fast and penance instead of a feast. In the language of the time, Christmas had been reduced from a major holiday, the anchor point of a season of revelry, to a minor holiday, at most an occasion for contemplation. Shops and government offices were expected to stay open. Churches were expected to stay closed. The Ordinance of 1644 was the work of an unlikely coalition of Puritan hardliners and Scottish Presbyterians. From the first days of the Commonwealth the Scots had been demanding firm action on Christmas. Now they had their wish.

The suppression of Christmas was unpopular, but the Puritans had overwhelming force on their side. In Ealing, Canterbury, and other towns supporters of Christmas rioted in the streets. The riots were put down harshly.[2] On the night of December 24, town criers walked the streets of London, calling out at the stroke of midnight "No Christmas! No Christmas!"[3] Parliament sat in session that Christmas morning, as it would each Christmas until 1656. Across the country, Commonwealth soldiers spread out. Shopkeepers who had closed their establishments to celebrate the holiday with their families were interrupted by armed parties and informed, respectfully but firmly, that they were needed at their shops. Congregations who had gathered in church to observe the Nativity were disrupted by Commonwealth platoons. In the larger towns of England, Christmas observances were either abandoned or driven beneath the surface in the years immediately following the Ordinance of 1644.[4]

But the Puritans were far from done with Christmas. Encouraged by the apparent effectiveness of the Ordinance of 1644, Parliament pushed further. Additional ordinances forbade all observances of Christmas, Easter, and the English religious holiday of Whitsuntide.[5] The anti-holiday ordinances were enforced sporadically. Some ministers and members of their congregations who dared to gather for a Christmas service were arrested, pulled struggling from their churches, and thrown into gaol.[6]

Though the Puritans were not without popular support, many common people straddled the fence, willing to endorse most of Cromwell's programs but bitterly resentful of the Puritan campaign against Christmas. The holiday became a rallying point for reactionaries. Royalists adopted Father Christmas as their mascot. Ten thousand men in Kent and Canterbury passed a resolution threatening that they would see the king back on his throne before they would willingly give up their Christmas.[7]

England's commonwealth period provides an abiding reminder of the mischief that can result when small cabals of people, fanatically wedded to a religious or political vision of the good, take up the tools of state coercion in order to create more quickly the society they imagine. It is a lesson today's Eastern Europeans wish their ancestors had learned better in 1917. For myself, while I approve of the Puritans' distaste for Christmas, I utterly abjure the means they chose with which to oppose it.

By the late 1650s public tolerance for Puritan moral adventurism was declining. Yearnful longing for Christmas may have helped to pave the way for the restoration of the monarchy.[8] Upon his death on September

3, 1658, Cromwell was succeeded by his son Richard, who wisely abdicated the following year. The Commonwealth fell, and the Stuart monarchy was restored. Charles II, son of the king Cromwell had deposed and beheaded, returned from exile to reign once more.

What now of Christmas? For sixteen years England had known, at least *de jure,* "No Christmas! No Christmas!" An entire generation of children had grown up without the delightsome Christmas memories on which adult devotion to the holiday seems to depend. Social processes had subtly altered English folkways to fill the gap where the public celebration of Christmas used to be. Could it ever be the same again?

In a monarchy, it is never wise to answer such questions without consulting the monarch. Charles II had known poverty while he languished in exile. The experience changed him, and when he returned to the throne he was not anxious to reinstitute the lavish feasts and costly masques that his father had loved so well.

England had lost much of the Christmas habit. Think of it as Cromwell's last laugh. After the Restoration, Christmas became a holiday of indifferent stature, largely disconnected from religious associations. The dominant ways of "keeping Christmas" had degenerated into card playing and heavy drinking.[9]

Trouble with Christmas? In eighteenth-century England, Christmas could get you killed. For many the Puritan critique of the holiday still rang true. As individuals and in mobs, Puritans could still make their feelings known. A brief example from the New World may illustrate the point. In Boston on Christmas Day, 1706, a Puritan mob surrounded King's Chapel, an Anglican church. The protestors shouted threats and shattered the church's windows, all to stop the Nativity service going on inside.[10] In England, numerous sources report brawls, beatings, stabbings, and worse when persons of Puritan sympathies would encounter or deliberately disrupt Christmas celebrations in taverns and other places of public assembly. Eighteenth-century efforts to revive the Christmas ball with its mistletoe and ribaldry always courted the risk of a raid by angry Puritans. Manslaughter was the occasional result.

Small wonder that as the century wore on, Britons paid less attention to Christmas. In time, New Year's Day and even Valentine's Day were considered more important holidays.[11] As Stevens expresses it: "Christmas of the eighteenth century lost almost all of its religious meaning. Church services were conducted, but few people attended them. Many simply spent the day playing cards."[12]

By the end of the eighteenth century, Golby and Purdue report, the traditional twelve-day Christmas season was "moribund."[13] Wistfully *The*

Times of London noted in 1790 that: "Within the last half century this annual time of festivity has lost much of its original mirth and hospitality."[14]

During the eighteenth century, then, English Christmas had continued to lose ground. With the dawning of the nineteenth, its demise seemed only a matter of time: "Christmas, in the first decades of the nineteenth century, was neither a major event in the calendar nor a popular festival."[15]

The British holiday chroniclers Golby and Purdue scanned December issues of *The Times* from 1790 to 1835. In twenty of those forty-five years they found no mention of Christmas. In the remaining years, the holiday received minimal mention, perhaps a single short nostalgia piece. Their review of other early nineteenth-century British newspapers and magazines revealed the same pattern.[16]

By 1820, English culture had pulled the plug on Christmas. Few could have looked at the desiccated husk that was English Christmas circa 1820, and even imagined the altered festival that would rise from its bier in only a few years' time. But that is a matter for our next chapter. For now, another continent awaits.

Christians versus Christmas in the New World

In much of seventeenth- and eighteenth-century America, just as in England, the celebration of Christmas was almost utterly discarded.

The earliest successful English colony in the New World was established in Virginia in 1607 under the leadership of John Smith. Solid Cavaliers, Smith's colonists even named their settlement Jamestown. Of course, they were all Anglicans, Episcopalians in New World parlance. They valued Christmas and celebrated it avidly as soon as they could. Christmas was largely ignored during the miserable winter of 1607, when the inadequately provisioned colony almost starved. By the winter of 1608, things were looking up. The Jamestown colonists expressed their Cavalier sensibilities in a roisterous Christmas festival. They decorated their cabins with evergreens, burned Yule logs, and improvised festive meals from native foodstuffs. They celebrated by firing round after round into the air, launching a Southern tradition that is observed with guns and fireworks to this day.[17]

Another innovation of the Virginia colonists was eggnog. The frothy drink had been known for centuries, but the Jamestown colonists were the first to treat it specifically as a holiday beverage. The name is probably a corruption of the phrase "egg and grog," *grog* being a generic term for drinks based on rum.[18]

The Christmas traditions preserved or improvised by the Jamestown Cavaliers would spread across the South and define the way Christmas was observed in much of the territory below the Mason-Dixon line. But the South was not settled solely by Episcopalians. Religious groups that disapproved of Christmas were also represented. In particular, during colonial times most Baptist denominations disdained Christmas.

In New England, it would be a different story. The history of New England begins, oddly enough, in Holland. In the years before the English civil war, thousands of English Puritans had exiled themselves to Amsterdam to escape religious and political persecution at the hands of the Royalists. Then, as now, Dutch society was exceptionally tolerant. If the Puritans considered themselves lucky that the Dutch would put up with them, they did not relish some of the other customs that Dutch tolerance expected everyone, even English Puritans, to put up with. Twenty-two years before their compatriots would seize power in England, a small band of Puritans who had had their fill of Dutch tolerance set out across the Atlantic. They sought a haven in America where they could enjoy freedom of religion yet deny it to others. The name of their ship was the *Mayflower.* Americans know them, of course, as the Pilgrims, and our popular images tend to gloss over what a sullen, narrow little band they were.

Like all Puritans, the Massachusetts Bay colonists considered Christmas popish and bacchanalian. Landing late in the year, they spent their first Christmas day living aboard the *Mayflower.*[19] Work parties went ashore to start construction of the colony's first building. Governor William Bradford's diary for December 25, 1620, reads as follows:

> Monday, the 25th day. Some to fell timber, some to saw, some to rive [split logs], and some to carry, so no man rested all that day. We went to work on Plymouth's first building, the Common House, construction of which began on Christmas day.[20]

Well, at least he mentioned it.

Plymouth would not remain a Puritan enclave for long. In 1621 there arrived another ship, the *Fortune,* whose passengers were mostly young Englishmen of Anglican sympathies.[21] On Christmas 1621 they asked Bradford to excuse them from work because it went against their consciences to do work on their religious holiday. Bradford agreed, but his cooperative spirit evaporated when he saw how the Cavalier newcomers were spending their time off. They were engaging themselves, well, cavalierly. Encountering them on the street, Bradford found "lusty younge men . . . pitching ye barr, and some playing at stoole-ball and such like sports."[22] Angrily, Bradford broke up their games and commanded the young men to go indoors. If they would make use of religious liberty to exempt themselves from work on Christmas day, they would not spend their holiday in ways calculated to annoy dour Puritans still laboring at their chores.

In 1659—the very year the Commonwealth fell—the legislature of the Massachusetts Bay Colony passed a stringent law against the observance of Christmas. Even that dim glimmer of tolerance that had danced, however fleetingly, behind Governor Bradford's eyes was now extinguished:

> Whosoever shall be found observing any such day as Christmas and the like, either by forbearing labor, feasting, or any other way upon such account as aforesaid, every such person so offending shall pay for each offense five shillings as a fine to the country.[23]

In time, even the Puritan stranglehold on Massachusetts had to weaken. The anti-Christmas legislation was repealed in 1681.[24] Yet for most in Massachusetts, and many elsewhere in New England, Christmas would continue to receive short shrift for almost two hundred years.

In the 1680s Massachusetts had been saddled with the ultimate ignominy, an Anglican governor. Edmund Andros had been appointed to advance an unpopular and ultimately unsuccessful scheme to merge the New England colonies with those anti-Puritan bastions, New York and New Jersey. When, in 1686, Andros wanted to attend a Christmas church service, there was none to be found in all of Boston. He had to retain an Episcopal clergyman and stage the service in Boston Town Hall. Even then Andros required two soldiers to escort him safely to and from the service![25] The 1706 incident in which Boston Puritans rioted outside King's Chapel during the Christmas service has already been mentioned.

New England's Puritans expressed their disdain for the holiday in positive as well as in negative ways. From the earliest colonial days until well into the nineteenth century, it was unusual to find a shop closed, a factory idle, or a school empty in Massachusetts on Christmas Day.

By the time of the Revolutionary War, Christmas in America had become the same kind of religio-political litmus test it had been in England before the civil war. New England remained staunchly opposed to Christmas. The South remained strongly attached to it. Elsewhere, what you did or didn't do on Christmas told your neighbors more about you than you might have wanted them to know.

Some of these divisions were organized along denominational lines. Puritans, Baptists, Presbyterians, Methodists, and Quakers shared a distaste for Christmas. Members of the Church of England, the Dutch Reformed Church, the various Lutheran denominations, and the growing trickle of Roman Catholic immigrants kept Christmas vigorously. In other regions people tended to favor or disfavor Christmas according to social class, or along city dweller-country dweller lines. In New York City and the older Dutch-influenced communities surrounding it, Christmas tended to be more broadly popular than almost anywhere else outside the South. But even there, some churches took pride in sitting Christmas out.

In the mid-1700s, denominational confrontations over Christmas lost their urgency. Concern shifted from religious matters to the economic and political issues that would dominate popular consciousness during the American Revolution. If there was less energy for disagreements over the holiday, there was also less energy for resolving those disagreements. Positions remained frozen. Those who once loved Christmas still favored it; those who once despised it still disliked it.

No one in the years just before the Revolution would have found it easy to believe that Christmas would one day be the most important holiday in American life.

During the Revolutionary War, General George Washington put American ambivalence about Christmas to good use. The famous river crossing at Trenton was deliberately conducted on Christmas Eve. Washington knew that the Hessians, the German mercenaries who then formed the backbone of the Redcoat force, would be drunk or asleep after their Christmas revelry.

After the Revolution, Christmas lost more popularity, caught in postwar anti-British sentiment. Christmas was identified with Anglicanism, Toryism, and the Loyalists. As in England, Christmas customs temporarily forgotten proved difficult to revive. Once established among the fledgling nation's habits, practices that shortchanged the holiday proved difficult to eradicate. Though few American history texts bother to note it, the United States Congress sat in session on December 25, 1789. None of the lawmakers thought enough of Christmas to request a recess. In fact, *Congress sat on Christmas Day in all but three of the next sixty-seven years.* Only after 1856 would it be customary for Congress to adjourn on Christmas Day. Indeed, when it next convened on Christmas, in 1861 and 1862, the act was recognized as an emergency measure inspired by the Civil War.

If anti-British sentiment fueled public disdain for the holiday in the years after the Revolution, changes in immigration patterns helped to keep opposition to the holiday alive during the early nineteenth century. In the 1820s, long-established Americans of primarily Anglo-Saxon descent began to note with alarm the rising tide of immigrants from other parts of Europe. The Germans, Swedes, Finns, and Norwegians were largely Lutheran. Most of the Irish and southern Europeans were Catholic. One of the few characteristics the disparaged newcomers shared was their enthusiasm for Christmas. In the exclusionary "Know-Nothing" reaction that seized so many Anglo-Saxon Americans, ignoring Christmas or celebrating it very modestly was a mark of real Americanism.

Let us pause for a snapshot of Christmas in America in the mid-nineteenth century. It is a picture of a holiday near extinction—a holiday whose supporters could not have imagined the growth that lay in store for it.

The South's love affair with Christmas had successfully followed the western expansion, as this letter by an 1839 visitor to Texas attests:

> It is now 9 o'clock, P.M. and tomorrow's Christmas. The way the votaries of that jolly god Bacchus are "humping" it is curious. Fiddles groan under a heavy weight of oppression, and heel-taps suffer to the tune of "We Won't Go Home 'Till Morning" and now and then the discharge of firearms at a distance, remind me that merriment now despotic rules to the utter discomfiture of dull care, while I, O Jeminy! have nothing stronger wherewith to lash my cold sluggish blood than water.[26]

If the Southern custom of marking Christmas with gunpowder had been exported to Texas, it remained no less popular at home. An 1851 edition of the Wilmington, North Carolina, *Daily Journal* reported as follows:

> John Barleycorn retained his usual spirit . . . and our town authorities on Christmas generally let the boys have their way so far as mere noise is concerned. There was therefore much firing of crackers, rockets, sarpients, etc. and a good deal of cheering and shouting, but nothing worse and as the night wore on even these ceased and the town slept.[27]

In New England, the status remained starchily quo. Golby and Purdue describe a large manufacturing concern in Vermont whose owner kept the works open on Christmas Day every year until 1867.[28] Boston's public schools stayed open on Christmas Day until at least 1870. As late as 1874, New England-born Henry Ward Beecher could still tell an interviewer, "To me, Christmas is a foreign day."[29]

Even in New York City, Christmas killjoys were not hard to find. The *Daily Times* for December 26, 1855, reported: "The churches of the Presbyterians, Baptists and Methodists were not open on December 25. . . . They do not accept the Day as a Holy One. . . ."[30]

In 1879 the American novelist Joseph Conrad could report that in twenty years of almost continuous seafaring he had observed but a single Christmas observance on shipboard.[31] In 1893 a cattleman's newspaper in Miles City, Montana, thought nothing of noting that its offices would be open on December 25 and accepting subscription payments.[32]

As late as 1925 the editor of the *Catholic World* could still reminisce about "Christmas, a Catholic conquest" and write that

> Christmas was considered a "papist" festival. . . . Indeed, within the memory of living men, to ask for a holiday on Christmas was sufficient to warrant discharge from one's position, as well as to incur opprobrium as a "Romanist."[33]

The authentic Christmas whose origins we've been exploring is not the Christmas Americans celebrate today. Contemporary Christmas is so pervasive that we imagine that its traditions stretch unbroken to medieval Europe and even to Bethlehem. That is an illusion.

By the early nineteenth century old Christmas lay dying in the English-speaking world. By mid-century, it *had* died. The authentic English Christmas of boar's head and plum pudding, of mistletoe and caroling, of boy bishops and Father Christmas—the Christmas Anglo-Americans had always striven, however inaccurately, to celebrate—gave a little groan and flatlined. Had social and cultural development followed slightly different paths, today's average American might not even know what Christmas was.

The Christmas we celebrate today is a revival. So was Frankenstein's monster. Contemporary Christmas is not only new; to some degree, it is an accident. And from a certain perspective, it is politically incorrect. How did this happen? It is to the improbable story of a holiday's miraculous, yet culturally narrowing resurrection that we turn next.

Notes

1. H. G. Wells, *The Outline of History: The Whole Story of Man.* Rev. ed., ed. Raymond Postgate (Garden City, N.Y.: Doubleday, 1956), pp. 646–47.

2. Maymie Richardson Krythe, *All About Christmas* (New York: Harper and Brothers, 1954), p. 7.

3. Ibid.

4. J. M. Golby and A. W. Purdue, *The Making of the Modern Christmas* (Athens, Ga.: University of Georgia, 1986), p. 33.

5. Ibid., p. 35.

6. Krythe, p. 7.

7. Golby and Purdue, p. 33.

8. Ibid.

9. Krythe, p. 7.

10. Golby and Purdue, p. 35.

11. Ibid. p. 44.

12. Patricia Bunning Stevens, *Merry Christmas! A History of the Holiday* (New York: Macmillan, 1979), p. 127.

13. Golby and Purdue, p. 76.

14. Ibid., p. 40.

15. Ibid.

16. Ibid., pp. 40–42.

17. Golby and Purdue, pp. 34–35.

18. Stevens, p. 124.

19. Golby and Purdue, p. 35.

20. Stevens, p. 121.

21. Krythe, p. 8.

22. James Harwood Barnett, *The American Christmas: A Study in National Culture* (New York: Macmillan, 1954), p. 3.

23. Krythe, p. 9.

24. Golby and Purdue, p. 35; Barnett, p. 3.

25. Barnett, p. 3.

26. Ibid., p. 13.

27. Ibid., p. 12.

28. Golby and Purdue, p. 48.

29. Ibid., p. 35.

30. Barnett, p. 8.

31. Tristram Potter Coffin, *The Book of Christmas Folklore* (New York: Seabury, 1973), p. 173.

32. Ibid., p. 171.

33. James M. Gillis, *This Our Day: Approvals and Disapprovals* (New York: Paulist Press, 1933), p. 43.

8

Back From the Dead

When Christmas was reanimated, its perspective narrowed. The rich heritage of holiday traditions from all over Europe contributed little to the contemporary holiday except as they were refracted through the lenses of British and American sensibilities. The revival of Christmas was an Anglophone achievement, and it was performed by a handful of people. Advocates of political correctness who criticize the overrepresentation of "dead white European males" are missing a bet. With a lone exception, the resurrectors of Christmas were dead white *Anglophone* males. The exception does not make Christmas a multicultural bonanza. She was Victoria, the queen who smilingly oversaw one of the greatest orgies of bigotry, imperialism, and cultural arrogance the planet has ever witnessed. Is the Christmas we know truly so recent? Holiday historians J. M. Golby and A. W. Purdue put it this way: "The Christmas that we know and observe today is very much the creation of the Victorians in Britain and the United States."[1]

Contemporary Christmas—that is, the "standard issue" holiday that arose in Britain and America, crystallized into final form in the U.S., and has now spread all over the world—does not descend *directly* from any of its many international influences. Non-Anglophone customs inform the modern holiday to the degree that they colored British and American holiday practices roughly between 1830 and 1910 and engaged the imaginations of the handful of English-speaking Victorians who brought Christmas back to life.

Amazingly, only six famous Britons and Americans determined the form of our modern holiday. While they were at it, they supplied much of its content. I call these innovators the DWAMQs, pronounced "Dwamicks." The acronym stands for five "Dead White Anglophone Males and

96

a Queen." Everything that is essential about contemporary Christmas was pinched through the limited apertures of their individual understandings.*

What sort of festival did the DWAMQs create? The emerging holiday stressed charity, the celebration of the family, the indulgence of children, and a sharp nostalgia for Christmases past, whether they existed or not.[2] Indirectly, the DWAMQs gave Christmas "a centrality in the yearly cycle which it had never known before."[3]

In part because of the growing importance of Santa Claus, the Victorian Christmas inflated the importance of gift giving. Gift giving had long been associated with the holiday, yet not until Victorian days were gifts the anchor point. "The . . . contemporary emphasis on holiday gifts did not develop until the nineteenth century," reports James Harwood Barnett in a classic study of the holiday.[4]

Saint Nick of the Knickerbockers

Up to now we have discussed the resurrection of Christmas as though the old holiday died in 1850 and the revival debuted in 1851. Real life is less neat. Santa Claus, as distinct from old Saint Nicholas, was one of the most important of the "Victorian innovations"[5] that would shape the new holiday. The story of Santa Claus begins at the dawn of the nineteenth century. Appropriately, the oldest tradition of the "new Christmas" arose in the New World, not the Old.

At the turn of the nineteenth century, memories of the American Revolution were still fresh. The tensions that would lead to the War of 1812 were gathering. Things British being out of fashion, New Yorkers leapt to celebrate their city's Dutch heritage. To this end the New York Historical Society was founded in 1804 by one John Pintard. A born promoter, Pintard had already persuaded the fledgling nation to observe Washington's Birthday and the Fourth of July. Now he would concoct something truly special. Pintard burrowed into Dutch archives and brought back the children's tradition of *Sinter Claes*.[6]

It is doubtful that early nineteenth-century New Yorkers bothered observing the *Sinter Claes* tradition Pintard promoted, but they loved reading about it. One of the readers was surely Washington Irving (1783–1859). Irving, who would one day create *The Legend of Sleepy Hollow,* was already a leading figure on New York's literary scene. Though he didn't know it, he would also become the first of our DWAMQs.

---

*The DWAMQs: Washington Irving, Charles Dickens, Queen Victoria, Clement C. Moore, Thomas Nast, and Francis Church.

In 1809 Irving published an enormously influential work with the ponderous title *The History of New York from the Beginning of the World to the End of the Dutch Dynasty.* It was attributed to one Diedrich Knickerbocker, a pseudonym that fooled few among Irving's intended readers. It was a zany pastiche of truth and tall tales that portrayed "the early Dutch founders as lethargic and simple-minded folk,"[7] a "burlesque . . . in which torpid New Netherland burghers whiled away their days smoking long pipes and swilling immense tankards of ale."[8]

Despite its levity, the "Knickerbocker history" was often mistaken for real history. For example, New Yorkers accepted that the first Dutch ship to land in the New World had had a pipe-smoking Saint Nicholas as its figurehead. Irving meant the claim as satire, but generations of historians have solemnly repeated it as fact.

Saint Nicholas pops up more than two dozen times in the Knickerbocker history. Irving makes it seem that the Dutch founders of New York made his feast day the pivot around which rotated the entire year.

According to "Knickerbocker," each Saint Nicholas Eve children would anticipate the saint's arrival. He was said to course over the treetops on a magic horse and visit all the houses in New York, leaving gifts for the good children and switches for the bad ones.

There is even a passage in the Knickerbocker history that speaks of old Saint Nick "laying a finger beside his nose,"[9] a phrase that would reappear verbatim in the poem *A Visit From Saint Nicholas,* now better known as *The Night Before Christmas.*

Did Irving report a cult of Nicholas that actually existed in Nieuw Amsterdam? Did he exaggerate shamelessly? Or did he make it up? There are few better ways to start a pie fight among historians of Christmas than to ask how seriously the Nieuw Amsterdam Dutch took Saint Nicholas Day. James Harwood Barnett suggested that the colony all but closed down in December:

> In New York the Dutch settlers observed an extended holiday period which was both religious and secular in nature. Public offices closed during the Christmas season, which began during the early part of December. The Dutch celebrated Saint Nicholas (or Sinterklaas) Day on December sixth . . .[10]

But Patricia Bunning Stevens found the idea of a Nicholas cult in a colony dominated by the Dutch Reformed Church absurd:

> Both church and state in the little American colony were thoroughly Protestant. No doubt any open celebration of a saint's feast day would have been severely frowned on. If Saint Nicholas was alive and well and living in New

Amsterdam throughout the colonial period, he must often have been driven underground.[11]

Historian Charles W. Jones went for the jugular. Having studied the history and records of the Dutch colonies and found little evidence of a Saint Nicholas cult, he declared: "Without Washington Irving, there would be no Santa Claus." And again: "Santa Claus was *made* by Washington Irving" (italics in original).[12]

Which was it? When authorities disagree so violently, we may never know for sure. But we know Irving took great liberties with history elsewhere in the Knickerbocker account. It seems reasonable that Saint Nicholas meant less to the actual Dutch colonists than to Irving's Knickerbockers. If so, the contemporary figure of Santa Claus did not develop out of a real tradition. It grew out of a satire of a tradition—an ironic heritage, to say the least.

If Irving had contributed only the Knickerbocker history, his stature among the resurrectors of Christmas would be secure. But he would return to Christmas and Saint Nicholas. In his 1818 *Sketch Book* he described an "old fashioned" Christmas feast set at a fictional English manor. In later years American readers would consciously emulate the Bracebridge Hall Christmas of Irving's story as they struggled to recreate the holiday.[13]

Irving knew a rich vein when he found one. He teamed with his brother-in-law James K. Paulding to churn out a Christmas literature that would slither deep into the heart of American culture. One of Paulding's solo works, *The Book of Saint Nicholas*, fairly burst with manufactured Nicholas lore. It was wildly popular. In 1835 Irving himself helped to found a Saint Nicholas Society, the better to spread the growing, if largely synthetic, cult of Nicholas.[14]

Washington Irving was the first of our DWAMQs, and the only one whose contribution to the emerging holiday would not reach mature form in his own lifetime. Among the Dead White Anglo Males we will profile, only Irving actually did his best work in that condition.

We'll return to the evolution of Santa Claus in chapter nine. Now our story shifts to England, where the second and mightiest of the DWAMQs is about to change the course of holiday history with a stroke of his pen.

One Dickens of a DWAMQ

As early as the 1830s, references to Christmas in English media had begun to increase. The first ones shared a wistful quality of nostalgia for the joys of a holiday presumed long past.[15] Here and there, the holiday was stirring. The English government first recognized Christmas as a legal holiday in 1834. The decree was not binding in Scotland; even in England, the working classes ignored Christmas in droves, sticking instead to their favored New Year's observance.[16]

Still, though traditional Christmas lay dying, cultural forces were gathering for its revival. All England needed was a popular wordsmith who could kick start the engines of renewal. Who better than an insufferably popular author who could say of his own childhood: "Little Red Riding Hood was my first love. I felt that if I could have married Little Red Riding Hood, I should have known perfect bliss."[17]

Charles Dickens (1812–1870) lived to see his work reshape Christmas on both sides of the Atlantic. We'll get to the queen in a moment, but make no mistake, Dickens was the king of the DWAMQs.

The holiday had long fascinated Dickens. At age twenty-four he published a successful novel, *The Pickwick Papers* (1836), that depicted a lavish "traditional" Christmas at an English manor house. Like the Bracebridge Christmas of Irving's *Sketch Book,* the celebration Dickens described at his fictional Dingley Dell grazed its way through an idiosyncratic menu of archaic traditions. Christmas would be revived not as it had been, but as its dying echoes caught the fancy of those who controlled the machinery of renewal.

Seven years after *The Pickwick Papers* would come the work that made Dickens's reputation and left a permanent mark on Christmas. *A Christmas Carol* was written at feverish speed in the closing months of 1843. An indifferent success in print, it became a juggernaut when Dickens began reading it aloud on tour. Within a year of its release, crowds as big as thirty-five thousand were flocking to hear Dickens read the story of Marley, Scrooge, Cratchit, and Tiny Tim.[18]

Scrooge seems a harsh and peculiar figure to modern eyes. Dickens intended him as a cautionary character. But Scrooge appeared less extreme to Dickens's contemporaries than he does to us. Hard-hearted proprietors who abused their workers the way Scrooge exploited Bob Cratchit were a dime a dozen. Scrooge's view that charity was a wasted effort was widely shared; he is remarkable only in how openly he spoke his mind. Finally, Scrooge's contempt for Christmas was far from extraordinary. When Dickens wrote, doubtless many Londoners concurred with the famous judgment, "Bah, humbug!" Scrooge's plan to open for business on Christmas Day was nothing unusual, nor was his desire that Cratchit report to work. Choosing to work on Christmas was less bizarre, and having to work on Christmas less burdensome, in Dickens's time than either might seem today.

The final proof that Scrooge was not so far outside the mainstream of his day comes right from the story itself. What does Scrooge do on Christmas morning? He arises filled with joy and determines to give Bob Cratchit a turkey. Scrooge looks for an errand boy who can go to the butcher's and buy a turkey for him. In no time flat, he finds a little boy walking down the street who, *on Christmas morning,* has nothing better to do than to run an errand for a stranger. Scrooge gives the child some money without the slightest worry that the butcher's shop might be closed. His confidence is justified. The Cratchits sit down to a bountiful holiday feast that they could not have enjoyed if Scrooge's butcher had not done the very thing modern readers condemn Scrooge for considering: being open for business on Christmas morning!

To the audience Dickens wrote for, it made sense that a businessman as hard-hearted as Ebenezer Scrooge might also scorn Christmas. But the first readers of *A Christmas Carol* did not *equate* a disdain for Christmas with a selfish, evil, or stunted personality. Too many of their contemporaries neglected the holiday for us to imagine that. Dickens meant his audience to dislike Scrooge because Scrooge reviled charity, mistreated Cratchit, and was mean with his money. Dickens knew his readers would view those things negatively. Having established that they were true of Scrooge, Dickens next strove to transfer the readers' disapproval to another of Scrooge's characteristics, his contempt for Christmas. It did not come automatically. In 1843, pulling it off confronted Dickens with a storytelling challenge.

Today, by contrast, *A Christmas Carol* could be told in shorthand. Unlike Dickens's readers, modern audiences already hold the stereotype that people who do not celebrate Christmas are ruthless, hard-hearted, bereft of charity, unmoved by compassion—in a word, twisted. According to the stereotype, the reason Scrooge-like people are twisted is that they do not celebrate Christmas. Yet the *proof* that they are twisted is the same: they do not celebrate Christmas. This is the tail-eating logic of prejudice. Think of those old Southern towns where the townsfolk refused to employ blacks, then called them shiftless because they didn't have jobs.

Our contemporary negative stereotypes about people who do not celebrate Christmas are nothing more or less than bigotry. The stereotype on which that bigotry feeds was invented by Charles Dickens, and it was burned indelibly into contemporary consciousness by the success of *A Christmas Carol.* Dickens helped to make Christmas universal by creating an atmosphere in which people who did not care for the holiday no longer dared admit it.

The story of Scrooge became famous for its apparent power to persuade noncelebrators to jump on the Christmas bandwagon. Contemporary accounts abound in which stolid Victorians whose families had not kept Christmas in generations sent for their first holiday turkey after reading *A Christmas Carol.* Within weeks of the slender fable's debut, no lesser light than novelist William Makepeace Thackeray commented: "Had the book appeared a fortnight earlier, all the prize cattle would have been gobbled up in pure love and friendship, Epping denuded of sausages, and not a turkey left in Norfolk. . . ."[19]

Like Washington Irving, Dickens knew how to capitalize on success. To cash in on the fame of *A Christmas Carol,* he wrote Christmas novels in 1844, 1845, 1846, and 1848. The later books were financial successes, but none of them approached the long-term impact of *A Christmas Carol.*

That impact was almost incalculable. Dickens read the entire book aloud to spellbound audiences in England and the United States. Of one American reading Dickens wrote: "They took it so tremendously last night that I was stopped every five minutes. One poor young girl burst into a passion of grief about Tiny Tim and had to be taken out."[20]

Dickens singlehandedly reversed New Englanders' disapproval of the holiday. On Christmas Eve 1867 Dickens read *A Christmas Carol* aloud in Boston. Correspondence survives from a Vermont factory owner whose factory had always been open on Christmas. Attending that reading and hearing Dickens had melted the Vermonter's heart; he ordered that his factory close that Christmas and every Christmas thereafter.[21]

Dickens died in 1870. Christmas had been born anew in his wake. His influence left the holiday more sentimental in character and more universally observed than ever before. And whether Dickens intended it or not, his influence left Christmas far less tolerant of anyone who failed to appreciate its peculiar glories.

Anglicizing the *Tannenbaum*

No aspect of the contemporary Christmas is more ubiquitous than the home Christmas tree. It is popular to think of the Christmas tree as a German innovation, but today's tradition is descended from Britons' and Americans' enthusiastic response to the German custom.

What do we know about the home tree tradition? We have mentioned the paradise tree, trimmed with apples and flanked by tiny figures of Adam, Eve, and the serpent. The Christmas pyramid was a wooden frame with tiered shelves. Each shelf would be laden with evergreen branches, shiny baubles, and candles until the framing disappeared beneath a mantle of holiday finery. Sixteenth-century evidence attests to the custom in Germany and Alsace.[22]

At the same time, Germans had begun experimenting with indoor evergreen trees. The diary of a traveler in the 1500s tells of fir trees being taken into homes in Strasbourg and trimmed with paper roses, wafers, and fruit. By the late sixteenth century inarguable *tannenbaums* were appearing in German lands west of the Rhine. In a letter dated 1708 Lisolette von der Pfalz gave the first surviving description of an indoor tree trimmed with lighted candles in recounting her German childhood.

But the German custom would not evolve directly into our contemporary Christmas tree. First it must pass through English and American eyes. German merchants and diplomats living in eighteenth-century London had Christmas trees, but Britons did not imitate them.

What prompted Britons to make the *tannenbaum* their own? When Queen Anne died without issue in 1716, the Hanoverian line—German cousins of the royal family—succeeded to the British throne. With each generation, the royal family would receive a fresh infusion of German tradition as Windsor monarchs imported spouses from Germany. In 1761 King George III married the German Princess Charlotte. They would have thirteen children, so there was ample opportunity to use the new Christmas traditions Charlotte brought to the household. In 1818 William IV married another German, the Princess Adelaide. When, in 1837, Victoria assumed the throne at age eighteen, she married still another German, Albert of Saxe-Coburg-Gotha.

Here comes our Queen.

George III, William IV, and Victoria all celebrated Christmas with decorated indoor trees. But Britons had fallen in love with the teenage queen, and obsessed on the details of her life. She was a "royal" in the sense we know from supermarket tabloids. As early as 1840 she and Albert had a Christmas tree at Windsor Castle. In 1848 the *Illustrated London News* made Victoria's tree famous. It carried a romanticized engraving of Victoria, Albert, and a gaggle of children and their governess admiring their tree. By contemporary standards, the tree was bare and stubby. Yet that single illustration launched the Christmas tree phenomenon in England. In 1847 few English households had trees; by Christmas 1849 trees were everywhere. In 1854 Dickens, the King DWAMQ himself, wrote favorably of the queen's inadvertent innovation as a "pretty German toy" that had taken England by storm.[23] Seldom does even royalty wield such power.

The story of the Christmas tree in the United States would be more complicated. There is a report of a Christmas pyramid at Bethlehem, Pennsylvania, in 1747. The Hessians had makeshift trees in their camps. Between 1832 and 1851, records tell of trees in Cambridge and Wooster, Massachusetts; Philadelphia, Pennsylvania; Rochester, New York; Richmond, Virginia; and Cleveland, Ohio. James Harwood Barnett speculates that the American tree tradition sprung up independently of English custom and that the American version was genuinely a grass-roots phenomenon.[24] Other chroniclers disagree.

Queen Victoria seems to have played a role in establishing the Christmas tree on American shores. Remember that *London Illustrated News* engraving from 1848 that so captivated the British? In 1850 it was reprinted in *Godey's Lady's Book,* an influential volume of ideas for American housewives. The editors took Victoria down a peg or two. They retouched the engraving to remove her royal tiara and never told readers that she was the queen of England. The result was an evocative image of Yuletide family bliss, featuring an anonymous, attractive, obviously wealthy family whom American readers probably assumed to be Boston or New York society swells.

With these brief accounts of Washington Irving, Charles Dickens, and Queen Victoria, we suspend our census of DWAMQs to consider a sociological question. Santa Claus, Christmas as a universal holiday, and the Christmas tree are gargantuan cultural objects. How did three individuals, no matter who they were, manage to impress such personal stamps on these customs?

The DWAMQs could not have done it if society were not ready for the change. The Christmas tree meshed perfectly with growing Victorian preoccupations with home, family, and children. Older customs like wassailing made of Christmas a community experience for adults; the Christmas tree custom reunited the generations and stressed the primacy of the family.[25]

The Victorian mindset was ready to welcome Christmas back—on its own terms. As the nineteenth century progressed, certain of the old customs flowered once more. Others were distorted, still others cast away. In England, Christmas largely replaced New Year's as the day for holiday gift giving by 1870. Boxing Day was declared a bank holiday for the first time in 1871.[26]

Other aspects of old Christmas were apparently beyond reviving. Authentic wassailing, Yule logs, boar's head dinners, and the "Lord of Misrule" tradition failed to reestablish themselves.

On the other hand, some customs fairly leapt out of the grave. In the first half of the nineteenth century kissing under the mistletoe had been considered a diversion for rural folk or the lower classes. By 1850 it was a universal and beloved feature of holiday gatherings. Christmas mistletoe stands out as one of the only practices with an element of sexual frivolity that the strait-laced Victorians allowed. The famed American illustrator Thomas Nast thought nothing of drawing his own teenage daughter standing expectantly beneath the mistletoe, firelight illuminating her features from below, like a succubus. The effect was as close to an odalisque as one could get with a subject who was standing up and wearing a high-necked black dress—pretty racy stuff by Victorian standards. To publish a drawing of one's daughter in such a pose might have courted scandal under circumstances that did not involve the mistletoe.

It is also surprising how small a role the churches played in the Victorian revival. From its inception, contemporary Christmas was primarily a secular and commercial holiday. The parsons were as surprised as anyone else when after a century-long hiatus, the pews started filling up again on Christmas morning.

American history provides another barometer of the festival's revival. The first state to declare Christmas a legal holiday was Alabama in 1836. The reason for doing this was primarily commercial. Promissory notes could not be collected on a legal holiday, which eliminated the specter of homes being foreclosed or property seized for nonpayment of debts on Christmas.[27] Between 1845 and 1865 twenty-eight states made Christmas a legal holiday. Even Massachusetts gave in, in 1855, though it would be another fifteen years before Boston stopped opening its public schools on Christmas Day. After 1890, newly admitted states customarily recognized Christmas upon joining the Union.[28] Detail addicts may appreciate the table on the following page, which shows when each of the lower forty-eight states and the District of Columbia recognized Christmas Day.

Legal recognition may have come early on the state level, but state legislatures took years to take care of other housekeeping related to the holiday. By 1931, nine states had not yet required public schools to close on Christmas.[29]

Nostalgia by the Pound

How can one wax nostalgic about a holiday that is essentially new? For that matter, why bother? The renewal of Christmas was less a return to old ways than the grafting of an old name onto new traditions. One way to resolve the contradictions this created was to weave into the fabric of the new holiday a bittersweet, if misleading, preoccupation with its own antiquity. It wasn't easy, but Irving and Dickens had shown how to do it.

The Bracebridge Christmas of Irving's *Sketch Book* and Christmas at Dingley Dell in Dickens's *Pickwick Papers* shared an impressive, but utterly false, patina of age and tradition. A predigested nostalgia for non-existent Christmases past became a part of the holiday's mythic cargo.

If Lee Iacocca had tried to manufacture nostalgia by rhapsodizing about the Chrysler minivan he drove in high school, no one would believe

Recognition of Christmas by States

1836	Alabama	1863	Idaho
1838	Louisiana		North Dakota
	Arkansas	1864	Kentucky
1845	Connecticut	1865	Michigan
1848	Pennsylvania		Montana
1849	New York	1868	Kansas
	Virginia	1870	West Virginia
1850	Vermont		District of Columbia
	Georgia	1873	Nebraska
1851	California	1875	South Carolina
1852	Rhode Island		Indiana
1854	New Jersey	1876	New Mexico
1855	Delaware	1877	South Dakota
	Massachusetts		Missouri
1856	Minnesota	1879	Texas
1857	Ohio	1880	Mississippi
	Tennessee	1881	North Carolina
1858	Maine		Florida
1861	New Hampshire		Arizona
	Illinois	1882	Utah
	Nevada	1886	Wyoming
	Wisconsin	1888	Washington
	Colorado	1890	Oklahoma[30]
1862	Oregon		
	Maryland		
	Iowa		

him. Yet children's Christmas literature carved out an important place in mid-nineteenth-century Anglo culture by doing the same thing. As early as 1857, authors would romanticize the Christmas trees that had brightened the holidays of their solidly English childhoods. It posed no obstacle that they were fully grown adults writing just *nine years* after Christmas trees had become popular in England, so that their childhoods could only have included such trees if they were closet Germans.[31]

Not surprisingly, by the end of the nineteenth century, most people had lost sight of the gulf between the holdiay's actual history and socially mediated ideals of Christmas past. Only forty-one years after the custom became broadly popular in the United States, President Benjamin Harrison's 1891 Christmas tree—one of the first in the White House—would be described as an "old-fashioned Christmas tree for the grandchildren."

> The development of the Victorian Christmas, which was initiated by nostalgia for a half-imaginary recent past, was not a revival, for the Christmas which Victorians sought to recapture drew selectively upon many Christmases past; it was a symbiosis of an idealized past with the preoccupations of Victorians themselves and was so extensively refurbished and reinterpreted that it amounts to an invented tradition.[32]

We have seen that some of the most elementary principles of the contemporary Christmas were Victorian inventions, and that the number of "inventors" was astoundingly small. In chapter nine we will complete the census of DWAMQs, and trace the play of post-Christian influences to the present day.

Notes

1. J. M. Golby and A. W. Purdue, *The Making of the Modern Christmas* (Athens, Ga.: University of Georgia Press, 1986), p. 13.
2. Ibid., p. 12.
3. Ibid., p. 13.
4. James Harwood Barnett, *The American Christmas: A Study in National Culture* (New York: Macmillan, 1954), p. 80.
5. Golby and Purdue, p. 57.
6. Patricia Bunning Stevens, *Merry Christmas! A History of the Holiday* (New York: Macmillan, 1979), pp. 82–83.
7. David Maldwyn Ellis, James A. Frost, Harold C. Syrett, and Harry J. Carman, *A History of New York State* (Ithaca, N.Y.: Cornell University Press, 1967), p. 203.

8. David Maldwyn Ellis, *New York: State and City* (Ithaca, N.Y.: Cornell University Press, 1979), p. 148.

9. Tristram Potter Coffin, *The Book of Christmas Folklore* (New York: Seabury, 1973), p. 85.

10. Barnett, p. 4.

11. Stevens, p. 81.

12. Coffin, p. 85.

13. Golby and Purdue, pp. 42–43; Barnett, p. 104.

14. Coffin, pp. 85–86.

15. Golby and Purdue, p. 42.

16. Ibid., p. 76.

17. Charles Dickens quoted in Bruno Bettelheim, *The Uses of Enchantment* (New York: Knopf, 1976).

18. Stevens, p. 128.

19. William Makepeace Thackeray, writing in *Fraser's Magazine,* circa 1844, quoted in Coffin, p. 158.

20. Barnett, p. 16.

21. Golby and Purdue, p. 48.

22. Alexander Murray, "Medieval Christmas," *History Today* (December 1986): 35.

23. Golby and Purdue, p. 61.

24. Barnett, p. 11.

25. Golby and Purdue, p. 61.

26. Ibid., p. 76.

27. Barnett, p. 19.

28. Golby and Purdue, p. 76.

29. Barnett, p. 66.

30. Ibid., p. 20.

31. Golby and Purdue, p. 61.

32. Ibid., p. 44.

9

He Knows When You Are Sleeping

Three down, three to go. Not surprisingly, our three remaining DWAMQs are remembered for finishing the work begun by Washington Irving: refining the modern Santa Claus from the sometimes unpromising ore of the Saint Nicholas tradition. Their names are Clement Clarke Moore, Thomas Nast, and Francis Church.

When Moore Is Less

If Washington Irving was the only DWAMQ whose influence on the holiday peaked after his death, Clement Moore (1779–1863) holds a stranger distinction. He is the only DWAMQ who may be remembered for something he did not do. We will rattle the skeleton in Moore's closet presently, but first, the accepted facts of his biography.

Clement Clarke Moore was born already tied to the nation's history: His father was the clergyman who gave Alexander Hamilton communion after Hamilton was mortally wounded in his ill-advised duel with Aaron Burr. The younger Moore became a professor of Greek and Hebrew at New York City's General Theological Seminary. He fathered six children and by all accounts was a doting, if reserved, parent.

The works of which Clement Moore was proudest were a translation of the works of the Roman satirist Juvenal and a Hebrew dictionary. He also published poetry.[1] Of course, Clement Moore is best remembered for a children's bagatelle often called *The Night Before Christmas*. That is not its real name. And neither, some scholars believe, is Moore its real author.

A Visit From Saint Nicholas, as the ballad was first titled, made its premiere appearance in the *Sentinel* (Troy, New York) on December 23, 1823. Editor Orville L. Holley ran the composition anonymously. It lay unnoticed until 1829, when the *New York Morning Courier* reprinted it. The *Schenectady Whig* picked it up in 1832. Sometime in the 1830s, Troy lithographer Myron King published the first illustrated version. In 1837 it appeared in a collection of poems by New Yorkers, where Moore claimed authorship for the first time in print. In 1844 Moore included the work in a short anthology of his own poems.[2]

In 1849 and 1855 *A Visit From Saint Nicholas* was reprinted in two influential anthologies of American verse. After the Civil War it became a staple in school readers and holiday supplements, making its place in holiday culture secure.[3]

It is already apparent that the origins of *A Visit From Saint Nicholas* are mysterious. Assuming that Moore was the author, how did his most significant work turn up anonymously in a Troy, New York newspaper? The traditional explanation is that Moore had composed the ballad for the amusement of his children. Having memorized it, he would perform it for his family each year at Christmas time. If this is how *The Night Before Christmas* began, Moore must have composed it no later than 1822, suggesting that he might have been influenced by Irving's Knickerbocker history or by the Saint Nicholas doggerel churned out by Irving and James K. Paulding. The traditional account continues with Moore's wife, Eliza, setting down the text of the poem in a family album where it was spotted by an unknown friend of the family who recopied it and gave it to editor Orville Holley.[4] Today we have a word for friends of that sort. We call them "plagiarists."

In another popular explanation of the poem's origins, by 1822 Moore was performing *A Visit From Saint Nicholas* for other families around New York. Harriet Butler, daughter of a Troy clergyman, is said to have heard the ballad and copied it into her album. (No one in these stories has any trouble memorizing stanza after stanza of verse on first hearing.) The following autumn, she is said to have given the poem to Holley without revealing its source.[5]

Those are two of the traditional accounts. They share an assumption that Moore did, in fact, write *A Visit From Saint Nicholas*. Some historians question Moore's claim of authorship. Instead they propose that the true author was Henry Livingston, Jr. (1748–1828), a land surveyor and Revolutionary War veteran. The claim has long standing in Livingston's family; as late as the 1860s, a member of Livingston's family got into a "violent dispute" with one of Moore's grandsons over authorship of the poem.

Based on descriptions of Livingston and Moore by their contemporaries, Livingston certainly seems better suited temperamentally to be the true author. Moore was described as severe and pedantic. Livingston was apparently a cut-up who often improvised light-hearted poetry and peppered his youthful correspondence with doggerel of this character:

> To my dear brother Beekman: I sit down to write,
> Ten minutes past eight and a very cold night.
> Not far from me sits, with a baullancy cap on,
> Our very good cousin, Elizabeth Tappan.[6]

This ditty, presumably composed between 1660 and 1775, is written in the very meter *A Visit From Saint Nicholas* would later impress on the mind of every school child.

Moore had made suspicious claims of authorship before. His 1844 poetry anthology included thirty-seven compositions. Two were credited to his wife; of the rest, Moore claimed in his preface that all were "written by me." Yet two of the thirty-five works were credited in their own subtitles to other poets. Three others were direct translations from the Italian or Greek. "Perhaps," comments folklorist Tristram Potter Coffin, ". . . in the fashion of country singers, he felt anything he revised or touched up could be classified as his."[7]

Whoever wrote *The Night Before Christmas*—for once, I will follow convention and credit Moore—there is no exaggerating the ballad's importance. In a handful of verses, it completes almost the entire work of transforming Saint Nicholas into the modern Santa Claus. Every detail in *The Night Before Christmas* has been incorporated into our canonical Santa Claus myth.

In places, the ballad looked to the past: The image of Santa "laying a finger aside of his nose" came straight out of Irving's Knickerbocker history. Elsewhere, *The Night Before Christmas* pushed the Santa myth squarely into the future. Moore dispensed with Saint Nicholas Eve, attaching Santa Claus to Christmas Eve. He swept away the horse and wagon associated with Saint Nicholas, substituting the sleigh drawn by flying reindeer that figures so prominently in the contemporary Santa Claus myth. Even this appears to be derivative, since a children's holiday book, *The Children's Friend: A New-Year's Present, to Little Ones from Five to Twelve,* included the following couplet: "Old Sancte Claus with much delight / His reindeer drives this frosty night."[8]

Moore's most important achievement was to secularize Saint Nicholas. Gone were the gaunt silhouette, the towering height, the bishop's robes, and the mitered cap. In their place were pagan elements. Moore's Nicholas was short, rotund, and jolly—an elf, not a saint.

With *The Night Before Christmas,* Santa Claus was essentially complete. An 1842 editorial in a New York City publication makes clear how quickly the myth had caught on and how thoroughly observers of the period understood its pagan origins.

> Tomorrow will be Christmas, jolly rosy Christmas, the Saturnalia of children. Ah, how the little rogues long for the adventure of this day; for with it comes their generous friend Santa Claus with his sleigh, like the purse of Fortunatus, over-flowing with treasures.[9]

But the imaginations of children are not confined to words. The further evolution of Santa Claus would require the services of a fifth DWAMQ, illustrator Thomas Nast.

Santa Gets the Picture

A gaggle of artists strove to capture Santa Claus as the figure grew popular in the mid-nineteenth century. An 1843 engraving by illustrators Sherman and Smith showed an elfin Santa figure stuffing toys into children's stockings. He wore a fur coat and cap, but still a bishop's cross. In 1847 J. G. Chapman depicted a Cavalier Santa Claus in fur clothing and high boots, with a feather in his cap. Yet as late as the 1870s, a respected illustrator like New York's Fredericks could try to pass off as Santa Claus a stern-faced figure clad in the robes of a Druid priest, wearing a holly wreath on his forehead, and holding out a glass of wine.[10]

The job of creating a consensus vision of Santa Claus would fall, as did most of the image mongering of late nineteenth-century America, to the famed New York illustrator Thomas Nast (1840–1902).

Nast was born at Landau, Bavaria, the son of a military musician. Despairing of Europe's future, Nast's father sent the rest of his family to America while he served out his enlistment in an army band. Nast arrived in the United States in 1846 at age six. An unpromising student, he displayed one exceptional talent, drawing. He won a coveted illustrator's job at New York-based *Leslie's Magazine* when only fifteen years old.[11] At age twenty, Nast assumed the post he would hold for three decades: head cartoonist at the influential *Harper's Weekly*. From 1860 to 1890, Nast would revolutionize the craft of political cartooning. Nast invented both the Democratic party donkey *and* the GOP elephant. If he did not invent the figures of Uncle Sam and Columbia, the woman in Grecian robes who represented the purity and high seriousness of America to the nineteenth-century imagination, he unquestionably hammered them into their final forms.[12]

Nast's acerbic drawings influenced American history. Every U.S. presidential candidate whom Nast supported got elected. Nast's best-known encounter with American history came in 1871, when he almost single-handedly toppled from power Tammany Hall tyrant William Marcy "Boss" Tweed.[13]

Nast's treatment of the 300-pound Tweed was typical of his approach to social-commentary cartooning. In Nast's visual vocabulary, obesity almost always signaled moral infelicity. So did facial hair. An amazing engraving survives that shows King Death, a crowned skeleton, pinning a medal on Bacchus for having spread so much ruin and death among humankind. (See photo insert.) Bacchus is fat, with chubby cheeks, a full, snowy beard and moustache, and long white hair. He squints delightedly, his jolly face oddly familiar. Nast's Bacchus even wears a crown of holly, a token of paganism. All of these elements would recur in Thomas Nast's cartooning as symbols of the artist's disapproval. At least, they would until Nast poured them all into his influential vision of Santa Claus.

Nast's first drawing of Santa Claus appeared in an 1862 edition of *Harper's*. It was a Civil War propaganda cartoon in which Santa—about four feet tall and clad in the stars and stripes—drops off a sleighful of presents to a campful of good (that is, Union) soldiers.[14] Santa was altogether elfin in appearance. His sleigh was pulled by reindeer. He wore a plain fur cap, not the stylized sleeping cap of later depictions. In this early incarnation Santa actually looked a bit disreputable. (See photo insert.)

From that 1862 debut until 1886, Thomas Nast would continually return to the Santa Claus theme in holiday numbers of *Harper's*. Casting ever farther afield for activities in which Santa could be shown, Nast fleshed out the details in our contemporary Santa Claus myth that Clement Moore had failed to supply. It is in a Nast cartoon that we first see Santa reading children's letters, monitoring their behavior from a parapet with an old-fashioned telescope, and recording the names of good and bad children in immense books.[15] Nast also established Santa's North Pole headquarters. An 1882 cartoon shows the old elf perched atop a huge package labeled, "Christmas Box 1882, St. Nicholas, North Pole." Nine years later, Nast would treat *Harper's* readers to an insider's view of Santa's North Pole workshop.[16] Other classic engravings would show Santa Claus trimming a Christmas tree, flying through the skies in his sleigh, climbing down a chimney, stealing out of a Union household just in time for the war-weary man of the house to return home on Christmas leave, and taking down a little girl's Christmas list over the then newfangled telephone.

By 1886, Nast's style had fallen out of fashion. He was dismissed from *Harper's*. Unfortunate investments and a too-easy generosity ruined him financially. President Theodore Roosevelt took pity on the bankrupt artist and gave Nast a diplomatic appointment. Unfortunately, the only available posting was Grayaquil, Ecuador. Because of the threat of yellow fever, Nast left his family in the United States. Already in failing health, he contracted yellow fever after a brief period of service. Thomas Nast died of yellow fever alone in Grayaquil on December 7, 1892.[17]

The Nast-Moore Santa Claus was promptly seized upon by an army of writers and artists. Mrs. Claus was not long in appearing. She was introduced in 1889 in a children's book titled *Goody Santa Claus on a Sleigh Ride,* written by no less a literary figure than Katharine Lee Bates, lyricist of "America the Beautiful." In December 1901 the *Ladies' Home Journal* published a ballad by Ednah Proctor Clarke titled *The Revolt of Santa Claus.* In this poem Santa grew disgusted with human selfishness and decided to stop making his Christmas rounds. At last, his heart was softened by a delegation of children from many nations. Such themes would become common in what can only be described as a burgeoning "Santa exploitation literature." Popular sentimentalists who created characteristic—and lucrative—Santa Claus works included Bret Harte, Roark Bradford, James Lane Allen, John Macy, James Russell Lowell, Eugene Field, and even Louisa May Alcott.[18]

The American Santa Claus lost no time in leaping the Atlantic. As early as 1893, the *Illustrated London News* would run an engraving of two little girls hiding on the great stairway of a fashionable house "watching out for Santa Claus." That's all the time it took to establish Santa Claus in the land of Father Christmas. As late as 1912, the British scholar Clement A. Miles could still write: "Santa Klaus . . . has come to us via the United States . . . where he still has immense popularity."[19] Miles apparently expected the Santa Claus myth to evaporate not only in England but even in the United States. Unfortunately, he was wrong.

The figure of Santa Claus would undergo one more refinement before reaching its final modern form. That was provided in 1931, when illustrator Haddon Sundblom began to churn out colorful paintings of Santa Claus for the Coca-Cola Company. Sundblom made Santa taller and more robust, less like an elf and more like an overweight superhero.[20] In that form he has remained ever since.

Church Defends Blind Faith

The Moore/Nast Santa Claus differed from Saint Nicholas in ways that enhanced the figure's marketability as the holiday grew more secular. His appearance was more inviting than the sere and judgmental figure of Nicholas. His powers were magical rather than holy. Instead of the pale horse of Woden and Berchta, Santa's flying reindeer conveyed an exotic flavor of the far north as they seemingly explained Santa's ability to service the whole world in a single night. Taking care of all the good little boys and girls in the world was a job that required an impressive home base: hence, the mystical North Pole workshop at which Santa spied on the world's children and exploited the labor of his armies of elves.

From a metaphysical standpoint, the most important difference between Saint Nicholas and Santa Claus was the sort of existence that children were expected to impute to the two characters. Nicholas was a religious figure. The reality of Santa Claus was of a more mundane sort.

If little children were supposed to believe in the existence of Santa Claus as a literal fact, how should the culture finesse the inevitable moment when the child grew older and could no longer maintain that belief? In a Victorian society that otherwise lionized practicality, naturalism, and the world view of science, how could the same Santa myth hold different meanings for young children, adolescents, and adults?

Our sixth and final DWAMQ rose to this philosophical challenge. He dashed off his solution in an afternoon. No DWAMQ earned his or her place for doing less work! Yet the approach to the "Santa Claus dilemma" that Francis Church contributed has defined the way American families have treated the existence of Santa Claus for almost a century.

It all began in the fall of 1897, when the editors of the *New York Sun* received an unusual letter.

Dear Editor:

I am eight years old. Some of my little friends say there is no Santa Claus. Papa says "If you see it in The Sun it's so." Please tell me truth, is there a Santa Claus?

Virginia O'Hanlon
115 West 95th Street
New York City

Yes, Virginia, there was such a letter. Francis Church was one of the *Sun*'s editorial writers, and the reply he drafted to Virginia O'Hanlon's query leapt into the Christmas canon. It became one of the most widely reprinted passages in the history of American journalism, especially in truncated form with the third and fourth paragraphs removed.

Church's "Yes, Virginia" is seldom reprinted in its entirety. We will read it in its entirety, just like the readers of the *New York Sun* on September 21, 1897.

Virginia, your little friends are *wrong*. They have been affected by the skepticism of a skeptical age. They do not *believe* except they *see*. They think that nothing can be which is not comprehensible by their little minds. All minds, Virginia, whether they be men's or children's are little. In this great universe of ours man is a mere insect, an ant, in his intellect, as compared with the boundless world about him, as measured by the intelligence capable of grasping the whole of truth and knowledge.

Yes, Virginia, there *is* a Santa Claus. He exists as certainly as love, and generosity and devotion exist, and you know that they abound and give to your life its highest beauty and joy. Alas! How dreary would be the world if there were no Santa Claus! It would be as dreary as if there were no Virginias. There would be no childlike faith, then, no poetry, no romance to make tolerable this existence. We should have no enjoyment, except in sense and sight. The Eternal light with which childhood fills the world would be extinguished.

Not believe in *Santa Claus!* You might as well not believe in fairies! You might get your papa to hire men to watch in all the chimneys on Christmas Eve to catch Santa Claus, but even if they did not see Santa Claus coming down what would that prove? Nobody sees Santa Claus, but that is no sign that there is no Santa Claus. The most real things in the world are those that neither children nor men can see. Did you ever see fairies dancing on the lawn? Of course not, but that's no proof that they are not there. Nobody can conceive or imagine all the wonders there are unseen and unseeable in the world.

You tear apart a baby's rattle and see what makes the noise inside, but there is a veil covering the unseen world which not the strongest man, nor even the united strength of all the strongest men that ever lived, could tear apart. Only faith, fancy, poetry, love, romance, can push aside that curtain and view—and picture the supernal beauty and glory beyond. Is it all real? Ah, Virginia, in all this world there is nothing else real and abiding.

No Santa Claus! Thank God he lives, and he lives forever. A thousand years from now, Virginia, nay, ten times ten thousand years from now, he will continue to make glad the heart of childhood.[21]

Trying to cobble up an all-purpose Santa Claus dodge and make a deadline at the same time, Francis Church blended together strands of Christian mysticism, nineteenth-century Trascendentalism and Romanticism, and a broad distrust of scientific objectivity. The result was a disingenuous evasion.

Let's "deconstruct" Church's stonewalling whoppers sentence by sentence, including the passages one—understandably—seldom sees:

Virginia, your little friends are *wrong*. They have been affected by the skepticism of a skeptical age. They do not *believe* except they *see*.

What's wrong with that? Sounds like a sound beginning to me.

> They think that nothing can be which is not comprehensible by their little minds. All minds, Virginia, whether they be men's or children's are little. In this great universe of ours man is a mere insect, an ant, in his intellect, as compared with the boundless world about him, as measured by the intelligence capable of grasping the whole of truth and knowledge.

Here Church rings in a Christian attack upon the limitations of reason. Framed as a warning against intellectual *hubris,* it had been popular among nineteenth-century preachers and writers eager to defend Christianity against the mockery of rationalists. If such language is friendly to faith, it is hostile to science and serious inquiry. It belittles the very possibility of intersubjective human knowledge. Secular humanists would reject this line of argument out of hand. Today it should make as little headway among mainstream and liberal religious believers, who have largely made their peace with the "demon" of science.

> Yes, Virginia, there *is* a Santa Claus. He exists as certainly as love, and generosity and devotion exist, and you know that they abound and give to your life its highest beauty and joy.

Here Church improperly shifts his terms. He starts out with what appears to be a simple statement that Santa Claus exists, then sidesteps into a description of the "existence" of love, generosity, and devotion. What he fails to make clear, of course, is that those qualities exist in a secondary and metaphorical way, not at all the literal kind of "existence" shared by chairs, houses, the Liberty Bell, and (at the time, anyway) Virginia O'Hanlon and Francis Church. That was the kind of existence Virginia was asking about, and it was deceptive of Church to pretend to answer her question, then wriggle into the *demi-monde* of metaphor.

This is Church's solution to the problem of a literal Santa Claus, and it has been adopted by generations of parents. When children grew old enough to find naive belief in Santa unsatisfactory, one could simply shift the terms of the discussion. Parents could mumble something like "Santa Claus is the spirit of giving" and walk away, imagining that the child would have a transcendent experience of discovery and encounter a fulfilling new world of deeper meanings. The only problem is that children's minds don't think that way. Sociologist Warren Hagstrom describes language like Church's as "higher criticism," recalling the term used for scientific evaluation of the texts of the Bible. Adults interpret such language as "giving metaphorical interpretations to Santa." Kids don't see it that way! To them the weasel words are literal expressions of fact, simply another layer of concepts to accept, even if they are harder to understand. "Santa as the spirit of giving" is accepted literally, just like the older vision of "Santa as a physical creature who lives at the North Pole."

> Alas! How dreary would be the world if there were no Santa Claus! It would be as dreary as if there were no Virginias. There would be no childlike faith, then, no poetry, no romance to make tolerable this existence.

Here Church issues a veiled threat—what, no Virginias?—and hopes that its emotional resonancc will conceal its irrelevance. Virginia asked what was true, not what was tolerable.

> We should have no enjoyment, except in sense and sight.

Have we enjoyment except in sense, which encompasses sight, hearing, smell, taste, and touch? Materialists would argue that this is precisely all there is to life. Issues like these had been thrashed out thoroughly by the 1890s. Even when pretending to write for an eight-year-old, Church cheated in thinking he could *assume* such a concept instead of arguing for it.

> The Eternal light with which childhood fills the world would be extinguished.

Hang on, Church almost jumps the tracks with this one. The "Eternal" with a capital E prepares the reader for some appeal to Christian doctrine. But Church stops short; in Christian doctrine the "eternal light" is not thought to enter the world primarily through the institution of childhood. Church feints toward Christianity in order to dignify the far less focused brand of spirituality that he actually means to evoke. In Church's time it was called "New Thought" and associated with names like Helena Blavatsky, P. D. Ouspensky, Annie Besant, and others. In our time we call it "New Age." In any age it is claptrap, and Church will appeal to it far more openly before he is through.

> Not believe in *Santa Claus!* You might as well not believe in fairies!

Okay, Frank. You've got a deal.

> You might get your papa to hire men to watch in all the chimneys on Christmas Eve to catch Santa Claus, but even if they did not see Santa Claus coming down what would that prove?

Strictly speaking, it wouldn't prove there was no Santa Claus. No amount of negative evidence can truly prove a proposition as sweeping as "There is no Santa Claus," because in theory Santa Claus can always be lurking in the next place you might look. But if one attaches as much importance as Virginia presumably did to the hypothesis that "Santa Claus comes down all the chimneys on Christmas Eve," then the test Church proposes would go a long way toward disconfirming it.

Nobody sees Santa Claus, but that is no sign that there is no Santa Claus.

Sure, and ignorance is strength. If the existence of Santa Claus is consistent with a complete lack of evidence for Santa Claus, how would you distinguish a world in which Santa Claus existed from one in which he did not? Church skates away from this contradiction by feinting once more toward unfocused spirituality.

The most real things in the world are those that neither children nor men can see. Did you ever see fairies dancing on the lawn? Of course not, but that's no proof that they are not there. Nobody can conceive or imagine all the wonders there are unseen and unseeable in the world.

Again Church tries to settle an argument by bringing up fairies; strict Christian readers might find his preoccupation with creatures of pagan myth disconcerting. Again he alludes to impossibility of disproving any proposition, no matter how stupid it may be. Is intellect that helpless? Of course, says Church, and to prove it he returns to the limitations-of-reason theme.

You tear apart a baby's rattle and see what makes the noise inside, but there is a veil covering the unseen world which not the strongest man, nor even the united strength of all the strongest men that ever lived, could tear apart. Only faith, fancy, poetry, love, romance, can push aside that curtain and view—and picture the supernal beauty and glory beyond. Is it all real? Ah, Virginia, in all this world there is nothing else real and abiding.

Let me make sure I've got this straight. In all the world nothing can be more real than the unreal. No amount of strength and determination can answer the big questions, but with enough faith, fancy, and romance all confusion can be brushed aside. After close to a hundred years of being raised on that, no wonder 94 percent of Americans are scientifically illiterate and more than half believe in such lunacy as extra-sensory perception![22]

No Santa Claus! Thank God he lives, and he lives forever. A thousand years from now, Virginia, nay, ten times ten thousand years from now, he will continue to make glad the heart of childhood.

Quick, it's near the end. Mention God so uncritical readers will recall this mixed bag of spiritualism and anti-intellectualism in a warm Christian light. Close with a ringing affirmation that sounds important but offers no serious prospect of ever being confirmed or denied, and clock out. Another day, another editorial.

In fairness to Francis Church, he was just writing a puff piece. He never dreamed that generations of parents would actually attempt to manage an important part of their relationships with their growing children by the incoherent guidelines he offered.

At the same time, when we pick apart Church's reply this way we begin to understand the downside of having moved Saint Nicholas/Santa Claus outside the religious sphere. If Santa's reality is open to criticism like any other truth claim, adults quickly paint themselves into a corner. To preserve the belief in Santa, parents must invest heavily in double-talk that has the effect of stunting children's development of critical thinking skills. Hand in hand with this goes the disturbing requirement that parents lie to their children about Santa's existence. Some parents not only lie, but go to absurd lengths to fabricate supporting "evidence." This is insidious stuff, and we will examine it much more closely in chapter ten.

After the DWAMQs

Our census of the DWAMQs is complete. Five dead white Anglo males and a queen—Washington Irving, Charles Dickens, Clement Clarke Moore, Thomas Nast, Francis Church, and Queen Victoria—provided almost all the raw material English and American society needed to construct the contemporary Christmas festival. Some, like Victoria, did their work in-advertently. Some, like Church, did it quickly. Some, like Moore, may have borrowed much of it from somebody else. But these six people were indispensable to the evolution of Christmas as we know it today. If even one of them had never lived, Christmas would be different. It might not even exist at all. It was truly that close.

Now let's refocus and take a look at the ways the holiday traditions established by the DWAMQs filled out. Numerous independent customs have arisen to attach themselves to the cultural preoccupation that is Christmas.

The poinsettia was introduced to the United States in 1828 by Joel R. Poinsett of Charleston, South Carolina. A former congressman and an amateur botanist, Poinsett was then serving as U.S. Minister to Mexico, where the flower originated. With luck, a poinsettia could be persuaded to open its scarlet petals on Christmas day, a Holy Grail that generations of gardeners pursued, much as lovers stalk the simultaneous orgasm.[23]

In England after the turn of the twentieth century, a sixty-year tradition of attending concerts, stage shows, and sporting events on Christmas faded. Christmas now seemed more appropriate for family activities than public gatherings. Shops and commercial enterprises finally began closing on Christmas. British daily newspapers stopped issuing Christmas editions for the first time in 1912. By 1919 British author Evelyn Waugh could write in his diary, "Like birthdays, Christmas gets duller and duller. Soon it will merely be a day when the shops are inconveniently shut."[24]

Electric light was a natural companion to the Christmas tree. A vice president of Thomas Alva Edison's electric light company had the first electrically lighted tree, in 1882. Appalled by the deaths, injuries, and damages caused each year by trees decorated with candles, reformers pressed for wide adoption of electric lights. Insurance companies joined their campaign against the candle. In 1895 President Grover Cleveland put the first electric lights on a White House Christmas tree. The first giant outdoor "community Christmas tree" appeared at Pasadena, California, in 1909. New York followed in 1912, Philadelphia in 1913. In 1923 President Calvin Coolidge lit the first community tree in Washington, D.C. Quite the Christmas booster, Coolidge would also deliver the first presidential Christmas address, in 1927.

The first community tree in Britain rose in Trafalgar Square, London, in 1947. As early as 1951 there were reports of families in Puerto Rico and the Philippines celebrating Christmas with evergreen trees and artificial snow, both "as rare in the islands as they are in Judea."

In 1954 President Dwight D. Eisenhower greatly expanded the national tree lighting ceremony, inviting representatives of twenty-seven countries to join in what he dubbed the "Pageant for Peace."[25] The expanded ceremony would become a recurrent focus of church-state separation controversies, particularly after the addition of a manger scene.

Several popular Christmas carols have surprising histories. The carol began as a medieval round that was danced and sung. It is pre-Christian, and early ones were not connected with Christmas. In medieval times, most were lewd.[26]

The lyrics of "Joy to the World" were composed by Isaac Watts in 1748. Not until 1872, almost a century and a quarter later, did Lowell Mason recognize that it lent itself to a melody borrowed from Handel's *Messiah*.[27]

"Jingle Bells" was composed in 1857 by James Pierpont. The son of a noted abolitionist, the young Pierpont found a nasty way to rebel: He moved to Georgia and joined the Confederate Army. A ne'er-do-well, Pierpont was constantly broke, but he lived to see his nephew John Pierpont Morgan become one of America's wealthiest business magnates.[28]

Not until 1859 did John W. Hopkins, Jr., write "We Three Kings of Orient Are," a carol often thought to be of more ancient origin.[29]

The lyrics of "I Heard the Bells on Christmas Day" were composed in December 1863 by the great American poet Henry Wadsworth Longfellow. It is set to "Waltham," an English traditional song. The text was written immediately after Longfellow learned that his son, a lieutenant in the Union Army, had been badly wounded in the Civil War. It mixes equal parts of hope and trepidation for the future.[30]

"Away in a Manger" was probably composed by an anonymous Pennsylvania Dutch poet. One of Luther's hymns, *Von Himmel Ham Der Engel Schar,* treats a similar theme and may have inspired the anonymous writer, but we have no stronger reason than tradition for thinking so. The carol was unknown in Germany before the contemporary version spread from America. "Away in a Manger" did not appear in print until 1885. In that year *A Little Children's Book: For Schools and Families* was published in Philadelphia. Even this volume included only the text. Not until 1887 would J. R. Murray compose the better known musical setting. Murray erroneously credited Luther for the lyrics in the first published arrangement. In Catholic circles, the preferred tune was James E. Spillman's melody "Flow Gently, Sweet Afton," a setting of a poem by Robert Burns. Perhaps Catholics changed the melody because of a rumor that Luther had written the *music.* "Away in a Manger" is a classic example of the power Christmas folkways have to make recent additions seem ancient.[31]

How about "Little Drummer Boy"? It has to be old; that "pa rum pum pum pum" device is straight out of medieval French folk songs. Yet "Drummer Boy" was composed in the early 1940s by Katharine Kennicott Davis, a professional songwriter who consciously lifted the drum-sound motif from early French music.[32]

Red Nose or Red Face?

The most intriguing story behind a recent Christmas standard must be that of "Rudolph the Red-Nosed Reindeer." It made the last permanent addition to the Santa Claus's canonical entourage. There is not a suggestion of tradition or primitive origin in the story of "Rudolph."

In 1939 Robert May was a staff copywriter for Montgomery Ward. The chain needed something for its Santa Clauses to give away, so May cobbled up the verse story of Rudolph. He consciously borrowed from other popular children's stories, especially "The Ugly Duckling." Children could identify with the hapless Rudolph, whose physical difference made him an outcast. But the psychology cut deeper. May made Santa Claus fallible; Santa could not make his way around the world on that foggy Christmas Eve without Rudolph's help. The tale encouraged children to imagine themselves saving Christmas, and to imagine their parents in the dependent Santa Claus role. Rudolph as "a child figure able to aid the parents" was an appealing alter ego indeed.

In 1939 the *ersatz* elves at Ward's gave away almost two and a half million copies of Rudolph's story. Ward's used it again in 1946, when more than three and a half million copies were distributed. By 1947 Ward's was done with "Rudolph." May requested and was granted the copyright. Desperate for promotion, in 1949 May sent the poem to songwriter Johnny Marks. Gene Autry recorded it in a country style; Bing Crosby recorded it almost simultaneously with a conventional band backing him up. The two recordings quickly sold fifty million records. "Rudolph the Red-Nosed Reindeer" was for years the music industry's biggest-selling title.

In 1951 May attempted a sequel, "Rudolph's Second Christmas," but it did not live up to the impact of its predecessor. In due time, animated TV specials, cartoons, and TV spots featuring Rudolph made the naso-fluorescent ungulate an indispensable citizen of the North Pole.[33]

Our survey is almost complete. A few additional items should suffice to show how much of the furniture of our "traditional, old-fashioned" Christmas is of recent origin. For example, the U.S. postal system has marketed commemorative Christmas stamps for only thirty years. No Christmas stamp was issued by any government until 1937. In 1943 war-torn Hungary issued the first Christmas set, showing the whole Nativity story. In 1959 the Vatican issued a three-stamp set based on Raphael's *Nativity*.

In 1962 the United States issued its first Christmas stamp. The completely secular design featured a green wreath and red candles. Not until 1966 would the Post Office go over the line and issue a stamp bearing an image of the Madonna and Child. Church-state separation groups complained, and Americans United for Separation of Church and State filed a lawsuit that was ultimately unsuccessful. In 1970 the U.S. Postal Service adopted the practical, if constitutionally dubious, policy it has followed from that day forward: issuing two Christmas stamps each year, one religious in tone, the other secular.

And Scrooge Begat the Grinch

A final distinguishing characteristic of modern Christmas is a growing mean-spiritedness toward those who do not celebrate the holiday. Such attitudes are not altogether new. Holiday historian Maymie Richardson Krythe preserves a charming ditty that reflects Old English attitudes toward holiday spoilsports:

> Whosoever against Holly do cry
> In a rope shall be hung full high.
> Alleluia![34]

"Alleluia!"?

A Christmas Carol introduced millions to a virulent new negative stereotype of the noncelebrator. To call someone "Scrooge" is "a severe indictment," as James Harwood Barnett observed.[35] Unable to find a better way to condemn David and Sharon Schoo, the "home alone" parents accused of leaving their young daughters unsupervised while they vacationed in Acapulco, a bystander who witnessed their arrest at O'Hare International Airport hissed "Scrooge!"[36]

Yet American culture has produced an even more sinister figure in the Grinch of Dr. Seuss's children's classic, *How the Grinch Stole Christmas.*[37] This 1957 picture book became an overnight success. No Christmas innovation other than Rudolph has been so quickly accepted into the holiday's canon.

The sour old Grinch lives on a mountain high above Whoville, a city filled with insufferably happy, childlike beings called Whos. Irritated by the sound of Christmas carols from Whoville, the Grinch gets the "wonderful awful idea" of ruining their Christmas for good. In this he goes one step beyond Scrooge. The Grinch not only disdains the holiday, but schemes to destroy it!

The story gave Christmas lore something it had lacked since the festival became secular: a villain. Herod didn't do it for modern children, and repellent as he was, Scrooge was not fundamentally evil. With *How the Grinch Stole Christmas,* we see "the transformation of the Scrooge figure into an active perpetrator of evil."[38]

Having stolen all of the Whos' Christmas paraphernalia, the Grinch prepares to throw it off the top of a tall mountain when he hears the sound of distant voices raised in song. Undeterred, the Whos are gaily singing carols! The Grinch is touched; his heart "grows ten sizes" and he scrambles back down to Whoville to return everyone's decorations.

In an analysis by Thomas Burns, the Grinch represents adults' threat to children that Santa Claus won't reward them at Christmas if they misbehave. The Grinch's climactic loss of resolve represents the triumph of the child: "The parental ogre is defeated and the presents are reclaimed by the childlike community of Whoville."[39]

With such charming stuff we teach our children to despise anyone whose feelings toward the holiday deviate from the mainstream attitude of terrierlike adulation. For most, it begins in childhood. American culture has a multitude of ways to acquaint children with negative views of Christmas abstainers. *A Christmas Carol* and *The Grinch* are high on the list, but for sheer audacity I've never seen anything to match a lavishly illustrated children's book that came out in 1982. *The Santa Claus Book* by Alden Perkes purports to tell young readers everything they ever wanted to know about the jolly old elf. Some of it is breathtakingly ingenious; it never occurred to me to wonder how the elves plan their surprise parties. Somewhere between the machine Santa uses to read children's minds and the diagram of how airflow around a reindeer's antlers generates lift there lurks a breathtaking attack upon noncelebrators of the holiday. (See photo insert.) Under the headline "What Happens to Non-Believers?" Perkes presents two drawings of an adult male. In the first drawing, the man is dapper, happy, and healthy; in the second, he is disheveled and apparently near clinical depression. The text claims that the drawings are photographs which were taken a short time apart, and that such drastic symptoms *in an adult* were the result of ceasing to believe in Santa Claus. Thoughtfully, Perkes even suggests that the poor man might die soon.[40]

The mischief this passage might work on a gullible young reader is difficult to overstate. First, it claims that belief in Santa Claus is a necessity not only for Christmas cheer but for health and life itself. Second, it claims that the belief is as necessary for adults as for children. What fears might lance the mind of a child of eight or nine who knows that his parents don't believe in Santa Claus? Will they die too?

Selections like these may be extreme, but they exemplify the defensiveness and anger with which partisans of contemporary Christmas often defend their holiday. Confronted with such venom, I cannot help wondering what else Christmas has to hide.

In the next chapter, we'll find out.

Notes

1. For Moore's biography, see Tristram Potter Coffin, *The Book of Christmas Folklore* (New York: Seabury, 1973), p. 87; Patricia Bunning Stevens, *Merry Christmas! A History of the Holiday* (New York: Macmillan, 1979), p. 83; and

J. M. Golby and A. W. Purdue, *The Making of the Modern Christmas* (Athens, Ga.: University of Georgia Press, 1986), p. 71.

2. Stevens, p. 87.

3. Coffin, pp. 90–91.

4. Thomas Nast St. Hill, *Thomas Nast's Christmas Drawings for the Human Race* (New York: Harper and Row, 1971), p. 6.

5. Coffin, p. 88.

6. Ibid., p. 90.

7. Ibid., p. 88.

8. Ibid., p. 91.

9. James Harwood Barnett, *The American Christmas: A Study in National Culture* (New York: Macmillan, 1954), p. 14.

10. Ibid., p. 28.

11. St. Hill, p. 1.

12. Stevens, p. 87.

13. Russell Belk, "A Child's Christmas in America: Santa Claus as Deity, Consumption as Religion," *Journal of American Culture* (Spring 1987): 91.

14. St. Hill, p. 9.

15. Stevens, p. 87.

16. Rebecca Jones, "A Treasury of Trivia for Christmas," *Rocky Mountain News,* December 25, 1992.

17. St. Hill, p. 122.

18. Coffin, p. 93; Barnett, pp. 30–31, 104.

19. Clement A. Miles, *Christmas in Ritual and Tradition, Christian and Pagan* (London: Fisher Unwin, 1912).

20. Stevens, p. 88.

21. *New York Sun,* September 21, 1897, reprinted in Coffin, pp. 93–94.

22. For scientific illiteracy, see Carl Sagan, "Why We Need to Understand Science," *Skeptical Inquirer* (Spring 1990): 264. For ESP, see George H. Gallup, Jr., and Frank Newport, "Belief in Paranormal Phenomena Among Adult Americans," *Skeptical Inquirer* (Winter 1991): 139.

23. Stevens, p. 113.

24. Golby and Purdue, p. 105.

25. Stevens, pp. 108–109; for Puerto Rico and the Philippines, see Renzo Sereno, "Some Observations on the Santa Claus Custom," *Psychiatry* 14 (1951): 388.

26. Alexander Murray, "Medieval Christmas," *History Today* (December 1986): 38.

27. Coffin, p. 110.

28. Stevens, p. 144.

29. Barnett, p. 103.

30. Stevens, p. 140.

31. Coffin, p. 110; Stevens, p. 140; Maymie Richardson Krythe, *All About Christmas* (New York: Harper and Brothers, 1954), p. 152.

32. Stevens, p. 145.

33. Stevens, p. 88; Coffin, p. 95; Barnett, p. 114.

34. Krythe, p. 48.

35. Barnett, p. 82.

36. Anna Quindlen, "Not a Movie," *New York Times,* January 3, 1993.

37. Theodore Seuss Geisel, *How the Grinch Stole Christmas* (New York: Random House, 1957).

38. Thomas A. Burns, "Dr. Seuss's *How the Grinch Stole Christmas:* Its Recent Acceptance into the American Popular Christmas Tradition," *New York Folklore* (Winter 1976): 198.

39. Ibid., p. 201.

40. Alden Perkes, *The Santa Claus Book* (Secaucus, N.J.: Lyle Stuart, 1982), p. 90.

10

Ho Ho Ho? No No No!

John Lennon once said that the Beatles were bigger than Jesus Christ. He was wrong. That honor belongs to Santa Claus. An estimated 85 percent of American four-year-olds believe in Santa.[1] Only 82 percent of adults in a recent poll told Gallup that they were Christians.[2] Among their respective target audiences, Santa outpulls Jesus by a nose.

According to a study by Norman M. Prentice, Martin Manosevitz, and Laura Hubbes, belief in Santa Claus peaks at age four at the afore-mentioned 85 percent. By age six, only 65 percent believe. By age eight, a mere 25 percent cling to the myth.[3] Yet Santa-related behaviors continue long after most children stop believing in Santa Claus. John G. Richardson and Carl H. Simpson found that letter-writing to Santa peaked between ages six and seven, when belief was already slipping.[4] At age eight, Richardson and Simpson reported more children writing to Santa Claus than Prentice and his colleagues had found believing in the jolly old elf. This is no statistical fluke. The Prentice study itself measured children's likelihood of leaving small gifts *for* Santa—snacks, family snap-shots, and the like—before retiring on Christmas Eve. Three-quarters of the eight-year-olds reported leaving gifts, even though only one-quarter of them believed in Santa.[5] Even if we make the generous assumption that all the eight-year-olds who believed left gifts, why did two-thirds of the eight-year-olds who left gifts leave them for a recipient they did not believe in?

Little serious research has been done on the Santa Claus myth and its psychological and developmental implications. It is a perplexing omission, considering the importance of belief in Santa to American children. A strong taboo discourages inquiry into Christmas traditions. How strong is the taboo? Popular attitudes leave no room for pity when adults blow the whistle on Santa Claus. "Any adult who dares tell a child the objective truth on the matter" of Santa Claus "is considered worse than blasphemous," wrote psychiatrist Renzo Sereno with regret.[6] Novelist and playwright W. J. Locke expressed the same sentiment with an attitude closer to bloodlust: "He who would destroy a child's faith in Father Christmas, and thus annihilate the exquisite poetry of childhood, should be kept chained up beyond the reach of his fellow men."[7]

If the Santa Claus myth is beneficial, why does it need such powerful defenses? In this chapter we will discover that the Santa myth does its share of harm. No matter how they feel about the rest of the Christmas observance, parents would do well to do away with Santa Claus. This is not a new suggestion. In the first few decades of this century, open criticism of Santa was much more common, and better accepted, than today. The attacks were so routine that in 1923, an editor at *Collier's* could write:

> Who's for Santa Claus? . . . What with . . . folks who believe that elfs [*sic*], goblins, and fairies of whatever species are no fit company for their children, the annual balloting has at times been uncomfortably close.[8]

Those were the days! Today, critics face longer odds. Perhaps the Santa Claus myth has become what biologist Richard Dawkins would call a "virus of the mind," a self-perpetuating belief system that alters our thinking so that we behave in ways that protect the belief system, whether belief in Santa is beneficial or harmful.[9]

How harmful can the Santa Claus myth be? Minorities in the mental health, child development, and educational communities have always found fault with it. They warn that despite good intentions, parents who initiate their kids into the cult of the Claus may obstruct their growth toward cognitive and emotional independence. The myth may stunt youngsters' capacity for critical thinking. Savvy parents should aim to free—better, to spare—their children from belief in Santa Claus. Pick up your idol-smashing hammers, gentle readers. We're heading for the North Pole.

Ten Reasons Why Thoughtful People Should "Just Say No" to Santa Claus

(1) *To teach and perpetuate the Santa Claus myth, parents must lie to their children.* This is no innocent "sharing of fantasy," as defenders claim. It is a lie, and one in which parents are always caught, eroding children's trust at a critical time.

(2) *The Santa Claus myth exploits characteristic weaknesses in young children's thinking, perhaps obstructing their passage to later stages of cognitive development.*

(3) *To buoy belief, adults stage elaborate deceptions, laying traps for the child's developing intellect.*

(4) *The myth encourages lazy parenting and promotes unhealthy fear.* The Santa Claus myth lends itself too easily as a tool of unearned and deceitful parental influence. Its desperate embrace by parents indicates family-wide dysfunction.

(5) *The number of characteristics that Santa Claus shares with God and Jesus verges on the blasphemous.* This should worry religious parents who want their children to worship just one God. It should also raise a red flag for infidel parents, who might prefer that their children worship none.

(6) *The Santa myth harms children's cognitive and emotional development and damages family dynamics.*

(7) *The Santa myth stunts moral development because it encourages children to judge themselves globally, as good or bad* persons, *rather than to judge positive or negative behavior.*

(8) *The myth promotes selfish and acquisitive attitudes among children.* Often it does this in subtle and disturbing ways that few parents recognize.

(9) *Children may not enjoy the Santa Claus drama as much as parental nostalgia suggests.*

(10) *Contemporary authorities who defend the Santa myth on psychotherapeutic grounds fail to make a convincing case.* Generally their defenses founder in contradictions, because to justify the myth they must advance propositions that *they* would criticize in any other context.

These are serious charges. If they are true, parents might feel compelled to rethink their stance toward the Santa tradition. What is the evidence?

To teach and perpetuate the Santa Claus myth, parents must lie to their children.
There is no candy coating this one. Teaching kids about Santa is not an exercise in fantasy. It is a lie. Lying and fantasy differ because, paraphrasing Coleridge, fantasy demands a willing—and therefore con-

scious—suspension of disbelief, "which is precisely what is absent in ordinary deception."[10] There is no conscious disbelief with the Santa Claus myth. Children buy it hook, line, and jingle bell. Now and again this is acknowledged; *New York Times* commentator Anna Quindlen took to the pages of *Redbook* to agonize over perpetuating "the lie we tell for love."[11] Writing in *Parents* magazine, Ann Banks wondered whether the Santa myth was worth its price. At the core of her discomfort: "I mind the lies."[12]

How did *you* feel when you first learned there was no Santa Claus? Be honest. Fight the ameliorative nostalgia adults bring to this question.

Susan is a Florida atheist, formerly a Jew, whose parents kept a conventional Christmas all through her childhood. Here's how she recalls it: "I felt betrayed. I was angry about being lied to. I was angry at my parents. It was not until years later that I realized the relationship between Santa Claus and God."[13]

Susan has the courage to remember it all. When I learned the truth, I felt betrayed. My parents had taught me not to lie; how could they have lied to me so elaborately for so many years about something they knew to be a central part of my childhood? When we paper over our own pain at the loss of Santa Claus, we make it easier for us later to inflict the same pain on our children. "I remembered when my parents confessed [that there was no Santa Claus] and how betrayed I felt," wrote Banks.[14] Yet it did not occur to her to break the cycle of deception until it was too late.

The lies parents must tell to initiate kids into the Santa tradition are whoppers. What follows is only a sampling:

- A benign force reigns over the world from a headquarters at the North Pole.

- Santa sees—and records—everything that happens. On the upside, nothing is overlooked. On the downside, no child has privacy.

- Every child receives his or her just deserts each year, based on a global judgment whether the child has been "good" or "bad."

- Santa physically visits every family with children in the world in one night.

- Since Santa is the source of all the bounty of Christmas, holiday cheer originates outside of the family and is unrelated to the family's emotional or economic health.

Some of the lies are uncomfortably reminiscent of a childlike view of God, and we'll get to that later. Whatever else may be said about these "facts," one thing is undeniable: All of them are false. Teaching them to children burdens young minds with ideas about the world that are radically untrue.

Nonsense, argue defenders of the myth. Few children take Santa Claus lore so seriously. Most recognize it as pleasant make-believe. The available research contradicts this genial view. Prentice and his colleagues found no relationship between children's belief in Santa Claus and their inclination toward other fantasy-related behaviors, for example, having imaginary friends, daydreaming, or identifying with characters from fairy tales.[15] These children did not regard Santa Claus as a fantasy figure. They thought he was real, "an actual fact, like the existence of a wheelbarrow in the back yard."[16]

Discovering later in childhood that cherished visions of Santa were false often causes further damage. The loss of belief "leaves a cynical disillusionment which occasionally shows up among the trauma in case-histories of maladjusted adults," wrote John Shlien in an oft-quoted study.[17] Philosopher Judith Boss observed:

> Because of the special bond that exists between parents and children, and because of the great power a parent has over a child, deception within a family is particularly destructive of trust.[18]

In 1945 psychiatrist Janet Rioch urged parents to prevent the traumatic loss of a literal belief in Santa Claus by presenting Santa only as "shared make-believe."[19] In 1972 Dr. Lee Salk, director of pediatric psychology at the New York Hospital-Cornell Medical Center, sounded the same refrain: "A child should be told from the beginning that Santa is a make believe person or it might create an early credibility gap between parent and child."[20]

Teaching Santa Claus as make-believe may not be possible in a culture as determined as is ours to present him as real. But at least the desire to do so, and thereby stop the lying, is a step in the right direction.

The Santa Claus myth exploits characteristic weaknesses in young children's thinking, perhaps obstructing their passage to later stages of cognitive development.

Parents who lie about Santa Claus catch their children at a vulnerable time. Youngsters have trouble distinguishing fantasy from reality as it is. Pioneer child psychologist Jean Piaget suggested that between the ages of two and seven, children are in what he called a "pre-operational" stage of cognitive development. They may understand the significance of lying, but they can accept—or create—great distortions of reality without feeling that any deception is involved.[21] Young minds need to be plastic. Child psychologist Bruno Bettelheim stressed that children's minds work differently from those of adults:

> Too many parents want their children's minds to function as their own do— as if mature understanding of ourselves and our world . . . did not have to develop as slowly as our bodies and minds.[22]

Recent research suggests that the Santa Claus myth attracts the young because it exploits the same cognitive predispositions that help children learn religion. A growing number of scientists suspect that the mind's development, like the body's, may follow an inherited timetable. Very young children have a dazzling capacity to learn language that fades around age four. Is there a "golden time" in childhood for the acquisition of religious ideas? Biologist E. O. Wilson and others have speculated that religious beliefs had adaptive value for early humans. Perhaps early religion improved group cohesiveness and helped tribal groups withstand adversity.[23] If so, young children might very well be predisposed to acquire religious ideas on a timetable mediated by biological evolution.

Young minds might embrace religious ideas of varying complexity at characteristic ages. A 1991 study by child psychologist Fritz K. Oser explored this process.[24] At the ages when belief in Santa peaks, Oser found that children tend to hold a blend of two naive religious views. The simplest imagines God as a distant, powerful ultimate being and a stern, unpredictable judge. This view is also characteristic of some of the earliest known religions. Oser called it Stage One. At the next level, God is still imagined as an external judge, but the Stage Two deity can be influenced by good behavior. Such ideas echo the religions of sacrifice, familiar from ancient history and the pages of the Old Testament. In children he studied, Oser found that Stage One views were already giving way to Stage Two concepts by the age of seven. Stage Two thinking tended to peak at age eleven or twelve.[25] There are later stages, of course, but they come too late in life to affect the way children come to believe in Santa Claus.

The figure of Santa Claus combines aspects of the Stage One and Stage Two religious world views. Like the Stage One God, Santa Claus is external and powerful. He observes from a distance and metes out justice (presents or coal) based on what he sees.

Like the more advanced Stage Two God, Santa Claus can be bought. Children learn that they can purchase Santa's blessing and guarantee themselves a merry Christmas by "being good."

If you wanted to snare the religious imaginations of children passing between Stage One and Stage Two, you could scarcely do better than to craft the Santa Claus myth. It resembles authentic, age-appropriate religious ideas closely enough to seize a "royal road" into the developing psyche, exploiting the mechanisms of religious learning much as an opiate exploits the brain's endorphin receptors. The Santa Claus myth is a "mind virus" of great power. It was shaped either by social forces or by design, or by both to exert the maximum possible influence on young minds.

To what end is that influence used? According to stereotype, the Santa myth has positive effects. It is said to help children outgrow the selfishness of early childhood and develop adult ideas about generosity and giving. Research suggests otherwise. When educational psychologists David J. Dixon and Harry L. Hom sought links between charitable acts by children and their belief in Santa Claus, they came up dry. Strong belief in Santa was not correlated with generous behavior.[26] So much for the idea that parents can justify lying about Santa because it makes their children better people.

So what is the Santa Claus myth good for? What *do* parents, children, and society get in return for allowing youngsters' religious curiosity to be so spectacularly abused? Amazingly, almost nothing. Like a true virus, the Santa Claus myth turns the wheels of society toward purposes unrelated to human welfare. It exploits the nascent religious sensibilities of children, if such there be. It compels parents to tell, and later to defend, insupportable lies. At the end, the Santa Claus myth benefits only itself.

To buoy belief, adults stage elaborate deceptions, laying traps for the child's developing intellect.

Disillusioned eight-year-olds don't just learn that their parents lied to them, they learn that society invested tremendous energies to drag out the lie a little longer. No one can be trusted.

Deception about Santa begins at home. Kids begin to notice how many Santas there are at the mall. They spot the present from Santa that is wrapped with the same paper as a gift from Mom and Dad. They ask how Santa can visit every house in the world in one night. It gets harder to confine the kids to their rooms after lights-out on Christmas Eve—time parents need to set the stage for the drama of Christmas morning. As the lies become more elaborate, and correspondingly harder to keep straight, some parents begin to feel "like a burned-out secret agent ready to come in from the cold."[27]

Take it from one who learned the hard way. Parents have a bigger problem when their believing children *don't* ask embarrassing questions about Santa Claus. A bright but sickly only child, I often spent weeks cut off from other children my age. Books were my companions, and I struggled to find answers to my questions on my own. Parents, teachers, even priests and nuns had told me years before to believe in Santa Claus, so I did. I maintained the illusion until I was ten, an inordinately long time. Yet I had been a bright child. I probably asked "How can this be true?" earlier and more intensely than many of my peers. Why did I go on believing?

Caught between my questions and my determination to believe, I defended my increasingly rickety belief in Santa Claus by creating *epicycles*. The term comes from the history of astronomy. Before Copernicus, when the earth was considered the center of the universe, astronomers tried to account for the heavenly bodies' motions around the earth. Since, except for the moon, heavenly bodies *don't* revolve around the earth, this effort had understandably contradictory results. To resolve the disagreements, astronomers postulated "epicycles," literally, smaller circles within the great circles the celestial bodies supposedly swept around the unmoving earth. Astronomical data piled up, and the circles acquired circles within circles within circles. It took the combined efforts of Copernicus, Kepler, Newton, and Galileo to pry the learned away from their geocentric model of the universe and its epicycles.

When I was ten, belief in Santa was my "geocentric model." Name a flaw in the myth and I had an epicycle ready for it. How can Santa possibly build all those toys? The elves had traded their workbenches for modern assembly lines. How does he know if you've been bad or good? Electronic surveillance. Who were those Santas at the mall? They were "Santa's helpers"—no abstract concept, but a literal hierarchy as complex as that of the cherubim, seraphim, principles, powers, thrones, and dominations. What about other children who no longer believed in Santa Claus and who mocked me for clinging to the myth? I knew the answer to that. It was the same answer the nuns had taught me in order to explain why Protestant and Jewish kids stubbornly clung to their religions. Those who believed differently from me were evil.

No wonder my certainty exploded so violently when at last it had to be shouted in my face that there is no Santa Claus. I came away shattered, but with a visceral understanding of the mechanisms by which cultists and crackpots can hold baseless beliefs with immovable conviction.

Adults go to foolish lengths outside the home, too, to protect the Santa Claus myth. In 1914 John D. Gluck organized the Santa Claus Association in New York City. Its purpose was literally "to preserve children's faith in Santa Claus." The association got kids' letters to Santa from the post office and used donated funds to fill selected requests. Amid growing questions about how the association raised and spent its money, the post office pulled the plug in 1928. Belatedly realizing the illegality of handing first class mail to third parties, the postmaster ordered that no more letters to Santa be released.[28]

In December 1927 West Virginia Superior Court Judge John H. Hatcher issued a famous opinion, "Ex Parte Santa Claus." This unsolicited verdict found in favor of the Santa Claus myth and against unnamed individuals who sought its reform. Legal scholars assume that the opinion was written tongue-in-cheek. One hopes so, because in writing it Hatcher announced his willingness to junk first the theory of evolution and then the Constitution, if that's what it took to preserve the Santa myth.[29]

During World War II, labor leader John L. Lewis called a coal miners' strike just before Christmas. NBC opened its radio newscast with the words, "John L. Lewis just shot Santa Claus." In the next hour thirty thousand calls inundated the network's switchboards. A Texas boy despaired and downed a bottle of castor oil. So frightening was the reaction that NBC hurriedly staged an "interview with Santa Claus" to reassure Americans that the jolly old elf was still alive. The actor portraying Santa Claus reported that "John L. Lewis just missed me," which Lewis would describe years later as the foulest blow of all.[30]

In 1948 Boston's city council asked the mayor to allow only one costumed Santa in the city, and to confine *him* to Boston Common. "There is a Santa on every corner," complained one council member, "and children are beginning to wonder."[31] The mayor did not comply. The next year public outrage forced a Michigan thrift to retract a billboard that read, "There is no Santa Claus. Work—Earn—Save."[32] Then there was the prankster who almost got a Wiconsin hunter killed. The hunter had stopped for some errand, leaving his car parked with a good-sized buck over its fender. The prankster painted the deer's nose red, found some youngsters on their way home from school and told them, "There's Rudolph!" When the hunter finished his errand and returned to his truck, some fifty children attacked him. Some threw snowballs at the man they thought had killed Rudolph the Red-Nosed Reindeer. Others hurled rocks. According to a Milwaukee newspaper, the hunter barely "escaped with his life."[33]

With the golden age of the shopping mall, organized deception in support of the Santa myth went into high gear. Today's kids don't find Santa on some tacky throne in a corner of the toy department. He reigns mid-mall over a dazzling "winter wonderland" with acres of fake snow, dozens of animated figures, and thousands of lights. Afterward, kids can visit an outdoor reindeer petting zoo, take in the "festival of trees" at a convention center, and finally settle in to watch an endless parade of television specials detailing the antics of the elves and reindeer.

*   *   *

Whether efforts to protect the Santa lie occur in public or at home, their result is the same. As boys and girls detect successive contradictions in the myth, always to get smokescreened by fast-talking adults, they learn to distrust their own observations and their powers of deduction. In place of independent discovery, they learn to settle for the leaden substitute of data presented by authority figures and learned by rote. What may be lost is the capacity to distinguish verifiable facts from ungrounded claims, wishful thinking, and deception. Too often children keep faith in Santa Claus until they have lost faith in inquiry. Major General Brock Chisholm, Canada's Surgeon General during World War II, often cited two "pathological sore spots" in public thinking: the continued demand for highrise hotels without a thirteenth floor and the survival of the Santa Claus myth.

> There is no sound psychological reason that I know for children not enjoying the Santa Claus myth as long as they know that it is not true. [But] if a child at four or five years of age can believe that one person can come down all the chimneys of the world in one night, and can fly through the air with reindeer and a sleigh and necessarily a heavy load, the child's whole relationship with reality and whole ability to think clearly in terms of cause and effect have been seriously damaged. . . . He will have learned that to think in relation to the evidence of his own eyes leads only to confusion and fear. The fear is engendered by a very real insecurity produced when evidence is presented to the child that he cannot trust his own parents.
>
> For the intelligent child the results of belief in Santa are obvious. If these things can happen and do happen, then so can anything else happen quite free of any laws of gravity, time or space. . . . There are, of course, great varieties of personality distortion that can be produced by this situation.[34]

After we spend our children's formative years lying about Santa Claus and sabotaging their early efforts to unravel the myth for themselves, we stand before them revealed not merely as liars, but as the architects of an elaborate deception. Yet we are unashamed. Should we wonder when our children grow up as quick to lie as we were, or when they stumble into adulthood even easier to deceive than we? What an awful place the world must be if no lesser deception than the Santa Claus myth will awaken any spirit of generosity and kindness. Children can hardly be blamed for growing up to prefer magical thinking, paranormal beliefs, or exotic sectarian creeds to reality and critical thinking, or for grasping at any glittering lie to "add a tinsel splendour to the plain straight road of our life."[35]

The myth encourages lazy parenting and promotes unhealthy fear.
Children see Santa as an all-seeing judge who holds in one hand the

carrot of Christmas cheer, in the other a stick shaped like a lump of coal. The temptation for parents to abuse the myth is strong. "Mothers get a lot of mileage out of Christmas," Erma Bombeck once observed.[36] Parents do not imagine the damage they may do when they use the Claus as a club.

Do parents ever make good on the threat to give bad children coal or withhold gifts? In their famous "Middletown" studies, sociologist Theodore Caplow and his co-workers did not find a single instance of coal-giving among almost four hundred Muncie, Indiana, families. They did not find a case where gifts had been withheld. Yet a neighbor child and playmate of mine received coal in place of gifts in the early 1960s. Other anecdotes suggest that the practice is rare, but not extinct.

Ultimately, it does not matter how many "bad" children receive coal or are denied gifts. What matters is that most American children grow up believing that it *can* happen to them. The Santa myth teaches kids that they live in a world without privacy. The idea of a watcher who overlooks not a single forbidden action or a single wayward thought— even one parents miss—can hardly fail to terrify some children.

The image of Santa as Big Brother also makes the holidays less spontaneous for some tykes than the nostalgic parent might like to believe. As Sereno has noted, if Santa's gifts are a *quid pro quo,* then good behavior becomes a calculated investment for which the child is paid on Christmas morning. "The Santa myth implies a mutual obligation punctiliously discharged."[37]

Little serious research has probed the Santa Claus myth as a tool of parental control—that taboo again. Students of the holiday must settle for a 1964 study of parents who form "coalitions with God."[38] These parents extract obedience by threatening children with divine punishment. The children believe that God sees what they do, knows what they think, and punishes wrong actions. Viewed like this, God is the equivalent of Santa Claus. Child psychologist Clyde Z. Nunn found that at least one parent used the "coalition with God" strategy in 65 percent of the households he studied. It usually made children behave. But if they followed the rules, they were slow to *commit* to them. Nunn also cautioned that parents who used "coalitions with God" might create a sense of worthlessness in their children by offering them only conditional love and regard.[39]

Nunn's work leads us to two conclusions. First, if parents can harm their children by claiming that God is their back-up, using Santa Claus that way is probably harmful, too. Second, we live in a strange world where it is easier to publish research critical of God than research critical of Santa Claus.

*   *   *

The number of characteristics that Santa Claus shares with God and Jesus verges on the blasphemous.

Now and then someone dares to say it. In 1991 the pastor of a non-denominational church in Redstone, Colorado, forbade the children's choir to sing "Santa Claus is Coming to Town" because it suggests that Santa is all-knowing.[40] The Santa Claus myth parallels Christian ideas about God and Jesus in countless ways. Perhaps the old elf is less secular than we thought.

Conservative American Christians have often distrusted Santa. Zion City, Illinois, founded as a near-theocracy by a conservative Protestant sect, banned Santa Claus in 1921. Between 1927 and 1950, several prominent evangelists condemned the Santa Claus tradition.[41]

Research studies, personal anecdotes, and press reports illustrate the links between Santa Claus, God, and Jesus in the popular mind. One psychologist told reporter June Bingham that children's belief in Santa Claus "lays the groundwork for later belief in God." In the same article Arnold Gesell, director of the Yale Clinic of Child Development, revealed that three-year-olds he had studied understood the concept of Santa Claus before they knew the concept of God.[42] John Shlien reported that four- and five-year-olds would not eat candies shaped like Santa Claus, a behavior thought to show reverence. Another writer complained in the 1930s about overhearing his daughter praying to Santa Claus.[43]

Sociologist Russell Belk, who viewed Santa as an American god of consumption and an "unintentional parody of Jesus Christ," compiled a stunning list of parallels between Santa Claus and Jesus. I present only a handful, and add some of my own on the following page.[44]

Idaho secular humanist Ralph Nielsen circulates an "anti-tract" that pokes devastating fun at the parallels between Santa and Jesus:

DO YOU BELIEVE IN SANTA CLAUS?

For many years millions of people have believed in Santa Claus. Today millions more believe in him. Why do so many claim Santa Claus as their personal friend? Because they have found that the true way to know Santa is to believe in him. And the only way to receive his gifts is to become like little children and have complete faith in him.

Of course some people—agnostics, atheists, freethinkers, liberals, and secular humanists—claim that Santa Claus is a mythical being invented by humans. But these scoffers and doubters will never destroy people's faith in him, for as long as people believe in free gifts, they will believe in Santa Claus.

SANTA CLAUS	JESUS
MIRACLES	

Flying reindeer	Angels
Covering the world in one night	Bringing the Word to all nations
Bottomless bag of toys	Loaves and fishes

PARALLEL ELEMENTS

Elves	Apostles
Letters to Santa	Prayers (especially pledges of good behavior in return for favors)
Milk and cookies	Bread and wine
Immortal	Immortal
All-seeing, all-knowing	All-seeing, all-knowing
Rewards and punishes behavior	Rewards and punishes behavior
Lives at white, pure North Pole	Lives in white, pure heaven

OPPOSITES

Fat	Thin
Jolly	Serene
Creature of winter	Lived in deserts
Brings toys, luxuries	Brings health, spiritual necessities

Human gifts have to be made out of earthly materials; Santa creates his gifts out of nothing. Human gifts have to be paid for; Santa gives us his gifts for free. Some people think that he needs to be reminded of what they would like, but Santa already knows what we need. All we have to know is that Santa Claus is alive and loves us. All we have to do is make a personal commitment to believe in him. So won't you, too, accept Santa's offer of free gifts?

Just kneel down, bow your head, close your eyes, and reverently say to yourself:

Dear Santa Claus, I truly believe in you and want you for my personal friend. Let me humbly accept your gifts, not because I deserve them, but because it is your will that I should receive them. Let me not doubt, but increase my faith; for the harder I believe in you, the more real you become, Amen.[45]

If the parallels between Santa and Jesus or God disturb you, draw cold comfort from one major difference between them. When parents share religious beliefs with their children—or beliefs in astrology, spiritualism, New Age, and "alternative" creeds—they generally hold the beliefs themselves. Where Santa Claus is concerned, parents are persuading their children to accept as fact a legend that, in their own minds, consists of little more than repressed memories of their own childhood disappointments.[46]

The Santa myth harms children's cognitive and emotional development and damages family dynamics.

Psychiatrist Jule Eisenbud treated a patient who had envied her older brother. She had thought he enjoyed too much parental attention, and so implored Santa to make her into a boy. When Santa failed to deliver, she tumbled into a chasm of disillusionment that her parents never understood, plunging at last onto the therapist's couch.[47] Such dire results are exceptional. But even when the Santa myth does not harm children in obvious ways, it has subtler effects that worry authorities on child development:

> Telling children to be "good" so that Santa will be pleased and give them presents is a holdover from an earlier age with another view of child development. That approach is counterproductive—not only because it encourages children to look outside themselves for standards, but because the words "good" and "bad" convey little information, especially to young children.[48]

Other critics focus not on children, but on the adults whose support keeps the myth alive. Santa beliefs persist, one sociologist observed, "because they have meaning for adults as well as children—or rather, because they have meaning for adults in their relations to children."[49] Eric R. Wolf and his colleagues speculated that adults encourage belief in Santa in order to enforce upon their children their own distorted, nostalgic vision of a "golden age of childhood."[50] Sereno described adults' perpetuation of the Santa myth as a projection of their ongoing quest for transcendental certainty. They impose the myth on their children, he suggested, for the same reasons that they seek meaning, comfort, and reassurance in religion or mystical ideas.[51]

Sociologist Warren Hagstrom hinted that Santa serves parents as a scapegoat. If a child has fixed his or her heart on a gift the parent cannot afford, or receives the wrong present because a Christmas list was misunderstood, the parent can always resort to the callow argument that "Santa knows best." Hagstrom also stressed the usefulness of Santa Claus in allowing parents to give gifts without appearing to demand anything in return.[52] As social psychologist Barry Schwartz noted, accepting a gift for which one cannot reciprocate is an admission of social inferiority that even a child can understand.[53]

Sereno suggested that adults use the figure of Santa Claus as a buffer because they are unsure whether they deserve their children's love. The casualty of this attitude is often love itself. Parents

> need the reassurance of such deceitful acts in order to secure from their children the feelings and the conduct which should be their right and their duty to expect. Instead of letting their love flow, the parents attempt to strike a bargain. . . . The child . . . begins to nourish doubts about the love of his parents, and resents being obligated to a mythical ludicrous stranger, rather than being tied by love to those he loves most. . . . [P]arental love—diffused through a maze of pointless and never explained ceremonies—is wholly lost.[54]

Surely, with our society's wealth of cultural traditions, it should be possible to find ways of celebrating Christmas, even ways of making the holiday magical for children, that do not flirt with elements drawn from such emotionally twisted subtexts.

The Santa myth stunts moral development because it encourages children to judge themselves globally, as good or bad persons, *rather than to judge positive or negative behavior.*

The Santa myth is usually taught to children as moral shorthand. "He knows if you've been bad or good" compresses a sheaf of simplifying assumptions that adults take for granted. Children miss the jumps. If a merry Christmas depends on being a good boy or girl, they will struggle to be good even if they are not sure what "good" or "bad" means. And they will strive to be "good" even if they do not understand the distinction between being a "good child" and being a child who usually does good things.

The distinction matters. Do we want to teach our children to evaluate their behaviors, to see which can be improved? Or do we want them to score themselves *as persons?* Most child psychologists prefer the first strategy. When it is time to judge actions, positive or negative evaluations are applied to the acts, not to the child's personhood. It is healthy to explain to a child why he or she has done a foolish thing but hurtful to say that because of that behavior, he or she is a foolish child.

The Santa Claus myth gets it backward. Christmas morning is the biggest report card of the year. Presents—or coal? A year's worth of behavior funnels into that stocking; either you *were* a good child or you *were* a bad child. Several years ago I invited Albert Ellis, a famed psychotherapist and developer of Rational-Emotive Therapy, to address the probable impact of the Santa Claus myth on children's moral development. Ellis responded:

> The myth implies that the child who misbehaves or thinks improperly during the year is not only one whose behavior is poor but is a rotten child who is undeserving of any reward at the end of the year.
>
> My contention would be that whenever you rate anyone as a human or person and whenever you find that person deserving or undeserving, you are making a grave philosophic and practical error. There are really no good or bad people, but only people who do good and bad things. And the Santa Claus myth strongly implies that the person, rather than his or her behavior, is good and bad. Because of these implications I would definitely say that the Santa Claus myth, along with other myths, is definitely pernicious to people's completely and unconditionally accepting themselves as humans, whether or not they do good or bad acts.[55]

The myth promotes selfish and acquisitive attitudes among children.

Beyond the usual complaints about holiday materialism, the Santa Claus myth prepares children to become docile members of consumer culture. In a study of children's letters to Santa Claus, kids *always* asked Santa for material items, not new skills, intangible benefits for other family members, or good health. By contrast, when the same children listed their desires in contexts not associated with Santa Claus, fewer than half of their requests concerned material objects.[56]

In his masterful account of Santa Claus as a god of consumption, Belk showed that the myth "teaches us that we deserve what we get" and also teaches "the American ethic that we . . . get what we deserve."[57] If this is the basis of the American tradition of self-reliance and self-help, it is also the basis of social Darwinist ideas that the poor do not deserve the wealth of the rich. Such thinking may deepen the depression often felt when poor people cannot afford a materially indulgent Christmas.

Belk suggested that the function of the Santa Claus myth, indeed, of contemporary Christmas, is to shape children into good consumers. The conditioning starts early. Ideas of unending plenty and of unmotivated gifts are made the centers of the child's emotional universe. The myth teaches that life is so full of free lunches, there may not be enough noontimes to eat them all. In this way kids are groomed to assume their roles as American consumers, grasping for happiness with each new purchase. The final step is the idea of payback. According to the Santa myth, virtue is not its own reward, but if we are good enough a reward will eventually appear. Thus seduced, we are ready for an adulthood in which we "reward ourselves for doing well by buying ourselves things."[58]

The figure of Santa Claus plays a central and disturbing role in bending children toward sterile consumerist values. Parents should think twice about exposing kids to its influence.

Children may not enjoy the Santa Claus drama as much as parental nostalgia suggests.

Parents' gauzy memories of Christmases past may not be the best guide for deciding what is best for their children. Research suggests that children, especially young ones, approach the figure of Santa Claus with anxiety. Gesell found that children reacted to department store Santa Clauses with fear until age three.[59] Sereno noted "patent discomfort" in a group of kindergartners waiting to visit Santa.[60] In 1948 *Life* published a famous photo of children shrinking from a department store Santa Claus.[61] In the same year, the Parents Institute launched a program to train New York City department store Santas to be more solicitous toward frightened children. Wanna-be Clauses were taught not to put kids on the spot with direct questions like "Have you been good?"[62] And not a moment too soon because Sereno reported on his work with troubled adults that

> Most instances of total recall of an early experience with Santa, once analyzed, reveal only fear and loneliness and lack of faith in parental love. . . . In several cases there was a frank admission of fear.[63]

I must pause here to anticipate an objection. If the Santa Claus myth has such negative consequences for children, why do parents perpetuate it? They were children themselves. Always the pessimist, Sereno suggested parents' motive might lie in a desire, overt or hidden, for revenge: "The child . . . grows up ready to exact from his children the same toll of anxiety and deceit which has been exacted from him."[64]

Rational motives may be unnecessary to explain why sincerely loving parents initiate their children in the Santa myth. Perhaps parents pass on the myth for the same reason that men and women abused in any way as children are more likely to abuse their own kids. The "Stockholm Syndrome," in which kidnap victims and hostages identify with their abductors, has been closely studied. Physicians who bore killing workloads as interns and residents are often among the first to oppose reforms of internship and residency work rules. Almost the only people to raise their voices in defense of fraternity hazing on college campuses have been former Greeks. The psychology behind it all seems to be a reluctance to see others reach goals one attained in one's own life without undergoing the same privations. Maybe "Santa survivors" do the same thing. Perhaps they defend the holiday in order to say, "Dammit, I sweated bullets every Christmas Eve wondering whether this would be the year I got the lump of coal I deserved. If that was good enough for me, it's good enough for my kids."

Speculative? Bet on it. Much more research into the Santa Claus myth needs to be done. Yet that prickly taboo protects the myth from scientific examination. In some ways, the near-obsolescence of classical psychoanalysis is regrettable. For all its Freudian dogmatism, analytic culture was iconoclastic. It nurtured free inquiry into all myths, including the Santa myth. Some of what Sereno, Eisenbud, Chisholm, Rioch, and others had to say may seem quirky to modern ears. But it is often the only Santa criticism we have. Psychotherapy and its assumptions have largely pushed analytic culture aside. Professionals trained in therapeutic culture treat Santa more kindly than their Freudian predecessors. But can they justify their preference?

Contemporary authorities who defend the Santa myth on psychotherapeutic grounds fail to make a convincing case.

One of Santa's best-known defenders was the late child psychologist Bruno Bettelheim. Bettelheim argued that fantasy and myth could be positive influences on child development. In 1971 a popular women's magazine asked Bettelheim for his opinion on Santa Claus. His response turned out to be one of the therapeutic culture's definitive defenses of the Santa myth. Urging parents not to uproot children's belief in Santa, he warned:

> The small child should be able to believe in Santa. . . . Parental insistence on denying the impossible dream makes the world a terribly unfriendly place. . . . To hate reality is a likely consequence of being forced to give up fantasies too early.[65]

Strong stuff, this, and a passage the friends of Santa often repeat. But does it hold up? After searching the literature, Boss could find no support for Bettelheim's theory that children denied the Santa Claus myth or weaned from it too young grew up "to hate reality."[66] But we don't need other sources to dismantle Bettelheim's defense of Santa Claus.

One of Bettelheim's favorite themes was that myth, fantasy, and fairy tales help children to develop identity, values, and a sense of their roles in the world. What distinguishes real myths from other things we tell our kids? Subtly, myths let the reader or listener know that the stories to come aren't quite true. The Brothers Grimm launched their fairy tales with a hearty "Once upon a time." George Lucas, who applied the theories of Joseph Campbell in crafting his enormously successful *Star Wars* films, opened each picture with "A long time ago, in a galaxy far, far away."

Bettelheim argued that true fairy stories always begin with such a distancing device; even young readers grasp its cue that the story's real burden lies beneath the surface.

The trouble with the Santa Claus myth—and the thing that Bettelheim overlooked in defending it—is that it lacks a distancing device. As Prentice and his colleagues showed in their research, Santa is viewed not as myth or metaphor, but as fact.

Elsewhere in his writings, Bettelheim warned against telling children fantastic stories as plain truth. In his book *The Uses of Enchantment* he argued that the fairy tale's power lay in its other-than-literal qualities. Real myths require the child to do interpretive work, fueling healthy development. Bettelheim described the case of a troubled man who told his daughter "Cinderella" not as a fairy tale, but as an ongoing real-world drama with himself as the prince and his daughter as Cinderella. Several years of this distorted the daughter's development and turned her against her mother. Bettelheim also told of a child who read *The Little Engine That Could* and decided optimism and perseverance would always lead to success. Tackling hopelessly complex tasks with the same naive "I-*think*-I-can, I-*think*-I-can" attitude, the child suffered frustration after frustration. Defeat, disillusionment, and lost self-esteem followed. It could have been avoided if the too-simple moral of a literal story in fairy tale's clothing had not inspired the child to form self-defeating expectations.[67]

The Santa Claus myth is the same sort of literal story in fairy tale's clothing. Parents deny it, and Christmas tradition encourages the false claim that adults meant Santa as a symbol all along. Church's "Yes, Virginia" is often used this way. It seldom works. Ann Banks recalled her parents' effort to mollify her by reading Francis Church with a terse, "Sure. I knew when I'd been had." But that's all parents have to deflect the anger of adolescents who have just learned they've been lied to.[68]

If the Santa Claus myth ever operated as a fairy tale in the Bettelheimian sense, it no longer does. American culture treats the figure of Santa Claus too literally for the myth to function as a true fable. It is time for mental health and child development professionals to reopen their minds and ask whether the Santa myth is good for children.

Closing Arguments in the Case Against Claus

Striving to judge the Santa controversy, we possess mountains of assertion, anthills of proof. The need for more research is clear. Yet already it seems reckless simply to *assume* that the Santa Claus myth is wholly benign. To perpetuate a taboo against its serious, critical examination—

King Death's Distribution of Prizes. In this little-seen Thomas Nast cartoon, a crowned skeleton recognizes Bacchus for outstanding service in filling the halls of the dead. Note the resemblance between Bacchus and Santa Claus. In addition to the rotundity and facial resemblance, Bacchus is crowned with holly, carries a holly garland, and wears a garment made of fur.

Seeing Santa Claus. A wild-eyed Santa prepares to go down another chimney. Neither he nor his reindeer have noticed the two spying youngsters. Apparently Nast set little stock in Santa's supposed powers to avoid the gaze of wakeful children.

Santa Takes Sides. Nast's first Santa Claus cartoon for *Harper's,* 1862. Santa wears the Stars and Stripes and bestows gifts on a camp of good (that is, Union) soldiers. Sleigh and reindeer are already fully developed; Santa's hat would be elongated by later artists before reaching its canonical form.

What Happens to Nonbelievers

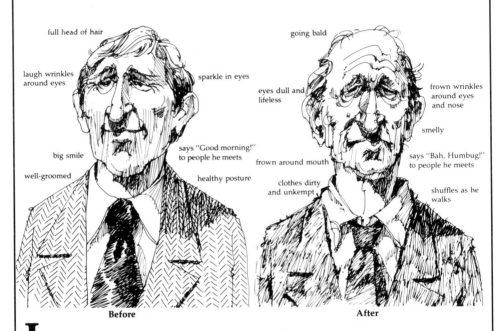

full head of hair

going bald

laugh wrinkles around eyes

sparkle in eyes

eyes dull and lifeless

frown wrinkles around eyes and nose

smelly

big smile

says "Good morning!" to people he meets

frown around mouth

says "Bah, Humbug!" to people he meets

well-groomed

healthy posture

clothes dirty and unkempt

shuffles as he walks

Before

After

It's strange but true: some people don't believe there is a Santa Claus. It's hard to explain why. But when a person stops believing, some very sad things begin to happen.

Shown here is a Before and After picture of the same person, to demonstrate what happens to nonbelievers. The person who believed (Before) was happy and healthy. But when he stopped believing (After), he began to suffer from the Scrooge Syndrome. He

quickly went downhill, and, if he's typical, he'll die much younger than the believer. (The second picture was taken only two weeks after the first!)

Sources:
—*Annual Report of the Surgeon General of the United States*, 1959, in Archives, Library of Congress, Washington, D.C.
—"Symposium on the 'Scrooge Syndrome,' " Cambridge Symposia Series, 1911, reported in *British Lancer*, 123:10:400–439.

How to Hate Skeptics. This page from a 1982 children's book strengthens negative stereotypes of those who do not celebrate the holiday. Note the claim that disbelief in Santa leads to quick deterioration and early death *among adults*. Of the two sources listed in the footnotes, one was irrelevant, the other did not exist. From *The Santa Claus Book* by Alden Perkes. Copyright © 1982 by Information Design. Published by arrangement with Carol Publishing Group. A Lyle Stuart Book. Used by permission.

or to ostracize those who choose on the basis of the evidence already in hand to have nothing to do with it—seems irresponsible.

What's to be done with the figure of Santa Claus?

"Perhaps we might stuff him and put him in a museum and label him as an extinct species which was popular during the days of Queen Victoria,"[69] so satirist George Ade suggested with a smirk in the 1920s. In the same era, playwright George Bernard Shaw sounded less playful when he snorted, "Santa Claus be blowed!"[70]

What can parents do? I present a modest proposal: Actively discourage children from believing in Santa Claus and from joining activities that reinforce the myth. A Santa Claus boycott may come easily to parents who celebrate the holiday half-heartedly, or who cherry-pick elements from a variety of traditions. But I would advise parents who keep a traditional Christmas to steer clear of Santa Claus too. Here are some starting points:

- *Tell your kids that the Santa Claus myth is not true.*

- *Make clear to children that it is parents and relatives, not super- natural visitors, who put those presents under the Christmas tree.*

- *Do not call Santa Claus a metaphor, an allegory, or "the spirit of giving." Just say that Santa Claus is a false belief that other people sometimes teach their children.* Present it as you might a peculiar religious doctrine: If other children believe in Santa, that is their right, and their sincerity in so believing it oughtn't to be impugned. But none of that requires entertaining for a moment the idea that belief in Santa Claus is either true or beneficial.

- *Tell children why Santa Claus has no place in your household.* Instill elementary principles of critical thinking: a realistic outlook, a respect for truth, and an appreciation for cause and effect.

- *Encourage (or at least permit) children to share their Santa skep- ticism with friends, at school, and during recreational activities.* This is vital even if it leads to confrontations with neighbors, relatives, or teachers who accuse your kids of "ruining other children's Christ- mas." Should this occur, defend your children's open iconoclasm. Challenge critics who stoop to such negative stereotypes as "Scrooge" and "Grinch." Most important, be sure children know that—and how—you supported them in their stance.

This position may seem radical, but it is supported by the available research, limited as it may be. Two things we *do* know: First, active discouragement works. In Prentice's study, no Christian child believed in

Santa Claus whose parents discouraged the belief and did so consistently. Belief in Santa can be prevented if parents stick to their guns.[71]

Second, anything less than active discouragement may fail to immunize children against the undesirable aspects of the myth. If parents leave a place in the family's celebration for a sanitized Santa, they can be sure that friends, school, and the media will supply the grubby parts. One hearing of "Santa Claus is Coming to Town" can undo years of patient effort to spare a child the fear of Santa as Big Brother. So pervasive is Santa Claus lore, and so powerfully does the larger culture endorse it, that thoughtful parents may find doing away with Santa Claus altogether the only solution.

What price are we paying for lying to children about Santa Claus? It may be steeper than we think. Because the myth panders to childhood credulity, some have implicated it in the rising incidence of scientific illiteracy among the young. Because it encourages children to build their world views on authority, not on independent thinking, others have related it to the abysmal judgment supposedly displayed by young adults. Can parents honestly be surprised when children do not consult them before experimenting with sex, drugs, crime, or destructive relationships—so soon after parents have made it clear that children cannot trust them to provide accurate knowledge of the world? A Christian parent put the issue clearly in a letter to the editor:

> Certainly we can't get away with lies for seven to ten years and then expect children to "outgrow" Santa . . . then suddenly expect them to believe us when we mention high intensity moral issues.
>   Simply being honest with our children, in my opinion, would outweigh anything Santa ever brought.[72]

The Santa story is a lie told almost universally in the United States and, indeed, in every country to which contemporary Christmas has spread. In all these lands it is now a principal rite of passage for preadolescents to discover that the most cherished belief of their childhood was an elaborate parental lie. If *that* defines us, I shudder to think what kind of people we are becoming.

In a society otherwise eager to lessen its reliance on magical beliefs, the vitality of the Santa custom stands as a grotesque indictment. Reflecting on the general decline of folk mysticism, Gamaliel Bradford penned these words in 1945:

The fairies are gone . . . the witches are gone . . . the ghosts are gone. Santa Claus alone still lingers with us. For heaven's sake, let us keep him as long as we can.[73]

Bradford blew it. For heaven's sake, let's finish the job!

Notes

1. Norman M. Prentice, Martin Manosevitz, and Laura Hubbs, "Imaginary Figures of Early Childhood: Santa Claus, Easter Bunny, and the Tooth Fairy," *American Journal of Orthopsychiatry* (October 1978): 618 ff.

2. Princeton Religion Research Center, "Religions of the World," *Emerging Trends* (January 1993): 3.

3. Prentice, Manosevitz, and Hubbs, pp. 621–22.

4. John G. Richardson and Carl H. Simpson, "Children, Gender and Social Structure: An Analysis of the Contents of Letters to Santa Claus," *Child Development,* no. 53 (1982): 430.

5. Prentice, Manosevitz, and Hubbs, p. 624.

6. Renzo Sereno, "Some Observations on the Santa Claus Custom," *Psychiatry* 14 (1951): 392.

7. Perriton Maxwell, "What I Think of Santa Claus: Signed Confessions Obtained by Perriton Maxwell From Eighteen Famous Writers," *Collier's Weekly* (December 15, 1923): 10.

8. Ibid.

9. Elena M. Watson, "Viruses of the Mind, and the 'Awe Factor,' " *Skeptical Inquirer* (Spring 1993): 233; Richard Dawkins, "Viruses of the Mind," *Free Inquiry* (Summer 1993), pp. 34–41.

10. Sissela Bok, *Lying: Moral Choice in Public and Private Life* (New York: Random House, 1978), p. 218.

11. Anna Quindlen, "The Lie We Tell for Love," *Redbook* (December 1991): 36–39.

12. Ann Banks, "Santa and the Truth," *Parents* (December 1990): 94.

13. Personal correspondence.

14. Banks, p. 96.

15. Prentice, Manosevitz, and Hubbs, p. 623.

16. Dorothy Canfield, quoted in Maxwell, p. 11.

17. John Shlien, "Santa Claus: The Myth in America," *Etc.: A Journal of General Semantics* (Summer 1959): 396.

18. Judith Boss, "Is Santa Claus Corrupting Our Children's Morals?" *Free Inquiry* (Fall 1991): 26.

19. Catherine Mackenzie, "Is Santa a Menace?" *New York Times Magazine* (December 23, 1945).

20. Dee Wedemeyer, "The Santa Myth: Even the Experts Can't Agree," *Houston Post,* December 2, 1972.

21. Boss, p. 24, citing Jean Piaget, *The Moral Judgment of the Child* (New York: Free Press, 1965), pp. 164–66.

22. Bruno Bettelheim, *The Uses of Enchantment* (New York: Knopf, 1976).

23. For discussions of these concepts, see Edmund O. Wilson, *Sociobiology: The New Synthesis* (Cambridge, Mass.: Belknap, 1975) and Charles J. Lumsden and Edmund O. Wilson, *Promethean Fire: Reflections on the Origins of Mind* (Cambridge, Mass.: Harvard, 1983).

24. Fritz K. Oser, "The Development of Religious Judgment," *New Directions in Child Development* (Summer 1991): 5–25. Oser focused only on stages in the development of religious sensibilities. Correlations between those stages and the belief in Santa Claus are wholly my own inferences.

25. Ibid., pp. 10, 16.

26. David J. Dixon and Harry L. Hom, "The Role of Fantasy Figures in the Regulation of Young Children's Behavior: Santa Claus, the Easter Bunny, and Donations," *Contemporary Educational Psychology* 9 (1984): 14–18.

27. Banks, "Santa and the Truth," p. 96.

28. James Harwood Barnett, *The American Christmas: A Study in National Culture* (New York: Macmillan, 1954), pp. 32–33.

29. Ibid., p. 37.

30. Warren O. Hagstrom, "What is the Meaning of Santa Claus?" *American Sociologist* (November 1966): 251; Shlien, p. 396.

31. Hartford *Courant,* December 22, 1948.

32. Barnett, p. 35.

33. Ibid., pp. 112–13.

34. "Road to War Seen in Mass Neuroses," *New York Times,* October 26, 1946; "Atomic Age Explodes Santa Claus Myth, Makes Fantasy Folly, Psychiatrist Says," *New York Times,* November 7, 1945.

35. William Kingdon Clifford, "The Ethics of Belief" (1877), anthologized in Walter Kaufmann, *Religion From Tolstoy to Camus* (New York: Harper and Row, 1964).

36. Erma Bombeck, "Those Wonderful Yule Threats," *Buffalo News,* December 17, 1987.

37. Sereno, p. 398.

38. Clyde Z. Nunn, "Child Control Through a 'Coalition with God,' " *Child Development* 35 (1964): 417–32.

39. Hagstrom, p. 251.

40. "Santa Claus is Not Coming to Town," *Free Inquiry* (Spring 1992): 61.

41. Barnett, pp. 39–40. Zion City, Illinois, founded by the Catholic Apostolic Church (a Protestant sect), later became Zion, Illinois. A holdover of the city's almost-theocratic past was the presence of a cross and other Christian symbols on the municipal seal. In 1992 these were ordered removed by the U.S. Supreme Court in response to a suit brought by Illinois atheist activist Rob Sherman.

42. June Bingham, "Santa and the Debate Over Him Go On and On," *New York Times Magazine* (December 18, 1949): 49.

43. Russell Belk, "A Child's Christmas in America: Santa Claus as Deity, Consumption as Religion," *Journal of American Culture* (Spring 1987): 90–91.

44. Ibid.

45. Ralph Nielsen, *Do You Believe in Santa Claus?* (Des Moines, Iowa: Humanists of Idaho, 1992).

46. Boss, p. 26.

47. Jule Eisenbud, "Negative Reactions to Christmas," *Psychoanalytic Quarterly* 10 (1951): 639–45.

48. Steven A. Gelb, "Christmas Programming in Schools: Unintended Consequences," *Childhood Education* (October 1987): 9–13.

49. Hagstrom, p. 250.

50. Eric R. Wolf, et al., "Santa Claus: Notes on a Collective Representation," anthologized in Robert A. Manners, ed., *Process and Pattern in Culture: Essays in Honor of Julian H. Steward* (Chicago: Aldine, 1964), pp. 147–55.

51. Sereno, p. 396.

52. Hagstrom, p. 252.

53. Barry Schwartz, "Social Psychology of the Gift," *American Journal of Sociology* 73, no. 1 (1967): 4.

54. Sereno, p. 390.

55. Albert Ellis, correspondence, September 9, 1985. First published in Thomas Flynn, "Should a Humanist Celebrate Christmas?" *Free Inquiry* (Winter 1985–86): 45.

56. Richardson and Simpson, "Children, Gender, and Social Structure: An Analysis of the Contents of Letters to Santa Claus," *Child Development* 53 (1982): 423–26, summarized in Belk, p. 93.

57. Belk, p. 95.

58. Ibid.

59. Bingham, p. 13.

60. Sereno, p. 390.

61. Barnett, p. 36.

62. Bingham, p. 13 ff.

63. Sereno, p. 391.

64. Ibid.

65. Bruno Bettelheim, "Dialogue with Mothers," *Ladies' Home Journal* 12, no. 88 (1971): 15–16.

66. Boss, p. 27.

67. Bettelheim, *The Uses of Enchantment,* pp. 126–31.

68. Banks, p. 96.

69. Maxwell, p. 10.

70. Ibid.

71. Prentice, Manosevitz, and Hubbs, p. 625.

72. Deborah D. Keel, "Dispel Childhood Myths," letter to the editor in the *Buffalo News,* December 14, 1987.

73. Gamaliel Bradford, "Santa Claus: A Psychograph," in Edward Wagen-knecht, *The Fireside Book of Christmas Stories* (Indianapolis: Bobbs-Merril, 1945), p. 275.

Part Two

The Trouble with Christmas Present and Yet to Come

Introduction

Trouble Ahead

This is a good spot to pause and sum up the argument so far. We have seen that most of our contemporary Christmas traditions come to us from decidedly pre-Christian roots. If many of our Christmas traditions came to us from the pre-Christian religions of Egypt and Rome, another rich trove of pre-Christian custom hails from pagan northern Europe. Then there are the traditions centered on eating, drinking, and the element of play. Deep in its heart Christmas remains a harvest festival, and much of its lore expresses the element of play at the end of a long growing season.[1]

One of the great ironies of Christmas is how little of its content is truly Christian. Once we dispose of the pre-Christian elements, most of what remains is post-Christian, rather than authentically Christian, in origin. What is there about the contemporary Christmas that we can view as authentically Christian? Besides midnight mass there is, amazingly, almost nothing else.

Here we hurtle into the blank wall of paradox. Though almost nothing about Christmas is uniquely Christian, we cannot reduce Christmas wholly to a secular festival.

> [T]here is no doubt that even the folk attributes of Christmas are embedded in a matrix of beliefs and customs related to Christianity. Furthermore, some of the folk symbols have acquired a semi-religious meaning through long association with Nativity accounts. Thus, the Christmas tree, though originally derived from pagan midwinter festivals, has acquired overtones of Christian significance. . . .[2]

Rather than confront the paradox, it is tempting to shake one's head tolerantly at the rich and magnificent folly that is humankind and say

155

yes to it all. The temptation might be irresistible were it not for the millions of non-Christian Americans who have become trapped in the paradox, who sometimes see even red-nosed reindeer and construction-paper snowflakes as veiled threats to their religious identities. And what about the nonreligious, for whom secular and sacred Christmas symbols smack equally of creedal intrusion into their lives?

Christian Americans may be genuinely puzzled when non-Christians complain that Christmas is not their holiday. "What are they bitching about?" Christians ask. "We throw this great party, and they get to crash."

" 'Crash' isn't the word," non-Christians retort. "You don't get invited to Christmas. You get drafted." From a secular humanist perspective, Christians are viewing the world as happy imperialists. They see their own ways as universals and are helpless to imagine how others fail to find their holiday as enjoyable as they do. Yet almost four in ten respondents to a Gallup poll said they found Christmas a "strongly religious holiday."[3] There is no question which religion is meant.

> There can be no doubt about the fundamental importance of Christianity in the American Christmas cult.[4]

> Even in its secularized form, Christmas is not religiously neutral. It is still Christian.[5]

"Christmas isn't my holiday," wrote a Jewish college student in a teen magazine. For her, full participation in Christmas would mean accepting Jesus as the Son of God. "I can't do that and still be who I am."[6]

Some will say that I am trying to have my rhetorical cake and eat it too. Exposing the holiday's non-Christian roots, I attack its credentials as a Christian feast. But then I claim that to make Christmas a universal holiday is unfair to non-Christian minorities. Which is it? Not Christian enough, or too Christian?

The answer is "both." Christmas is both non-Christian to the core, and Christian to the core. The paradox does not lie in my arguments; it lies in the holiday itself.

If Christmas can never escape its associations with the Christian religion, its future in an increasingly multicultural America looks grim. The United States is becoming more ethnically and culturally diverse. The fairest and most appropriate response to cultural diversity would be for the custodians of Christmas to retreat a few steps from the pinnacle their festival attained a century and a half ago. It is time to end the Victorian experiment with a universal Christmas. Celebrators should be content to keep Christmas as the central holiday of their particular communities, without expecting the whole of the larger culture to join their party. We should set our sights on a future in which Christmas is one holiday among many. We need to create a future in which noncelebrants, from the non-Christian to the utterly nonreligious, can pass the festival by without courting a stigma. Christmas enthusiasts need to learn why it is no less savage to call someone a "Scrooge" or "Grinch" than to revile members of other minorities with epithets such as "nigger," "fag," "kike," "cripple," or "retard." These are the issues that will concern us in the chapters that follow.

Notes

1. John Huizinga, *Homo Ludens: A Study of the Play Element in Culture* (Boston: Beacon Press, 1944).

2. James Harwood Barnett, *The American Christmas: A Study in National Culture* (New York: Macmillan, 1954), p. 69.

3. Robert Bezilla, ed., *Religion in America* (Princeton, N.J.: Princeton Religion Research Center, 1993), p. 46.

4. Barnett, p. 139.

5. Lawrence A. Hoffman, "Being a Jew at Christmas Time," *Cross Currents* (Fall 1992): 363.

6. Lisa Spierer, "Christmas Rift: It's a Nice Holiday But It's Not Mine," *Seventeen* (December 1991): 26.

11

Christmas and the Old Outsiders: The Jews

A thoroughly assimilated Jewish novelist watched from her car with her children as Christians filed into a nearby church during the holiday season:

> As our nameless and forgotten recent forebears stood in their villages of the Ukraine and Lithuania looking at the village church, so too are we aliens, outsiders in a Christian world. . . .[1]

In spite of the promise of the Constitution, in spite of the lip service Americans pay to pluralism, non-Christians still feel like outsiders at Christmas time. Few American Jews become as irate as the Pensacola, Florida, lawyer who allegedly bought a sword and brandished it in a shopping mall because the mall's gift-wrap booth had no Chanukah paper.[2] Yet non-Christian Americans have cause for anger. Our nation has failed in its early commitment to be open toward all religions. Instead, it has become a land where Christians and nominal Christians enjoy special privileges. The oppression non-Christians experience may be overt; more often it is subtle. But it is always visible at Christmas time.

It wasn't always this way. Contrary to what most people assume, Revolutionary-era America was lustily irreligious. Only 17 percent of the colonial population belonged to churches, compared to more than 60 percent today.[3] By the 1790s one could scarcely find a Christian—one who'd admit it, anyway—among students at New England's handful of colleges.[4] The early Republic separated church from state more zealously than today. The 1797 Treaty of Tripoli announced that "the Government of the United States is not, in any sense, founded on the Christian religion." Not an aberration, the treaty was negotiated under George Washington and approved by the Senate under John Adams.[5] In 1810 Congress passed a law requiring Sunday mail delivery. For the postal system even to appear to honor the Christian Sabbath was unacceptable. Twenty years later, in 1830, a Senate committee report advanced this simple logic for rejecting Sunday closing laws:

> The Constitution regards the conscience of the Jew as sacred as that of the Christian, and gives no more authority to adopt a measure affecting the conscience of a solitary individual than that of a whole community. . . . It is the duty of this government to affirm to all, to the Jew or Gentile, Pagan, or Christian, the protection and advantage of our benignant institutions on Sunday.[6]

We have lost so much! Modern-day conservatives bray that the United States was founded a Christian nation. On the contrary, the founders' original vision of religious neutrality has eroded with the passing years. Since the Revolution, the United States has become, on balance, less hospitable toward religious minorities.[7] If conditions have improved recently for non-Christian Americans, two groups deserve most of the credit. They are the religious outgroups that have been established the longest in American life: the Jews and the infidels. In the twentieth century, both groups scored significant victories for the rights of religious "minorities." Until perhaps 1950, Jewish organizations mounted this effort almost alone. Thereafter atheists, agnostics, secular humanists, and Christians so liberal in creed as to be effectively infidels matched or outpaced Jewish groups in fighting for freedom of religion. Members of both groups made immense contributions and helped to smooth the way for new non-Judaeo-Christian religious groups now taking their places in the American mainstream.

More recently Muslims, Hindus, Buddhists, and other non-Judaeo-Christians have attained large numbers, assumed high profiles, and begun independently to agitate for their rights. They will enjoy broader opportunities than their predecessors and confront different problems. For that reason I have chosen to divide religious outgroups into two broad categories. In this chapter and the next, I focus on Jews and infidels and their collisions with the Christmas tradition. I call them the "Old Outsiders." In chapter thirteen I will treat the remaining, increasingly visible outgroups. I call them the "New Outsiders."

Since the 1830s, Christmas has been a favorite pretext for limiting the rights of non-Christian outgroups and attacking their place in society. The Old Outsiders' battles for liberation have often taken the form of campaigns against Christmas or, at least, against certain forms of holiday observance. American Jews and infidels have paid a high price for their successes. We will understand how high when we see how each Old Outsider group has accommodated to December's holiday of obligation.

Jews and Judaism in the United States

In 1850 there were perhaps five thousand Jews in the United States and millions in Europe.[8] Repelled by pogroms and discrimination and attracted by images of American opportunity, some two and a half million Jews would stream to the United States by 1924.[9] After World War II and the Holocaust, there would be only about five thousand Jews in Poland and Hungary and millions in the United States.[10] Today, America's population of about five and a half million Jews is the largest number of Jews ever to live in a single political jurisdiction.[11] Despite massive migration to Israel after 1948, there remain almost twice as many Jews in the United States as in Israel.

American Jewry is diverse. Some Jews believe the word describes their religion. Others feel it captures their ethnicity or heritage, without binding them to specific religious convictions. Some American Jews believe that an atheist of Jewish heritage is authentically Jewish. There is even an organization put together along congregational lines devoted to "secular humanistic Judaism."

The remaining question—and a matter of some gravity in Jewish circles—is, How many ethnic Jews remain religiously active? If we define "religious Jewishness" minimally as joining a synagogue, sending children to Hebrew school, or supporting Jewish charities, only about half of American ethnic Jews are active in the U.S. Jewish community.[12] A controversial study of the nation's religious makeup conducted in 1991 by Barry Kosmin and Seymour Lachman of the City University of New York (CUNY) confirmed this figure.[13] Kosmin and Lachman surveyed 113,000 American adults and asked them to state their religious affiliation. Their ambitious methodology was unlike previous studies that had relied on information supplied by church organizations. The CUNY study found far fewer members of several non-Christian groups, including Jews, than earlier studies had led demographers to expect. We'll say more about the CUNY study; its findings about some non-Christian groups strain credulity. But the CUNY figure of about three million self-identified Jews fits. They probably represent the half of the nation's ethnic Jews who remain religiously active.[14]

Jews and the Melting Pot

Early Jewish immigrants to the United States retained an emotional attachment to a homeland, either to the European country they had left or to a then-imagined Zion. First- and second-generation Jewish immigrants constituted what sociologist Edna Bonacich called a "middleman minority." They tended to concentrate in careers that demanded little capital but offered high liquidity, perhaps insurance lest they have to move again. American Jews tended to segregate themselves, to resist marriage outside the community, to establish their own schools, and generally to resist assimilation.[15] Of course, they invested tremendous energy in maintaining their community's religious tradition.

Yet the "melting pot" had an almost irresistible power. Nineteenth-century America assumed that newcomers would shed their ethnicities in the course of becoming American. Some American Jews accepted the idea avidly. In the melting pot's glare they saw a fire that could burn away the bigotry they had crossed the Atlantic to escape. Jewish-American writer Israel Zangwill penned this breathless passage in 1908:

America is God's Crucible, the great Melting-Pot where all races of Europe are melting and reforming! Here you stand, good folk; think I, when I see them at Ellis Island, here you stand in your fifty blood hatreds and rivalries. But you won't be long like that, brothers, for these are the fires of God you've come to—these are the fires of God. A fig for your feuds and vendettas! Germans and Frenchmen, Irishmen and Englishmen, Jews and Russians— into the Crucible with you all! God is making the American![16]

To modern eyes this is ironic. Today we are more conscious of the motives of old New England Yankees like educator Ellwood P. Cubberly, who thought relentless assimilation would make immigrants more civilized, which is to say, more like Ellwood P. Cubberly:

Everywhere these people tend to settle in little groups or settlements, and to set up here their national manners, customs, and observances. Our task is to break up these groups or settlements, to assimilate and amalgamate these people as a part of our American race, and to implant in their children, as far as can be done, the Anglo-Saxon conception of righteousness, law and order, and popular government. . . .[17]

Takes your breath away, doesn't it? Few sociologists challenged the melting pot concept until the late 1960s.[18] Then, the success of the Black Power movement forced a reevaluation. In its angry celebration of African Americans' differences, Black Power caught sociologists flat-footed. Suddenly, they realized that ethnicity might not be dysfunctional after all. Ethnographer Stephan Thernstrom captured the new paradigm: "It is generally assumed that maintenance of ethnicity is desirable, that preservation of differences is healthy, that loss of group identity is to be deplored."[19]

Overnight, assertive ethnicity was cool; it became popular to understand intergroup relations as matters of conflict and power, and to view the resulting dialogue as healthy.[20] Almost as suddenly, the ethic of assimilation was eclipsed by the ethic of pluralism.

But the American Jewish community of the early twentieth century had a lot of assimilating to do before that bright day would dawn. Some think it dawned too late.

A funny thing happened on American Jews' way to the multicultural society. Years after other Americans gave up on the melting pot, some say the American Jewish community had started to melt down. By the early 1980s, only 24 percent of Jews were reporting weekly attendance at synagogue. (Forty-five percent of Christians attended church weekly during the same period.) In Rochester, New York, in 1980 only 2 percent of Jews claimed weekly synagogue attendance.[21] Intermarriage soared. As recently as the 1960s, less than 10 percent of American Jews married non-Jews; today the rate is closer to 50 percent. A recent Denver, Colorado, study found that more than 70 percent of Jews between the ages of eighteen and twenty-nine had married non-Jews.[22] Harvard sociologist Elihu Bergman predicted that by the year 2076 the American Jewish community might be as small as ten thousand. Under more optimistic assumptions he was unable to project a community larger than one million.[23] Other Jewish thinkers warn that the previous peak of Jewish assimilation occurred not in the United States but among the Jews of Germany in the 1920s, hardly an encouraging sign.[24]

Might today's upsurge in assimilation be, as one Jewish writer termed it, "the end of American Jewish history"?[25] Here comes the tough question. What if it is? I am not one of those who believes that "respecting diversity" means forcing members of outgroups to manifest their ethnic identities whether they want to or not. Yet millions find Jewish-American identity satisfying, and would choose to remain part of a vibrant American Jewish community if it continued to exist.

In its struggles for a respected place in Gentile society, has the American Jewish community sacrificed too much? Has it made compromises with the Christian ingroup that endanger its authenticity and integrity? Will future historians look back on the last few decades as the time when American Jews put a Jewish identity out of reach for many who might otherwise order their lives by its traditions? It is hard not to think so when we consider American Jewish culture's responses to Christmas.

The "December Dilemma"

"December is the cruelest month." So began a classic 1950 polemic against Christmas in *Commentary*.[26] The holiday season has forced American Jews to choose from three main alternatives, each with its own price.

(1) Ignore Christmas. One can go to work, keep one's business open, or devise family activities designed to create the illusion that Christmas is just another day.

(2) Split the difference. One can magnify some aspect of Jewish life, usually Chanukah, in order to disguise or compensate for any perceived loss in forgoing Christmas.

(3) Acculturate. Celebrate Christmas in almost complete form. One can pretend that Christmas is not only non-Christian in its origins, but also in its cultural significance. Down this path lie different kinds of "secular Christmas."

Just Say No

If one takes one's Judaism seriously, the strategy of ignoring Christmas altogether has logic on its side. There are sound historic reasons to maintain strict separation between Jewish life and the inescapably Christian holiday. Writing in 1939, Rabbi Louis Witt summed up the case against Christmas in stirring words:

> For years I, as a rabbi, like all rabbis, denounced with all the oratorical fervor and fury at my command this celebration of Christmas by my own people. I called it a shameful aping of alien gods. I stigmatized the Jew who was guilty of it as a renegade. . . . I drew the picture of Jewish brethren in fanatic lands through the centuries enduring horror and massacre on the very day on which Christ was born and cursing the day in the madness of their despair, and I asked with dramatic climax: "How can any Jew even in blessed America celebrate such a day?"[27]

This hard-line approach has adherents. Many Orthodox ignore the holiday. For them, the refusal to celebrate Christmas is just another case of Jews bearing adversity to protect their heritage. This approach is not restricted to the Orthodox. As recently as 1973, the rabbi of a major New York Reform Temple could declare: "Notwithstanding the commercialization and secularization of the holiday, it [Christmas] remains a deeply

Christian celebration, and, as such, has no place in the home life of a Jewish family."[28]

I am not a Jew. But from my secular perspective, I cannot see how American Jews can in conscience celebrate the Christian feast of the incarnation of the son of God and remain true to their own religious identity and traditions.

Swimming upstream is difficult. It is doubly, perhaps trebly, difficult for contemporary, assimilated Jewish families with children. Objections such as "Why can't we do what everyone else does?" and "All the other kids have it!" cut deep. Insidiously, the holiday season tries to force Jewish parents into its orbit by striking at their children.

Jewish parents understandably fret that their children may seem "different" to Christian peers if they ignore the holiday altogether. They worry that if children sit out the holiday, their socialization may be delayed or degraded. Yet when Jewish children are *not* prepared to resist the winter holiday's relentless Christianity, their very abilities to form a Jewish identity may be threatened. When Lisa Spierer was in grade school, she responded to the unchallenged Christmas decorations and Christmas observances in her school by concluding that she was not Jewish.[29]

American Jews might better serve their children by exposing them to the full scope of their differences, including the responses difference sometimes brings. Grace Goldin suggested as much, urging Jewish parents to keep their children Yule-free from the start. "[S]ooner or later," she wrote, Jews

> have to break the news to their children what kind of world this is, and the sooner the better. Christmas—or not having Christmas—is as good a place as any to begin.[30]

To many American Jews, especially ethnic Jews, resisting Christmas this resolutely is too much work and offers too little return. It is never easy to be different, but it is sometimes harder to be confused.

Chanukah on the Rack

Other American Jews respond to Christmas by "splitting the difference." The object split is usually Chanukah, which is grossly distorted to make it a better analogue of Christmas. Chanukah is the ancient festival of lights. Some authorities think that it, too, echoes the winter solstice. The menorah lights may represent an image of the sun, perhaps transmuted through a tradition that involved sacred bonfires.[31]

Splitting the middle often means adding a Christmas tree to one's

Chanukah observance. Middle splitters call their Christmas tree a "Chanukah bush" and hope no one will challenge their abuse of language. So popular is this compromise that today, most Americans think Chanukah *is* the "Jewish Christmas." But Chanukah was originally a minor Jewish festival.[32] The American Jewish Committee has declared that Chanukah "is not central to Judaism: Indeed, Jewish children are not required to absent themselves from school on this holiday."[33]

The Chanukah myth bears reviewing. If Chanukah is not the most important holiday on the Jewish calendar, it is, ironically, the holiday that deals most directly with the theme of Jews who must cope with the influence of a dominant, non-Jewish religion.

As the story begins, the Hebrews were residing in Syria. The Syrian ruler Antiochus followed the religion of the Greeks and was determined to make his Jewish subjects observe Greek rites. Menelaus, a turncoat high priest, bought his appointment by bribing Antiochus with temple vessels. Menelaus complied with demands that the Jews erect a statue of the king in the temple sanctuary, allow the sacrifice of pigs, and move worship from the temple chambers into the open air. Menelaus was so eager to please that he introduced the whole Greek pantheon, installing Yahweh among the gods of Olympus.

Flushed with this victory, Antiochus ordered Greek altars built throughout Palestine; pigs would be sacrificed on them. Soldiers would round up Jews and force them to eat the pig flesh. In the small town of Modin, an old priest named Mattathias resolved to tolerate this no more. At the next pig sacrifice, Mattathias slew the first Jew who reached for the pork, slew the lone Syrian solider present, and destroyed the altar. He fled with his five sons into the hills. Soon they were joined by many poor Jews.

The Jews fought with inspiration and frenzy. Thanks to a wise pronouncement by Mattathias, for the first time they fought on the Sabbath. This kept the Syrians from simply waiting for the seventh day, then slaughtering the unresisting rebels, a fate that had swallowed previous Jewish revolts.

When Mattathias died, command passed to his third son, Judah the Maccabee ("Hammer"), also known as Judas Maccabeus. After a four-year guerilla campaign, Judah was able to reenter an undefended Jerusalem and rebuild the temple. Only one day's supply of undefiled oil could be found with which to kindle the temple lights, but the day's supply of oil burned miraculously for eight days. At least, that is the story. It is the origin of the eight-day festival of Chanukah, in which another light is kindled on the menorah each evening.

Among American Jews, Chanukah has taken on many of the aspects of Christmas, including a preoccupation with children, a focus on gift giving, and a vast magnification of its importance on the calendar. "Chanukah is no longer a Jewish holiday," quipped one Jewish writer, "it's a major competitive winter sport."[34]

> If Chanukah comes earlier than Christmas, it's an inoculation; if later, an antidote; either way, we in our town violently amplify it . . . what used to be a festival of freedom becomes a festival of refuge.[35]

Sociologist Bruce L. Berg described the magnified Chanukah as a "means of insulation against the more prevalent Christmas . . . both as a shield, and as an integrating mechanism."[36] And so American Jews put electric menorahs in their windows, hoping their homes will seem as well decorated as those of Christians. They send "Season's Greetings" cards. Their children play Chanukah recordings, sing Chanukah hymns, and dress up as candles, *dreidels,* or the elephants ridden by the Syrian troops for Hadassah pageants that ape school Christmas pageants of forty years ago. Sometimes the figure of Judah Maccabee is even pressed into service as an alternate Santa Claus.

Call it "Chanukah Plus." Its conflicted nature is exemplified in that strangest of all Judaeo-Christian hybrids, the "Chanukah bush." Purists may choose a simple table-height tree, trimmed only with ornaments or paper medallions, reserving lights for the menorah. Others may opt for a tree that can only be distinguished from a Christmas tree by the number of points on its star.

Few Jewish writers have anything good to say about the Chanukah bush. One Jewish woman told a sociologist:

> The Jew who has a tree in an all-Jewish home is as much a hypocrite as if he'd have a cross on his wall. The Chanukah bush is degrading to the Jew, as far as I'm concerned. I feel it is a crutch for those who are ashamed or can't stand up for their ways.[37]

Yet American Jews who "split the middle" achieve two important goals. First, they reassure themselves and their children that they are full-fledged Americans, that nothing in the national culture is closed to them. Second, they reassure fellow Jews, themselves included, that they remain Jewish.

Members of the Christian ingroup culture should regret the profound distortion their overfed winter holiday has imposed on the authentic observances of so many in the American Jewish community. But the "bloating of Chanukah" will continue, as long as it reduces the strain American Jews feel between their Jewish identities and their desire to reinforce their place in the Christmas-obsessed American mainstream.

Collapsing Before Christmas

When Jews adopt the compromise of the Chanukah bush, they maintain a veneer of Jewish practice. Other Jews—almost certainly, a majority of nonpracticing or ethnic Jews—go a step further. They try to pretend that Christmas is a secular holiday, rationalizing away its Christian character. They put up not a Chanukah bush, but a full-blown Christmas tree. They exchange gifts, sing carols, teach their children about Santa Claus—the entire holiday round.

If American Jewish literature is any guide, many of the religious or ethnic Jews who choose this path are uncomfortable with it. Too often, they choose it out of a misguided belief that it is better for their children. "My son is aware that he's Jewish and knows what that means, but he would feel deprived if we didn't have Christmas," rationalized one Jewish parent.[38]

"We live in this country, not in Israel," agreed another. "It would be a shame to deprive my children and say, 'You can't have a Christmas tree because you're Jewish.' "[39] What better reason could one ask for?

Yet the magnetism of Christmas is strong. Even Rabbi Witt, who had preached so floridly against Jews who accommodate to the holiday, ultimately caved in. By 1939 he had taken to the pages of *Christian Century* to extol not "Chanukah Plus" but *Christmas,* complete except for the nativity story, as a fit celebration for Jews. Witt ridiculed fears about assimilation in language that is deeply disturbing to modern readers, who know that as this was being written the clouds of Holocaust were gathering in Europe:

> Already there are prophets of doom who, seeing the Jew become more and more like the majority in the environment, cry: "I told you so!" and lift their voices again in favor of "Back to the ghetto! Back to a national Jewish home! Back to racial Judaism!" That however, is in my eyes the way of defeatism and despair.[40]

On one level, Jews who try to celebrate Christmas without its Christian associations are trying to have their Cheshire cat without the smile. As we have seen time and again, Christmas is too deeply entwined with Christianity to secularize this way.

Social scientist Marden D. Paru observed that to most "religious Jews, not just the pietists, Christmas tree usage is an act of heresy."[41] Using the sharpest insult the vocabulary of Chanukah allows, Grace Goldin compared Jews who keep Christmas whole to Menelaus, the turncoat high priest:

In pre-Maccabean Jerusalem he built altars to the Greek gods before anybody ordered him to. . . . Nowadays he puts a Christmas tree in his picture window and scatters Christmas cards all over the mantelpiece.[42]

Anne Roiphe once published an article in the *New York Times* extolling her family's thoroughly "secular" Christmas. The result was scattered ostracism in the Jewish community. Later, Roiphe came to regret her acceptance of Christmas and strove to reverse it.[43]

Outright acceptance of Christmas seems to be a minority stance among American Jews. In one study, about 10 percent of American Jews polled had literal Christmas trees. Compared to the community as a whole, Jews who kept Christmas were more likely to be younger, to have young children, and to be of the third generation: that is, their grandparents had immigrated to the United States.[44] Significantly, they were also less likely to be religiously active. American Jews who trimmed Christmas trees were only half as likely to light Sabbath candles as their coreligionists who did not keep Christmas.[45]

Time and again, Jewish social scientists have begged American Jews to "become more aware of the inner contradiction involved in using the divisive symbols of religious identity of another group as their symbol of American unity."[46] Such is the power of contemporary Christmas, and the superficial appeal of caving into it, that this hasn't happened yet.

American Jews who keep Christmas complete also teach their children to believe in Santa Claus, with all the dangers that implies. Norman Prentice, dean of Santa studies, found that more than 23 percent of Jewish children believed strongly in Santa Claus. More than 40 percent believed somewhat. All told, Jewish children were almost half as likely as Christian children to believe in Santa, an appalling number.[47]

When Jewish parents mix Jewish and Christmas symbolism, the result is often confusion for the children. Susan from Florida spent her childhood in a nonpracticing, ethnically Jewish family in Queens. The family kept Christmas, generating predictable pressures for Susan:

At home we celebrated Christmas, not Chanukah. My parents would take my brothers and sisters to see the department store windows and the tree at Rockefeller Center. We also would go to Macy's to see Santa Claus, to tell him what we wanted for Christmas. The belief in Santa Claus was not discouraged.

On Christmas Eve we would hang up our stockings and set out milk and cookies for Santa. On Christmas morning we awoke to find the stockings filled, with lots of presents underneath.

. . . My Jewish friends' families celebrated Chanukah. I felt like I was two people. One was supposed to be Jewish, the other living in a Christian world that was supposed to be the enemy. I did not talk about Christmas with my friends. It was a code of silence. . . .

The season from Thanksgiving to after Christmas has always been a tough one for me. Once I became an atheist and worked out the important things in life—dying, etc.—I learned to look at that time of year as an observer.[48]

Other Jews emerged from the process more or less unscathed. If the holiday holds little significance for this ethnically Jewish atheist, it also poses little threat:

I celebrate Chanukah with my family, not because I believe in the story behind it, but out of respect for my heritage and because it's a time of good feelings.
. . . I have on occasion gone to this or that girlfriend's [Christian] church, for similar reasons. . . . I will never actively participate in a service. . . . I will not celebrate someone else's holiday as my own, as I feel no need to, but will give a nodding participation in one celebrated by someone who is close to me.[49]

Given a choice between the three alternatives—ignoring Christmas altogether, splitting the difference, or celebrating the Christian holiday almost complete—it seems clear to me that ignoring the holiday offers the best opportunity for American Jews who *choose* to express their culture seriously to do so in an authentic and consistent way.

Accepting Jewish Difference at Christmas Time

Christians claim that theirs is a tradition of tolerance and inclusion. Despite the historical evidence to the contrary, if contemporary American Christians want to live up to that ideal they might start by reducing the pressure mainstream institutions impose on American Jews at Christmas time.

We might begin at our television stations. Too often, stations try to leaven the drone of incessant Christmas messages by putting up the odd "Happy Holidays" slide. I once saw a TV station "Happy Holidays" message that included a cross, a star of David, the Islamic crescent and star, and, for good measure, Santa Claus in its artwork. Such efforts are usually more embarrassing than all-embracing: First, one wonders what Islamic December holiday the artist had in mind. Then there was the background music, a lush orchestral recording of the Protestant version of "Away in a Manger." Another favorite is the slide that wishes viewers a merry Christmas *and* a happy Chanukah. It seems safe to cover all the bases. But Christmas and Chanukah are not all of the bases. What about Muslims,

Buddhists, Hindus, and members of other non-Judaeo-Christian religions? What about hard-bitten infidels who don't celebrate anything at all this time of year?

The same basic criticism applies to libraries, public offices, commercial offices, shopping centers, and hospitals that treat Christmas as a "one size fits all" holiday and leave no respite for those who may not celebrate it. Those comfortable with the vocabulary of ageism, speciesism, lookism, and the like might choose to call this overemphasis on Christmas "Yule-ism." When governmental institutions engage in Yule-ism, it may violate the Constitution. When private institutions do it, it is simply bad taste.

Institutions have no monopoly on holiday boorishness. Lisa Spierer complained of the well-meaning insensitivity of individual Christians who assume that everybody celebrates their holidays. Of the bus driver who wished her a merry Christmas instead of the usual "nice day" and the butcher who wished her a happy Easter when she picked up the Passover turkey she wrote, "I know they're just being nice, but it offends me."[50]

Jews, Christmas, and the Schools

Christian-Jewish acrimony over the holidays often flares in the public schools. Some Christians can't understand Jewish sensitivities about holiday observances. Consider this Midwestern horror story from 1949. One of two Jewish students in a class of twenty-seven was singled out to trim a large Christmas tree at the entrance of the school. Teachers told the Jewish girl that they felt sorry for her because she had never trimmed a tree. Then she was assigned to write a report on Chanukah, which she delivered aloud before the third, fourth, and fifth grade classes. For good measure, she was made to repeat her report before a gaggle of visitors.[51] One hopes that such a performance would not be repeated today. Had it happened to a less garrulous child, the emotional toll could have been severe.

Other Jews clearly fared less well in the bad old days of American education. When a Denver newspaper ran an editorial lamenting the removal of Christmas trees from the Aurora, Colorado, public schools, an anguished Jew sent in this fierce and, to my mind, utterly accurate response:

> I am almost embarrassed by the total lack of sensitivity displayed in [the editorial]. I suppose it is too much to ask of a Christian to view things in the light of a non-Christian's experience.
> Perhaps had the writer had the youthful experience of many non-Christians of having to sing songs about a son of God they didn't believe in, or perhaps

had the writer been the one Jew in the group who had been mercilessly ribbed for refusing to put the Star of Bethlehem atop the class Christmas tree, he or she would be less prone to consider the Christmas tree "not a religious symbol."

To the millions of non-Christians in America, forced to celebrate a holiday that is contrived to commemorate someone we consider a false messiah, that innocent Christmas tree is just one more Christian religious symbol. And, it is just one more symbol of Christianity's attempts to make us all over in the Christian image.[52]

Friction between Jews and public school administrators over Christmas observance goes back to the early years of this century. In 1906 Jewish parents pulled thousands of grade school children out of the Brooklyn public schools to protest Christmas observances. The boycott succeeded; in 1907 New York City schools had no Christmas assemblies and no holiday decor other than trees and Santas.

After World War II, Jewish organizations issued policies on Jewish children and Christmas celebrations in the public schools. The Central Conference of American Rabbis urged parents to forbid their children to sing Christmas carols in holiday assemblies, but counseled them against making formal objections to the practice. The Rabbinical Assembly of America took a harder line, encouraging parents to complain or take legal action when necessary: "The practice of calling on Jewish children to join in the singing of Christmas carols, to take part in Christmas plays . . . must be regarded as an infringement on their rights as Americans."[53]

Controversy flared again in 1961. In Troy, New York, the school board voted to omit Jewish holidays from school pageants at the request of the Troy Jewish Community Council.[54] Hamden, Connecticut, was plunged into controversy when school superintendent David Wyllie tried to tone down Jewish and Christian religious elements in holiday plays.[55] At the same time, administrators in West Haven, Connecticut, refused a plea from that town's Jewish Community Council to curb Christian content in Christmas plays.[56] In 1988 a Hartwick, New York, Jewish parent lost a bid to force New York State to review its religious music policy after his daughter refused to sing "The First Noel" and other Christmas songs at a holiday concert.[57]

Jewish sensibilities have long been abused at Christmas time. If infidels and, today, non-Judaeo-Christians are shouldering a larger share of the burden, Jewish activists continue to resist holiday incursions by the dominant Christian culture.

A Perspective on Jews and Christmas

It is hardly my place to tell American Jews how to be Jewish. But as a former Christian who converted to that other Old Outsider group, the infidels, I think I can offer some useful advice: Just say no to Christmas! It is acceptable now, in a way that it was not decades ago, to assert your differences, to be conspicuous with your children in transmitting and expressing Judaism's understanding that the Christian emperor has no clothes. In the past, "submerging oneself in similarities has been seen as a surer road to survival than trying to cope with differences."[58]

This is no longer true. If the melting pot is not dead, it is optional in a way it was not when the grandparents of today's American Jews were seeking their place in the American mainstream.

As early as 1973, a correction against the old assimilationist attitudes was underway in the American Jewish community. "More Jews than ever before are not buying Christmas trees for the same reasons they're no longer bobbing their noses or changing their names," said the American Jewish Congress's Richard Cohen, perhaps optimistically.[59] Paul Cowan had a bestseller in *An Orphan in History,* a Jewish back-to-the-roots book that deplored the "amputation" that had separated American Jews from their history. Anne Roiphe, whose Christmas tree attracted such controversy, stopped celebrating the Gentile holiday. By 1981 she saw keeping Christmas as evidence of betrayal or, at best, self-deception.[60]

Susan in Florida reports that even her Christmas-keeping, ethnic-Jewish mother got the bug:

> As I got older all of a sudden being a Jew—the cultural part—became very important to my mother. My brothers had to be Bar Mitzvahed. My sister and I were threatened that if we did not marry nice Jewish boys she would not pay for our weddings. This was very confusing after years in which religion had not been important. In later years I look back at it all and it seems very silly indeed.[61]

If not silly, Susan's roller-coaster life within the American Jewish community certainly seems to have been needlessly complex: "We still celebrate Christmas. We all exchange gifts. It's no big deal."

Go figure.

Though different groups have responded to it in different ways, the net effect of the Jewish encounter with Christmas has almost certainly been negative for American Jews. It is still too early to speak of a Jewish movement to throw off accumulated Christmas accommodation. But increasing numbers of American Jews are coming to recognize that "If Christmas is accepted, a fundamental difference between Christianity and Judaism is lost and the Jewish religion loses some of its unique identity."[62]

Despite the expectation (or the hope?) of some Jewish commentators that Jewish discomfort with Christmas would lessen with time, most American Jews recognize something improper in being a Jew and accepting contemporary Christmas without complaint. Lisa Spierer's words in a popular teen magazine crystallize the strategy that every non-Christian outgroup ought to pursue at Christmas time:

> I'd like to ask for a little cultural sensitivity on the part of Christmas celebrants. During the winter holidays, try to be aware of those whose celebrations involve, instead of fir trees and manger scenes, menorahs and *dreidels*—nothing at all.[63]

American Jews have much to gain by standing up to Christmas. They have more to lose by continuing to let the Christmas juggernaut overrun their heritage. This militant clarion call from a 1937 article on ways to fight anti-Semitism seems to capture the right attitude:

> The first and most important thing for Jews is not to be driven into an attitude of retreat. Never back up! Never trim your sails. . . . Above all, avoid by all means . . . taking on protective coloration![64]

For American Jews, the trouble with Christmas is that it made protective coloration seem so attractive. American Jews need no longer hesitate to make their rejection of Christmas clear. Christmas is not their holiday; thanks in part to the tireless activism of their own community, they can say so without fear. It is time for more American Jews to join their fellow Old Outsiders, the infidels, and the New Outsider groups in making full use of the cultural latitude that American Jews have helped to create.

Notes

1. Anne Roiphe, *Generation Without Memory: A Jewish Journey in Christian America* (New York: Linden Press/Simon & Schuster, 1981), p. 10.
2. *USA Today,* December 24, 1992.
3. Roger Finke and Rodney Stark, *The Churching of America, 1776–1990: Winners and Losers in Our Religious Economy* (New Brunswick, N.J.: Rutgers University Press, 1992).
4. Albert Post, *Popular Freethought in America, 1825–1850* (New York: Columbia University Press, 1943), pp. 20–21.
5. *In 1962 Madalyn Murray O'Hair Kicked God, the Bible, and Prayer*

Out of School (Silver Spring, Md.: Americans United for Separation of Church and State, 1992), p. 9.

6. Shmuel A. Eisenstadt, "The Jewish Experience with Pluralism," *Society* (November–December 1990): 24.

7. I would like to strike the word "minority" from the rest of this discussion. Intercultural fairness is not a matter of counting noses; it has to do with whether one group is inappropriately subordinate to others. When small numbers of European colonizers administered vastly larger native populations, they were in the numerical minority. But no one would call them "oppressed." It seems more fitting to speak of *ingroups* and *outgroups,* the language on which I will standardize in this chapter. See Ricardo L. Garcia, "Cultural Diversity and Minority Rights: A Consummation Devoutly to Be Demurred," anthologized in James Lynch, Celia Modgil, and Sohan Modgil, eds., *Cultural Diversity and the Schools* (London: Falmer Press, 1992), p. 110.

8. Roiphe, p. 168.

9. Sara Bershtel and Allen Graubard, *Saving Remnants: Feeling Jewish in America* (New York: Free Press, 1992), p. 11.

10. Roiphe, p. 168.

11. *Statistical Abstract of the United States, 1992* (Washington, D.C.: Department of Commerce, Bureau of the Census, 1992), 112th edition.

12. Bershtel and Graubard, p. 94.

13. Barry Kosmin and Seymour Lachman, *National Survey of Religions Conducted by the National Survey of Religious Identification* (New York: City University of New York, 1991).

14. Vern L. Bullough, "Religion and the Polls," *Free Inquiry* (Summer 1991): 9.

15. Edna Bonacich, "A Theory of Middleman Minorities," *American Sociological Review* (October 1973): 273.

16. Israel Zangwill, *The Melting Pot* (1908), quoted in Bershtel and Graubard, p. 9.

17. Ellwood P. Cubberly, *Changing Conceptions of Education* (Boston: Houghton-Mifflin, 1909), pp. 15–16.

18. Philosopher Horace Kallen advocated pluralism over assimilation in the *Nation* as early as 1915. At the time, his was a voice in the wilderness. See Milton M. Gordon, "Assimilation in America: Theory and Reality," *Daedalus* (Spring 1961), anthologized in Norman R. Yetman and C. Hoy Steele, eds., *Majority and Minority: The Dynamics of Race and Ethnicity in American Life* (Boston: Allyn-Bacon, 1982), p. 232.

19. Bershtel and Graubard, p. 101.

20. Argument inspired by L. Paul Metzger, "American Sociology and Black Assimilation: Conflicting Perspectives," in *American Journal of Sociology* (January 1971), anthologized in Yetman and Steele, p. 298.

21. Bershtel and Graubard, pp. 99–100.

22. Ibid., pp. 12–13.

23. Ibid., p. 159.

24. Ibid., p. 80.

25. Ibid., p. 3.

26. Grace Goldin, "Christmas-Chanukah: December is the Cruelest Month," *Commentary* 10 (1950): 416.

27. Louis Witt, "The Jew Celebrates Christmas," *Christian Century* 56 (1939): 1497.

28. Nadine Brozan, "Jews at Christmastime: Is It Proper to Join In the Holiday?" *New York Times,* December 21, 1973.

29. Lisa Spierer, "Christmas Rift: It's a Nice Holiday But It's Not Mine," *Seventeen* (December 1991): 26.

30. Goldin, p. 417.

31. Gerald A. Larue, *Ancient Myth and Modern Life* (Long Beach, Calif.: Centerline Press, 1988, Expanded ed.), p. 258.

32. Walter M. Gerson, "Jews at Christmas Time: Role-Strain and Strain-Reducing Mechanisms," anthologized in Walter M. Gerson, *Social Problems in a Changing World: A Comparative Reader* (New York: T. Crowell, 1969), p. 73.

33. David L. Martin, "Strip the Halls of Boughs of Holly," *Learning* (December 1976): 29.

34. Goldin, p. 416.

35. Ibid., p. 417.

36. Berg, p. 147.

37. Gerson, p. 70.

38. Brozan, "Jews at Christmastime."

39. Ibid.

40. Witt, p. 1497.

41. Marden D. Paru, *"Tannenbaum* and the Jewish Problem," *Jewish Social Studies* 35, no. 3–4 (1973): 289.

42. Goldin, p. 419.

43. Roiphe, pp. 125–26.

44. Ibid.; see also Milton Katz, "The Meaning of the Christmas Tree to the American Jew," *Journal of Jewish Sociology* (June 1961): 130.

45. Paru, p. 287.

46. Katz, p. 136. See also Paru, pp. 283–84.

47. Norman M. Prentice and David M. Gordon, "Santa Claus and the Tooth Fairy for the Jewish Child and Parent," *Journal of Genetic Psychology* (June 1987): 147.

48. Personal correspondence.

49. Bulletin Board System (BBS) correspondence.

50. Spierer, p. 26.

51. Goldin, p. 417.

52. Letter to the editor, *Rocky Mountain News,* December 20, 1992.

53. James Harwood Barnett, *The American Christmas: A Study in National Culture* (New York: Macmillan, 1954), p. 68.

54. Unheadlined news item, *New York Times,* December 6, 1961.

55. "School Curbs Urged on Religious Fetes," *New York Times,* December 6, 1961.

56. Ibid.

57. "Challenge Denied on School Music," *Buffalo News,* October 13, 1988.

58. Jaime S. Wurzel, "Introduction," in Jaime S. Wurzel, ed., *Toward Multiculturalism* (Yarmouth, Maine: Intercultural Press, 1988), p. 1.

59. Brozan, "Jews at Christmastime."

60. Roiphe, p. 168; Bershtel and Graubard, p. 30.

61. Personal correspondence.

62. Gerson, p. 67.

63. Spierer, p. 26.

64. H. C. Engelbrecht, *How to Combat Anti-Semitism in America* (New York: Jewish Opinion Publishing, 1937), p. 14.

12

Christmas and the Old Outsiders: The Infidels

The other Old Outsider group consists of infidels, or the nonreligious. They call themselves atheists, agnostics, rationalists, freethinkers, and secular humanists. Christians often have their own names for them. Yet infidels have been part of the American scene from the beginning. If they emerged as an organized force later than American Jews, their presence as individuals goes back further in the nation's history. There were almost certainly more infidels than Jews in colonial America; today infidels may even outnumber African Americans.

That will surprise Christians who think unbelief is rare. They underestimate how many infidels they know because so many infidels are still in the closet. Christians often find it incomprehensible that infidels do not believe in an afterlife or in eternal reward or punishment. They wonder how the nonreligious can bear this life, knowing it is all they have. They wonder where infidels draw their values, if not from a selfish desire to spare themselves the torments of hell. Historically, humans have often based their values of right and wrong on sources other than religious belief. Far from being the norm, the way mainstream America identifies morality with religious belief is itself an historical oddity.[1]

In one sense, it is legitimate for Christians to ask these questions. Yet in another, they bespeak bigotry against unbelievers. I am always astounded by radio talk show hosts who nod when callers ask why as an atheist, I don't just go out raping, robbing, killing, and taking anything I want. I like to think they would respond differently if I were an African American and a caller asked me how I dealt with having natural rhythm and an insatiable appetite for sex.

Infidels may be the last minority against whom it is still safe to discriminate—an odd situation for the country's largest "religious minority."

177

In this chapter I will argue that infidels' anger, especially at Christmas time, can no longer be ignored. American infidels who have been holding back their indignation in an effort to "fit in" need to recognize that confrontation, not accommodation, is the way that outgroups now claim the respect due them in society.

Who are the infidels, and how many of them are there? One is quickly reduced to guesswork. Individual nonbelievers have not made themselves as visible as many American Jews. Social attitudes against unbelief have often been harsher than popular anti-Semitism, prompting infidels to conceal their disbelief. Infidelity also seems to go hand in hand with an individualistic, rather than a communitarian, orientation. As a result infidels tend not to be "joiners" and tend to be underrepresented on the membership rolls of infidel organizations.

A Capsule History of American Unbelief

Seasoned nonbelievers may want to skip this section. For the benefit of religious readers, I present a thumbnail history of unbelief in America that will help to put contemporary infidelity in perspective.

At the time of the American Revolution, open atheism was rare. Yet few among the educated would admit that they were Christian. A philosophy known as *deism* was then at the height of its influence. Deists emphasized reason. They rejected the idea of a personal God and disdained hope of life after death. All they retained of conventional religion was the image of God as the creator. The Deist God was an aloof watchmaker who had set the universe in motion, then turned away. He neither loved us nor cared for our sufferings. He was a wholly different sort of deity than the Christian God. When Jefferson wrote of "their Creator" and "Laws of Nature's and of Nature's God" in the Declaration of Independence, it was the apathetic God of Deism, not the Christian deity of the same name, that he invoked.

Prominent Deists included Benjamin Franklin and Thomas Jefferson. Jefferson once composed a revised version of the Bible, with all the supernatural claims removed. Ethan Allen (1737–1789), leader of the famed Green Mountain Boys, also wrote a bitterly anti-Christian tract titled *Reason: Only Oracle of Man*. Thomas Paine (1737–1809) is as well known for his devastating *Age of Reason* as for *The Crisis, Common Sense,* or *Rights of Man. Age of Reason* has probably converted more Americans to unbelief than any other work, which may be why Theodore Roosevelt erroneously tarred Paine as a "filthy little atheist." Also prominent in the Deistic movement were former preachers like Elihu Palmer (1764–1806), who played little role in the founding of the country but strongly influenced the young nation's religious thinking.

Ideologues who claim that the Founders intended to create a Christian nation need to account for the preponderance of Deists, rather than Christians, among the architects of liberty. Of course, they never do.

Deism retreated from center stage around 1810. Some fifteen years later, American infidelity entered a new chapter with the explosion of the freethought movement. At first, "freethought" simply meant the freedom to follow a line of inquiry wherever it led, even if it contradicted orthodox thinking. Any form of inquiry—political, economic, or moral, as well as religious—might be fair game for the freethinker. In time, "freethought" came to be associated specifically with free inquiry into the claims of the Christian faith. And since Christianity tended not to fare well under that sort of scrutiny, freethought ultimately came to mean not just inquiry, but outspoken criticism and rejection of Christianity.

Freethought activism flourished between 1825 and 1850. Among the major figures were reformer Frances "Fanny" Wright (1795–1852), who edited a radical publication called the *Free Enquirer,* and Robert Dale Owen (1801–1877), founder of the utopian community at New Harmony, Indiana. George Houston (?–1840) established a weekly freethought journal. Thomas Hertell (1771–1849), a New York State lawmaker and judge, agitated for a spectrum of liberal causes. Benjamin Offen (1772–1848) made his living lecturing on freethought subjects in New York City. Abner Kneeland (1774–1844) was prosecuted in a celebrated blasphemy trial. Ernestine Rose (1810–1892) combined freethought activism with a commitment to social reform and women's rights.[2]

Early nineteenth-century freethought was associated with a variety of radical and reformist causes, including woman suffrage, communalism, free love, utopianism, and socialism, though not all freethought leaders liked their politics so radical. Nineteenth-century freethought also differed from eighteenth-century Deism in its social character. If Deism attracted the educated elite, freethought had a strong popular component. It appealed to working-class immigrants from Germany and England who had belonged to strongly anticlerical fraternal organizations and labor movements in their homelands.

As always, it is difficult to move past the leadership to count individual freethinkers. Surely their numbers were dwarfed by the expanding rosters of the Christian churches. But the literature of the time makes clear that only the most insulated Christian could have ignored the existence of freethinkers and the freethought movement.

Freethought enjoyed a second period of growth between 1860 and 1900. This is often termed freethought's Golden Age. Leaders in this era included figures such as Benjamin Franklin Underwood (1839–1914), a full-time freethought lecturer who traveled the country challenging local clergy and edited two freethought periodicals. Robert Green Ingersoll (1833–1899) may be the most remarkable infidel in American history. He was simultaneously the Republican Party's most trusted political speechmaker, and a freethought firebrand who packed theaters across the country with four-hour lectures that savaged Christianity and its doctrines of eternal punishment. Some people loved Ingersoll, others hated him, but rare was the post–Civil War American who did not know his name. More people heard Ingersoll speak than would see or hear another human being until the advent of motion pictures, radio, and television. Though he was a household word in the late nineteenth century, he is almost forgotten today—a measure of the energy Christian Americans have exerted to erase his memory.[3] DeRobigne M. Bennett (1818–1882) founded the *Truth Seeker* in 1873. It became America's longest-running freethought publication. Bennett was also jailed by Anthony Comstock for sending information on birth control and sex through the mails. Samuel Porter Putnam (1838–1896), a former minister, traveled over one hundred thousand miles lecturing on freethought. He established a freethought magazine and led two national freethinker organizations. Charles B. Reynolds (1832–1896), another ex-minister, underwent one of the nation's last prosecutions for blasphemy in Boonton, New Jersey. He was defended by none other than Ingersoll, but was found guilty; Ingersoll paid his fine. John E. Remsburg (1848–1919) lectured on freethought in more than twelve hundred cities and towns and wrote three popular freethought books. Eugene M. McDonald (1855–1909) succeeded D. M. Bennett as editor of the *Truth Seeker,* and held that post for twenty-six years. Under his guidance the *Truth Seeker* became one of the country's leading reform papers.

Finally, no census of late nineteenth-century freethinkers is complete without a mention of Samuel Clemens, a.k.a. Mark Twain. Twain's acerbic wit is well known; what is less well known is how often he turned his wit upon popular religion with withering effect. *Letters From the Earth* is probably Twain's best-known antireligious book.

Freethought experienced a decline at the turn of the century; in part it was a casualty of its own successes. Thanks to the impact of Darwin and biblical criticism, much of the freethought critique entered the educated mainstream world view. It was no longer radical. Scientists, inventors, scholars, and other apostles of early twentieth-century modernity tended to take their irreligion for granted. Instead of criticizing religious teachings, figures like Luther Burbank, H. L. Mencken, Thomas Edison, and Clarence Darrow simply used unbelief as a springboard for accomplishments in other fields.

Still, organized freethought (which for the first time, began to refer to *itself* using the word "atheism") had its twentieth-century advocates. Joseph Lewis (1889–1968) was the best-known infidel between Ingersoll and Madalyn Murray O'Hair. He was the longtime president of the Freethinkers of America organization and editor of its magazine, the *Age of Reason.* In 1922 Emanuel Haldeman-Julius (1889–1951) purchased J. A. Wayland's socialist newspaper, the *Appeal,* and turned it into a publishing empire. Haldeman-Julius created the first paperbacks and almost singlehandedly invented direct-mail merchandising. His famous "Little Blue Books" put classics of world literature and influential freethought writings within the reach of every American. Millions of copies were sold by mail.

Lewis and Haldeman-Julius both suffered during the post–World War hysteria that equated atheism with communism. Despite the collapse of the Soviet Union, some American Christians continue to rant that infidels are closet Communists. This is the other great shibboleth of anti-infidel bigotry, and deserves a brief refutation here. It is true that some noted infidel leaders had socialist pasts. It is also true that the Marxist-Leninist leaders of the former Soviet Union professed to advocate atheism, though in practice they seemed more interested in establishing a religion of class struggle. But to charge that all American infidels were Communists was unjust and untrue. It was also laughably illogical. If all Communists are atheists, it does not follow that all atheists are Communists any more than since all cars have tires, it follows that all vehicles with tires are cars. (How about bicycles, little red wagons, and Boeing 767s?) But then, logic was never critically important to the McCarthyites.

The first of the contemporary infidel leaders came to prominence in 1963. Madalyn Murray O'Hair (1919–) brought *Murray* v. *Curlett,* the lawsuit that, together with *Abingdon School District* v. *Schempp,* helped to remove compulsory Bible reading from public schools. O'Hair went on to launch a controversial national atheist organization, which, though often rocked by acrimony of her own making, has made important gains for the nonreligious on certain fronts.

Contemporary infidelity has roots outside the freethought movement as well. In 1933 a small group of liberal Unitarian ministers issued a position paper called *The Humanist Manifesto.* Designed to set an agenda for a nontheistic religion capable of harmony with the world view of science, it became a catalyst for a humanist movement that advocated compassion, social activism, and nontheism. Humanism won the allegiance of international leaders of thought in the years following World War II.

In time, humanism moved away from its origins in liberal religion and moved closer to freethought. *Humanist Manifesto II* was authored by Paul Kurtz in 1973. It was signed by more than one hundred leading figures in science, politics, and the arts. It set a more secular tone than its predecessor. In addition, it explicitly preferred a democratic model over a socialistic one, perhaps reflecting the influence on Kurtz of his mentor Sidney Hook, the first major American intellectual to break with Utopian socialism. In 1980 Kurtz would publish *A Secular Humanist Declaration* and the break between secular humanism, liberal religion, and socialist intellectualism would be complete.

Today, cross-fertilization between humanism and freethought is growing. All told, infidelity is modestly healthy in the United States. Principal organizations include the Council for Democratic and Secular Humanism (CODESH), which publishes *Free Inquiry* magazine and has links with autonomous local groups in more than thirty major metropolitan areas. The Freedom from Religion Foundation (FFRF) combines a strong critique of organized religion with a feminist perspective. It has a network of chapters and many individual activists who have won significant legal victories for the nonreligious. The American Humanist Association (AHA) pursues an agenda midway between secular humanism and liberal religion; it has more than a score of chapters and publishes a national magazine. There are also local atheist groups in most parts of the country. Many are former chapters of Madalyn Murray O'Hair's American Atheists organization, cut adrift when Madalyn dissolved her chapter system early in the 1990s. Finally, several national publications serve the infidel community that do not operate membership organizations. The *American Rationalist* falls into this small but significant category. The *Truth Seeker* is still being published. Having cast off the racism and fringe preoccupations of its longtime editor, the late James Hervey Johnson, it has entered a period of renaissance.

Altogether, it has been estimated that there are about 178,000 infidels in the United States who belong to freethought, atheist, or secular humanist organizations or subscribe to "movement" publications.[4] This is only a fraction of the actual number of infidels in the United States. Pollsters have tried to measure the infidel population with inconsistent results. We saw that the City University of New York (CUNY) study in 1991 by Kosmin and Lachman did a good job of separating religious from ethnic American Jews.[5] The survey's estimates regarding American infidels have been more controversial. Kosmin and Lachman reported that 5 percent of their respondents claimed to have no religion. That would equal thirteen million Americans. Another .5 percent (about 1.2 million Americans) claimed to be agnostics. A tiny minority, equal to only about twenty-nine thousand persons nationwide, claimed specifically to be humanists.[6]

Many in the nonreligious movement believe Kosmin and Lachman have still undercounted America's infidels. Still, even if their modest figures are accurate, nonreligious Americans are at least twice as numerous as

Amcrican Jews. That is many, many more infidels than most Americans believe to exist!

Other polls suggest that the nonreligious population is larger yet. A recent Gallup poll reported that 9 percent of respondents were either atheists, agnostics, or expressed no religious preference.[7] That equates to *twenty-three million* nonreligious Americans—an awesomely large number.

Another study from Gallup's Princeton Religion Research Center (PRRC) sets the number higher still.[8] Digesting numerous Gallup and PRRC polls, PRRC claimed that the U.S. population includes 2 percent atheists (equal to 5.2 million people, 1.6 times the number of religiously observant Jews), another 2 percent agnostics (another 5.2 million), and 7 percent with no religious preference. That equates to 18.2 million Americans with no religion, six times the number of observant Jews. Put it all together, and 11 percent of the U.S. population is said to be either atheist, agnostic, or without a religious preference. That adds up to 28.6 million Americans. That is approximately equal to the population of African Americans, an outgroup everyone takes seriously.

Two other Gallup polls found even more infidels. A follow-up study found that 10 percent of respondents, rather than 7, reported no religious preference.[9] The Gallup Organization's benchmark *Religion in America* study for 1992, which used different survey methods, reports that 94 percent of Americans believe in God or a universal spirit.[10] That would suggest that 6 percent of Gallup's respondents—equivalent to 15.6 million Americans—are atheists or agnostics.

When the figures range this widely, it's hard to be sure what they say about American infidelity. They speak more loudly about the Gallup Organization's inconsistency in conducting the measurements. George Gallup himself is religious; in his foreword to *Religions of the World* he called for prayer to solve world problems. Infidel leaders, along with some professional demographers, have long suspected that Gallup poll questions are often worded to skew responses in favor of religion. So if you find the numbers we've just considered breathtakingly large, consider that these studies may *still* underreport the number of American infidels.

The "infidel community" is at least as numerous as the American Jewish community, including both observant and ethnic Jews; it is probably larger. It is also likely, though not proveable with current data, that infidels are the largest single minority group of any type (religious, racial, or ethnic) in American life.

America's nonreligious outgroup can no longer be dismissed. As most Americans know, in the last three to four decades it has taken a conspicuous place in the national debates over social values, ethical decision-making, and church-state separation.

Taking the Lead in Old Outsider Activism

Until the early 1960s, Jews rather than infidels led the way in opposing church-state entanglements associated with the Christmas season.[11] In some areas Jewish activism had been spectacularly successful. In others, it is suprising by contemporary standards how little was achieved. In 1954, after half a century of Jewish activism, James Harwood Barnett could still write: "Christmas observance in the public schools is accepted without question by most Christians, and a direct challenge to the legitimacy of the practice appears absurd to many."[12]

Today, the situation is different. Many Christians continue to oppose challenges to Christmas observance in the public schools. But far from being considered absurd, such complaints are now an expected sign of the season. What changed? We can look to a series of legal victories won by atheists and nonreligious former Christians. In the course of these achievements, infidels gradually overtook American Jews as the primary agitators for greater separation of church and state.

Ask most Americans about church-state lawsuits, and they'll tell you that Madalyn Murray O'Hair ejected God, prayer, and religion from the public schools. No one has worked harder to reinforce this impression than Madalyn herself, but it's not true. A wholly unrelated case, *Engel* v. *Vitale,* sparked the Supreme Court decision that did away with prayer led by teachers or principals in 1962, a year before Madalyn faced the high court. Even in 1963, Madalyn's suit *Murray* v. *Curlett* was the less important of two suits that the Court decided simultaneously. Both involved mandatory Bible readings. *Abingdon School District* v. *Schempp* was the more significant case. The youthful plaintiff, Ellory Schempp, was not an atheist. But neither was he a Jew; he was a Unitarian, and represented the growing significance of liberal churches in the "infidel" movement.[13]

In 1985 *Wallace* v. *Jaffree* pitted Alabama agnostic Ishmael Jaffree against a one-minute period of silence "for meditation or voluntary prayer" that Alabama authorities were attempting to escalate into a state-written prayer. Jaffree succeeded before the Supreme Court.

During the same period the Council for Democratic and Secular Humanism and its chairman, Paul Kurtz, brought a number of suits involving U.S. congressional chaplains.[14] *Kurtz* v. *Kennickel* ended the use of tax monies to print collections of prayers by Senate chaplains. *Kurtz* v. *Baker* secured a pledge by the then-Senate chaplain to refrain from making remarks during invocations that disparaged the nonreligious. But it failed to establish a right of infidel leaders to deliver "un-invocations" to open sessions of the House and Senate.

In 1989 Cambridge, Massachusetts, humanists erected a sign bearing quotes from Thomas Jefferson next to a Christmas crèche on the Cambridge Commons. In 1992 Freedom from Religion Foundation member Gene Kasmar succeeded in evicting an electric menorah from the grounds of the Minnesota State Capitol Building after three years of legal action. In the same year, Kasmar's effort to have the Bible banned as obscene by the Brooklyn, Minnesota, school board—intended to lampoon fundamentalist efforts to ban books such as *The Catcher in the Rye*—failed.

One of the longest-running comic operas in the history of freethought-Christmas confrontations began in Ottawa, Illinois, in 1956. At that time the town's retail merchant association commissioned sixteen paintings of the life of Jesus in connection with a "Put Christ Back in Christmas" display. The paintings were displayed in a public park from 1957 to 1969, and then lost. In 1980 they were found under a grandstand and erected annually in the same public park. In 1986 Freedom from Religion Foundation member Richard Rohrer complained about the paintings. In 1988 he sued, to be replaced by a Jane Doe plaintiff when business forced Rohrer to move out of Ottawa.

In 1989 a court ruled display of the paintings unconstitutional. On appeal, this ruling was termed "overbroad" and the park was ruled an open forum. In 1991 the paintings were displayed once more. When they went up in 1992, activists from the Freedom from Religion Foundation were ready. Taking advantage of the "open forum" the appeals court had acknowledged, they erected a banner of their own that said "Jesus Christ is a Myth."

The banner had to be replaced twice; apparently some of Ottawa's good Christians had trouble understanding what an open forum was. The first banner was stolen by a Sunday school teacher who said he wanted to take it to class and use it as the centerpiece of a lecture on tolerance. (You can't make up stuff like this.) The second banner was set afire by persons unknown. The third was defaced by a man in a Santa Claus suit who tried to obscure its message using paint-soaked rags on a long pole. At season's end, the Christian paintings were removed; freethought activists announced their determination to return if they were displayed the next year. Ottawa mayor Forest Buck got the message and announced that holiday displays of all types would be suspended in 1993.[15]

Recent legal actions by infidel activists in local communities have forced the removal of religious symbols and mottoes from municipal seals, challenged Nativity displays and other religious observances in public places, and precipitated a constitutional crisis in the state of Utah.

If Jewish activism in this area has been less conspicuous than that of infidels, it has hardly disappeared. In 1981 Towson, Maryland, stopped displaying a large electric menorah after an objection by Baltimore's Jewish

Council.[16] Jewish groups were prominent in a 1984 effort to prevent the Reagan administration from returning a crèche to the official Christmas Pageant of Peace held on the Ellipse, opposite the White House in Washington, D.C. And in *Lee* v. *Weisman,* it was a Jewish plaintiff who in 1992 persuaded the Supreme Court to end officially sanctioned prayers at public school graduations.

Still, the torch of church-state activism has partly passed from the Jewish to the infidel community over the last thirty-odd years. Why might this be? It may be that assimilation, including accommodation to Christmas, has blunted the militancy of the American Jewish community. Too often today, when Jewish groups go to court over holiday displays, they sue not to remove Christian symbols from the public square but to secure the right to place Jewish symbols alongside them. That strategy backfired spectacularly in 1992 in Cincinnati, Ohio. Lubavitcher Rabbi Sholom B. Kalmanson won the right to erect a menorah on the city's Fountain Square, which had previously been bare of sectarian holiday symbols. Ku Klux Klan activists used the Jewish victory as a precedent to demand (and receive!) their own right to display a controversial cross. If not for misplaced Jewish activism, we might have been spared the Klan's irritations in Cincinnati in December 1992.

Where Christmas is concerned and, indeed, wherever discussion turns to the separation of church and state, the wisest strategy is always *against* accommodation. Instead of fighting for "equal time," a better goal is to strip public facilities of holiday decorations that express a link to any sectarian religion. Private life has opportunities enough for those who want to engage in religious expression.

Infidels at Christmas Time

Where do the nonreligious stand on Christmas? I admit it: I am disappointed with many of my fellow unbelievers. Most infidels have been no less eager to accommodate to Christmas than assimilated Jews.

Infidel responses to Christmas fall into five categories:

(1) Keep Christmas complete.

(2) Keep Christmas in more or less conventional form, but inject an infidel component—perhaps in the spirit of a disclaimer.

(3) Observe most holiday traditions, but describe the holiday as the "winter solstice" rather than Christmas.

(4) Consciously craft an unconventional observance based on pagan solstice rites or on other sources as a counter to the Christian celebration rampant in society.

(5) Reject the holiday more or less completely. Far too few American infidels have given this option a fair try.

Infidels Who Keep Christmas Complete

Far too many infidels have simply surrendered to Christmas. Some find Yuletide irresistible; others think the holiday is not worth the effort of opposing it. Still others consider it cruel or impractical to deny their children Christmas when the holiday is so materially rewarding to their believing playmates. Infidels who keep Christmas may trim Christmas trees, decorate their homes in conventional ways, wish strangers "merry Christmas," sing carols, and perhaps even participate in a few religious exercises for ostensibly aesthetic reasons.

Whether Jewish or infidel, Old Outsiders who keep Christmas complete are trying to pretend that parts of contemporary Christmas can be divorced from the holiday's Christian roots. Why try the impossible? Bill, a Texas humanist, gives one of the most common and, in some ways, saddest reasons: "I have seven grandchildren and I would not suggest their parents try to raise them in our society today without a belief in Santa Claus."[17]

John from California picks up the same theme: "The main reason to carry on as usual is to keep the kids from being ostracized. Christians do that sometimes, you know."[18]

Charles, a secular humanist from Idaho, agrees:

> For my kids as they grew up, Christmas was a secular, nonreligious event of gift-giving and having a good time. But nonetheless it was observed as such, because the rest of society was doing it and I did not want my kids to be left out and alienated in a social sense.[19]

If some infidels cave in to Christmas because they fear that their children will be ostracized, others simply go overboard in the "live and let live" department, like this computer bulletin board correspondent:

> I see Christmas as an excuse to do what should be done all year long . . . to love one another and to show your feelings toward them . . . but if my loved ones need or want this holiday, I see no harm in it.[20]

You don't have to be an infidel to recognize that contemporary Christmas seldom has anything to do with "loving one another." Other nonbelievers see a practical value in exposing their children to the Yuletide madness. Bill from Texas, again:

> There is at least one value in children believing in Santa Claus. They could learn that belief, no matter how strong, does not make the thing believed in true. Why do adults who have learned the truth about Santa Claus put the same type of faith in a religion? Seems to me anyone with common horse sense would be able to relate the two.[21]

Infidels who keep Christmas complete are probably creating a legacy of confusion for their children rather than the atmosphere of acceptance they seek.

Infidels Who Keep Christmas but Inject a Freethought Component

Some infidels keep the holiday conventionally enough to spare themselves the stigma of seeming different. But they express their infidelity by putting a freethought twist on their celebration. David, a California atheist, puts it in sparkling terms:

> Although I am an atheist, I love Christmas and I don't concede that it is a religious holiday or celebration. My favorite holiday greeting is "Merry Christmas, God damn it." . . . I advocate an outspoken celebration with an explicit rejection of the religious elements.[22]

Neat trick, David. If only it could be done! I went through a phase where I sent atheist Christmas cards and gave "godless gifts." The day I tired of hearing "Look, he says he's an atheist but he still acknowledges the birthday of Jesus" was for me the beginning of wisdom. Still, David acknowledges that one cannot celebrate a "freethinking Christmas" without investing some energy in tweaking dominant Christian ideas about the holiday.

Molleen, a California secular humanist, puts an explicitly multicultural spin on her family's holiday observance. Raised a Jew, Molleen's husband is Japanese American. They kept Christmas for the sake of their daughter, but treated the holiday as an expanded New Year's celebration with overtones from a variety of cultures. Now that their daughter is in her late teens, Molleen and her husband are scaling back the celebration. One still wonders whether raising the child Yule-free might have given her development an even stronger multicultural flavor.

Other infidels seem to think that contemporary Christmas has become so secular that they can ignore its Christian aspects. Robert, a New York State humanist, describes his family's secularized tradition:

> The winter celebrations to our freethinking family were just holidays of feasting, merriment, and gift giving, devoid of any divine ceremony—enjoyed simply for their own sakes, no matter the derivation from mythology.[23]

A bulletin board correspondent amplified the theme:

> I'm pretty much an atheist and we celebrate Christmas. . . . I don't really think it affects . . . anyone's life that much. It's just turned into another birthday party where everyone gets presents.[24]

As you watch American culture turn itself inside out from Thanksgiving to New Year's, remind yourself that Christmas doesn't really "affect anyone's life that much." Dave, a Colorado humanist, paints a similarly optimistic picture:

> Christmas time helps bring out the best in most folks and the fact that Christmas is based on the so-called birthdate of an ambiguous if not fictitious Jesus shouldn't detract from all the goodwill it promotes and its positive worth to society.[25]

Perhaps it shouldn't; but it almost always does.

Arthur, a Minnesota atheist, takes the holiday very casually indeed. If there's a continuum between "laid back" and "laid out," I'm not altogether sure where he falls on it:

> I am one of those apparently rare atheists who isn't bothered in the least by Christmas, Easter, or any other holiday or event with religious overtones. As long as they don't force me into church, they can have as much fun as they like, and display Nativity scenes on public property for all I care.[26]

It may come as news to the Arthurs of the world, but there are leaders on the religious right who count on precisely this sort of complacency to create an atmosphere in which to undermine the rights of those who believe differently than they do. Christmas gives infidels a golden opportunity to show the world that they exist, to make sure they are not mistaken for Christians. It's a shame to see it thrown away.

Infidels Who Call Their Holiday the "Winter Solstice"

Some infidel activists believe that if they focus on the pagan aspects of contemporary Christmas, perhaps labeling their festival a "winter solstice" observance, they can be true to their principles without having to miss the party. Barbara Smoker, a usually gruff and outspoken freethinker who is sometimes called England's Madalyn Murray O'Hair, once commissioned a book to demonstrate the holiday's pagan roots so that infidels wouldn't have to feel guilty about celebrating it:

> Those of us who make no secret of our rejection of Christian doctrine are often subject to jibes [about being hypocrites for keeping Christmas] unless we are also, like Bernard Shaw, anti-Christmas ascetics, eager to do a normal day's work on December the twenty-fifth, avoiding the company of revellers. . . . Most of us do not aspire to such Shavian asceticism. Though concerned to appear consistent, we would hate to feel excluded from the general jollification.[27]

That makes about as much sense as advocates of big government cheating on their taxes, but it's a widely held view.

At other times, amazing energies are exerted to reassure Christians that yes, infidels actually like Christmas very much. At a recent Freedom from Religion Foundation conference, organizers requested that a Christmas tree be removed from an overcrowded meeting room so that more people could squeeze in to hear a popular speaker. A local television station trumpeted that the atheists had demanded the tree's removal because they hated Christmas. A San Antonio FFRF member rushed a letter to the editor to several newspapers: "If the [television] journalist had known anything at all about atheists, he/she would have known that most of them love Christmas trees."[28]

Though far too many infidels have Christmas trees, even I'm not sure how many love them. I suspect most regard their holiday conifers with resignation rather than enthusiasm. Unfortunately, they keep trimming them.

Infidels hungry for a celebration of their own at Christmas time often revive the winter solstice. The shortest day of the year in the Northern Hemisphere, it is also the day after which daylight continues to lengthen all through the spring. An authentic solstice revival might resemble this improvised ritual described by Elisabeth, an atheist who lives in Germany, where the pagan roots of Yule lie closer to the surface:

> To emphasize that [December] twenty-first was the darkest day of the year, my son was woken up [sic] at six A.M. Armed with a candle, he proceeded

through the darkened house, finding cryptic clues for a treasure hunt and puzzling over their meaning. Then, with a triumphant "Aha!", off he'd race to where he had figured out that the next clue would be. When he'd found all the treasures, he had a pancake breakfast lit only by a grate fire.

The solstice treasure hunt was atmospheric, action-packed, and intellectually challenging—and he felt sorry for the others who had to settle for presents lying under a tree four days later![29]

American infidel solstice observances are seldom either this creative, or as astronomically accurate. It strains credulity to think that modern nonbelievers armed with a scientific view of the world would seriously want to resurrect a festival from a religious tradition even more primitive than Christianity. Yet infidel leaders keep issuing sound bites like "The Christians stole the solstice from the pagans, and we're going to take it back," furnishing the spectacle of committed nonbelievers, many of whom spent years of their lives rejecting the Christian baggage of their upbringings, rushing to immerse themselves in sun worship.

A serious cult of the solstice seems inconceivable for people who understand the dynamics of the solar system and possess central heating. Yet the solstice is a growth industry among American infidels. Small companies have sprung up to publish solstice greeting cards. Shades of the Chanukah bush, some infidels have adopted the "solstice shrub," which is decorated with "just about anything."

The urge to reclaim the joys of Christmas from the matrix of Christianity is understandable. Gary, a Maryland secular humanist, describes the appeal of the solstice in moving language:

> Like most people, I enjoy the ambience of the winter holidays—the snow, the lights, the greenery. I refuse to give up this enjoyment just because the Christians have associated this season with their Jesus myth.[30]

What harm does it do for an infidel to keep the winter solstice, perhaps festooned with one's favorite remembered scraps of Christmas cheer? The solstice coincides so closely with Christmas, and shares so many of its elements, that from a short distance few observers can distinguish a solstice celebration from the conventional celebration of Christmas. When a secular humanist carefully says "happy holidays" to a stranger on a street corner, no point is made. The stranger interprets it as one more encounter with a good sheep who keeps Christmas—one more pebble atop the mountain of false evidence that Christmas is for everyone.

Celebrating the solstice is dangerous because it makes infidels invisible. Doing so may help individual infidels to make it through another

Christmas without stress. But it also provides grist for the mill of Christian Right pundits like Edward Grimsley:

> Nearly everyone makes merry at Christmas, but many people do not want to admit what they are doing when they observe the holiday. What they are doing, of course, is celebrating the birth of Jesus Christ.[31]

If Jesus Christ is not your savior, Christmas is not your holiday. Have the guts to sit it out without trying to sneak its echoes in through loopholes.

Infidels Who Craft Unconventional Observances to Counter the Christian Celebration

Some infidels try to defuse the impact of their accommodation to Christmas with humor. Sometimes it works. Here is Laurie, a Virginia atheist with a few Puritans on her family tree:

> The problem I have with sitting out holidays is that it would reenact the religious practices of some of my ancestors, so the message would be garbled. Besides, I like occasional gluttony, sloth, and lust just as much as the next person. . . . Today I plan to make some gingerbread *homunculi* and engage in a little ritual cannibalism. If I also make some sugar-cookie candles, bells, and five-pointed stars, and lounge around in my "ceremonial" fuzzy bathrobe while eating them, would it also constitute evidence of Satanic activity?[32]

Other nonbelievers bring an infectious energy and creativity to the creation of alternative holidays. Bob, an atheist living in Kentucky, has developed one of the cleverest "un-Christmases" for his family that I have ever seen. To fully appreciate the irony of what follows, you should know that Isaac Newton was not really born on Christmas Day, 1642. His Anglican parents engaged in a popular form of civil disobedience against Cromwell's hatred of Christmas: They listed December 25 on every birth certificate, regardless of actual date of the child's birth. Buckle your seat belts, here's Bob:

> As a family of atheists which includes children of ages two and seven, we have been at some pains to provide non-Christian celebrations within the family. It so happens that December 25 is the traditional birthday of Isaac Newton, and it is one of the biggest holidays of the year at our house.
> We have a weeping fig tree *(Ficus benjamina)* which we decorate with apples and we have a little Newton doll which we sit under the tree. ["Fig Newton," get it? Also consider the parallels to the old German Paradise tree.]

In the morning, when the children awaken, we gather at the tree and read [the classic story of the falling apple that supposedly inspired Newton to develop the theory of gravitation in 1666]. During the reading . . . my oldest child is holding a special apple above the Newton doll. At the completion of the reading she drops the apple onto the doll's head. Then we open the gifts which Isaac has left. . . .

We have sent out Newton's birthday cards to relatives and friends. We even received one in return! Newton has left notes for my children and has been known to drink a glass of milk left for him. My children thoroughly enjoy the celebration.[33]

If some infidels approach the holiday with creativity and pluck, others are simply overwhelmed by it. Inclined to sit out Christmas but unable to bring themselves to do so, they exist in uncomfortable stasis. Eve from Wisconsin writes that "I spent last Christmas pouting as usual. I always do":

Every year . . . I end up raining on the Christmas parade. The overwhelming guilt that sweeps down on me for merely going along with a tradition . . . is almost more than I can tolerate. And being the only one in my family who possesses my particular viewpoint makes the argument that much harder to win. I'm afraid we non-Christians are too soft on this issue. We have capitulated too much ground for wise debate. We have allowed our opponents far too much use of their power to convince us that we are . . . Scrooges because we view Christmas with a jaundiced eye!

. . . In the past, I have tried to rationalize . . . my inept attempts to express my views on the matter by pretending to celebrate only the "secular" aspect of Christmas, whatever that is. It didn't work—Christmas is Christmas no matter what label I place on it. Pretending, or allowing my opponents . . . to convince me that Christmas is the only day of the year when families can get together just doesn't seem a very fair argument. But nevertheless, it is the winning one.[34]

There is a solution to Eve's dilemma. It lies in taking the risks of open self-disclosure. Don't get trapped in half-measures; confront the Christian ingroup with the reality that in their midst live committed infidels who have the courage to march to their personal drummer, and take themselves seriously enough to march all the way to work on December 25.

Infidels Who Reject Christmas Completely

Our survey of infidels at Christmas is not solely a chronicle of compromise. A few nonreligious people follow the lead of philosopher George

Santayana and playwright George Bernard Shaw. Rose from Tennessee writes:

> I do not celebrate Christmas. I do not buy any presents, cards, or tree. . . .
> I am happy to be at peace in December (as much as possible).
>   . . . I do not celebrate any absurd "Solstice" or pagan celebration. I do
> not thrill to the thought that spring will come again. I know it's going to
> come again, a mere astronomical occurrence.[35]

Andy from Pennsylvania takes an uncompromising stance on all holidays. For him, there is too much to savor in each ordinary day to justify the fiction that any certain day is "special": "I stand on X-mas [his spelling] as I stand on all holidays: Most of them, and all of the religious ones, are a . . . waste of precious time."[36]

Aspasia from Washington is in her forties, athletic, single, and child-free by choice. She's so holistic it hurts, but beneath her New Age vocabulary she has found more satisfying uses for the holiday season than the usual round of excess, gluttony, and foolishness:

> There are two ways to seek the truth: One is to borrow knowledge, the other
> is to seek yourself. Of course, borrowing is easy, but whatsoever you borrow
> is never yours. . . .
>   To me, these so-called holidays are a time of self-reflection, rest, and
> most of all, self-care. *Solitude*. Solitude is good for the soul. I have discovered
> for me that during this time of year beginning around the Thanksgiving period,
> as a . . . creator of my own lifestyle, I commence by taking a singles cruise
> or a health cruise, or go to a weekend spa for self-care and pampering without
> guilt. . . . At the end of each year, I eagerly look forward to the new year—
> all rested and rejuvenated![37]

Michael from Tennessee finds nothing that appeals to him in contemporary Christmas or its infidel analogues.

> I'm baffled by the atheists who still love Christmas and do everything the
> Christians do, but call it "Solstice." . . . I feel no need to be a part of the
> secular Christmas culture, any more than I feel the need to be part of the
> Christian Christmas culture, or the less annoying, but no less silly . . . solstice
> culture.[38]

Charles from Oregon hints that if he did anything special during the holiday season, it might be a custom-built observance:

Christmas (or solstice) is not for us, I think. We should proceed to pick a "day" for ourselves, that would serve as a reminder to ourselves *and* to others that we exist. You get the picture: We need an "Un-Holy" day.

By the way, I don't do "Thanksgiving" either. Who is there to thank?[39]

Marilyn from New York State has no axe to grind. She just wishes that everyone would get off her case at holiday time:

No story. I just get tired of either (falsely) responding to the cheery "Merry Christmas" and trying to explain that I don't celebrate, or grumping like Scrooge—my usual option.[40]

Too few American infidels have given serious thought to boycotting the holiday altogether. It's an option with logic, consistency, and courage on its side. If Christmas makes you uncomfortable, give it a try.

Christmas and the Old Outsiders

In the last chapter we focused on Jewish responses to the Christmas juggernaut. In this one we have examined those of infidels. The common denominator has been accommodation to Christmas. Religious minorities for whom Christmas ought to be a nonevent have instead altered their own traditions or adopted practices that are alien and meaningless in the context of their own beliefs. Why have Jews and infidels surrendered so easily on this single issue?

- When Jews and infidels were making their places in American society, the rights of outgroups were less well understood than today. Cultural imposition and outright bigotry were considered normal.

- During the nineteenth and early twentieth centuries, assimilation was prized. Ethnicity was reviled. Unusual ethnic or philosophical identities cost more than they do today.

- Many of the multicultural assumptions we take for granted today had to be won by the Old Outsiders through patient argument, educational effort, or in the courts. Old Outsiders had to expend prodigious energies to move society toward its relatively tolerant stance today.

- Jews and infidels might have tolerated much cultural imposition by Christians because of the cultural elements they shared. Nineteenth-century Jewish immigrants had a scripture (what Christians

call the Old Testament) and much of European culture in common
with the Anglo-Saxon Christians who dominated U.S. society. Most
nonbelievers came from Christian backgrounds; steeped in Christian
scriptures, images, and ideas, they may have underestimated the
danger these posed to non-Christians' rights.

Today more than in the past, Old Outsiders need to remember that
they undercut their own position when they make themselves invisible.
Claiming to be non-Christian but still taking Christmas Day off work
may seem a small thing, but it can have a corrosive effect in the social
debate over minority rights.

As America's Old Outsiders contemplate their future, including what
they will do with themselves between future Thanksgivings and future New
Year's Days, three main points rise clearly into focus.

(1) *Assimilation is no longer the dominant goal of most minority
    groups.* If American Jews and infidels still find their December
    calendars being shaped by an "assimilation imperative" whose social
    power sputtered out more than a quarter-century ago, maybe they
    should reconsider their own collaboration in the process.

(2) *Now that assimilation is out, it's OK to be assertive about your
    differences.* Cultural imposition is out; cognitive choice is in. The
    newly visible outgroups that have followed Jews and infidels onto
    the national stage have learned the power of positive pushiness.
    African Americans owe much to Stokely Carmichael and Malcolm
    X, feminists to Kate Millett and Bella Abzug, gays to the deliberately
    outrageous activism of groups like ACT-UP and Queer Nation.
    In today's America, outgroups that are forthright about what makes
    them different get respect. If America's Jews and infidels are secure
    in their non-Christianity, now is the time to be *seen* treating
    Christianity's most popular holiday as "just another day."

(3) *Church-state separation, radically defined, must continue to be
    a focus of Old Outsider political and cultural activism.* Jews and
    infidels will always have a special role as guardians of the right
    not to be Christian in America. The Old Outsiders are in a unique
    position to know that "When folks take religion seriously, trouble
    is going to follow."[41]

Some of the historic compromises Jews and infidels have made with the
dominant Christian culture, especially in the area of the winter holiday,
no longer look like good ideas. Indeed, if we fail to set aside our Chanukah

bushes and solstice ceremonies, we risk losing our credibility as outgroups, entitled by virtue of our differences to the same social elbow room that other minorities claim.

Outgroups in a multicultural society are *expected* to be assertive about the things that make them different. If American Jews and infidels fail to do this at Christmas time, when their actions speak so loudly and are so well remembered by mainstream Americans, we will have given away our rights unilaterally and received nothing in return.

The "New Outsiders"—newly powerful religious minorities that are only now attracting the attention they deserve in American life—know the rules inside out. They *won't* settle for the compromises that have satisfied too many of the Old Outsiders. That's going to make for rougher holiday sledding for Christians who still cannot understand why American culture is no longer their private toy.

But that's a matter for another chapter.

Notes

1. For the historic independence of morality from religious thought, see Richard Taylor, *Good and Evil: A New Direction* (Buffalo, N.Y.: Prometheus Books, 1984).

2. See Albert Post, *Popular Freethought in America, 1825–1850* (New York: Columbia University Press, 1943). For more on Frances Wright and Robert Dale Owen, see Celia Morris, *Fanny Wright: Rebel in America* (Cambridge, Mass.: Harvard University Press, 1984).

3. For Robert Green Ingersoll, see Frank Smith, *Robert G. Ingersoll: A Life* (Buffalo, N.Y.: Prometheus Books, 1990); Clinton P. Farrell, ed., *The Writings of Robert G. Ingersoll* (Dresden, N.Y.: Dresden Publishing Co., 1900), 12 vols.

4. William B. Williamson, "Is the U.S.A. a Christian Nation?" *Free Inquiry* (Spring 1993): 33.

5. Barry Kosmin and Seymour Lachman, *National Survey of Religions Conducted by National Survey of Religious Identification* (New York: City University of New York, 1991).

6. Vern L. Bullough, "Religion and the Polls," *Free Inquiry* (Summer 1991): 9.

7. Williamson, p. 33.

8. "Religions of the World," *Emerging Trends* (January 1993): 2–3.

9. "Final 1992 Religious Preference Results," *Emerging Trends* (February 1993): 5.

10. Robert Bezilla, ed., *Religion in America* (Princeton, N.J.: Princeton Religion Research Center, 1993).

11. Leonard Gross, "The Jew and Christmas," *Look* (December 28, 1965): 12–14.

12. James Harwood Barnett, *The American Christmas: A Study in National Culture* (New York: Macmillan, 1954), p. 69.

13. Rob Boston, "Forever and Ever Amen," *Church and State* (June 1993): 128.

14. *"Free Inquiry* in Court: Half a Loaf," *Free Inquiry* (Winter 1986–87): 50.

15. *USA Today,* January 6, 1993.

16. "Christmas Conflicts, Again," *Church and State* (February 1982): 13.

17. Personal correspondence.

18. Ibid.

19. Ibid.

20. BBS correspondence.

21. Personal correspondence.

22. Ibid.

23. Ibid.

24. BBS correspondence.

25. Personal correspondence.

26. Ibid.

27. From the foreword by Barbara Smoker, in R. J. Condon, *Our Pagan Christmas* (reprint London: National Secular Society; Austin, Tex: American Atheist Press, undated), p. 1.

28. Jan King, "Atheists Love Christmas Trees," San Antonio *Express-News,* December 29, 1992. See also "Convention Update," *Freethought Today* (December 1992): 4.

29. Sylvia Brooks, "O Solstice Shrub, O Solstice Shrub," *Columbus* (Ohio) *Dispatch,* December 21, 1992.

30. Personal correspondence.

31. Edward Grimsley, "Be as Merry as Possible Under the Circumstances," *Conservative Chronicle,* December 18, 1992.

32. Personal correspondence.

33. Ibid.

34. Ibid.

35. Ibid.

36. Ibid.

37. Ibid.

38. Ibid.

39. Ibid.

40. BBS correspondence.

41. Fr. David Fulton, "Violent Events Affect Beliefs," *Newark Courier-News,* March 18, 1993.

13

Christmas and the New Outsiders

The "New Outsiders" are America's religious non-Judaeo-Christians: Muslims, Hindus, Buddhists, Confucianists, Shintos, Baha'is, Sikhs, adherents of Native American religions, Wiccans, and more. People who hold many of these belief systems have been part of our country since its beginning. Today they are they making their presence felt *as groups* in new ways.

Who are the New Outsiders? What does Christmas mean to them? A Jain bulletin board (BBS) correspondent offered this bitter summation of the New Outsider holiday experience:

> [T]he holiday season . . . is overemphasized and out of place. For example, religion of any kind, including the celebration of Christmas (including putting up trees, etc.) should *not* be allowed. [I assume public places are meant.] However, it is a Christian-dominant society and there is no way to prevent the overwhelming celebration of the holiday season. So, you cannot stop stores from selling trees and Christmas cards, and you cannot stop television from broadcasting Christmas specials; they are all in it to make money, and they will appeal to the majority market in any way they can. It would be good, however, to see more multicultural, and more interfaith, activities and promotions in the overall community.

A Baha'i BBS correspondent showed greater tolerance:

> As a Baha'i . . . as such, and at the recommendation of the national body of the Baha'i faith in the U.S., I *would* myself not have bothered with Christmas any more than I would have other major prophets of other religions. . . . And then, I married. My wife is Catholic. We get along fine in our religious discussion, however she put her foot down. She *would* have her holidays, so I agreed. . . .

While we still observe the holiday we do not get each other presents. [We give gifts to] everyone else in both families, yes, just not each other. What we do instead is take the money we would otherwise spend on [gifts for each other] and get presents for someone . . . that otherwise would have nothing. As for children, as it happens we don't have any, nor does it now appear likely we shall. However, since becoming a Baha'i is an elective process for each individual the ultimate choice would be . . . up to each one.

Here is another New Outsider voice, hailing not from an Eastern tradition but from Western paganism:

I'm a Wiccan . . . pagan, though I don't deal with the magick really . . . else I'd be grey, not white. . . . And no, I don't feel uncomfortable on holidays, because I celebrate Yule instead of Christmas, Samhain instead of Halloween, etc. I only feel uncomfortable if I get gifts that are thoughtless. . . .

This small sampling displays a degree of diversity—and between the lines, an impatience with Christian intrusiveness—that is new in American life. How numerous are the New Outsiders? The *American Encyclopedia of Religions* lists 12.7 million members of non-Judaeo-Christian religious groups, about 5 percent of the national population.[1] Chief among these are an estimated 5.5 million Muslims, perhaps 2 percent of the population. They attract an estimated thirty thousand converts per year,[2] and are served by more than 840 mosques and Islamic centers.

There may be one million Buddhists in the United States, including three hundred thousand members of Nichiren Soshu of America (NSA), two hundred thousand members (fifty thousand families) of the Church of Perfect Liberty, one hundred thousand members of the Buddhist Churches of America, and numerous smaller Buddhist groups.[3] Another one million Americans are estimated to practice Hinduism.[4]

By now, no one will be surprised to learn that these numbers are controversial. Larger projections of the Muslim population used to be popular. In 1990 the *Wall Street Journal* reported that U.S. Muslims were more numerous than Episcopalians, that more Muslims lived in America than in Libya, and that Muslims would outnumber American Jews before the year 2000. *Christianity Today* editor Terry Muck repeated that prediction in his book *Alien Gods on American Turf,* as did pundit Moorhead Kennedy in a 1993 column.[5] Confidence in the growth of U.S. Islam ran so high that one Muslim spokesperson declared: "We'd like people to start thinking of the U.S. as a Judeo-Christian-Islamic society." To that end New York City Muslim leaders have pressured banks and owners of office buildings to decorate for Ramadan, Islam's early-spring holy month, as they do for Christmas, Chanukah, Easter, and Passover.

Other reports suggest that the Muslim population explosion is a myth. Gallup's Princeton Religion Research Center recently claimed that Muslims make up less than 1 percent of the nation's population, half the previously accepted estimate.[6] In one 1990 Gallup study, only .2 percent of respondents claimed to be Muslim, equivalent to just 520,000 U.S. Muslims—only two-thirds the number who claimed to be Hindu![7] Kosmin and Lachman's controversial CUNY study predictably entered the fray with a surprising claim: this time, that most immigrants from Arab-speaking countries were Christian, not Muslim.[8]

Each time we think we have a handle on the statistics for any U.S. religious outgroup, along comes that CUNY study to upset the apple cart. Kosmin and Lachman's data suggest that previous measures have consistently overreported religious diversity. They even claimed that most Irish-Americans are Protestant, a finding ascribed to recent immigration from unstable, mostly Protestant Northern Ireland. Other demographers question the CUNY study's apparent implication that America remains a Protestant enclave after all.

How far can we trust the CUNY study? At first glance, its methodology—direct polling of more than one hundred thousand Americans—seems superior to anything done before. Gallup studies usually query fewer respondents, raising the possibility of sampling error. Standard reference works often rely on information from the national offices of the various denominations. Certain Eastern traditions don't attach much importance to nose counting. Few Buddhist sects have formal procedures for inducting members: "You're Buddhist if you think you are," a philosophy that complicates census-taking. While Hinduism has attracted numerous Western "seekers," few persons not born into the faith are accepted as full Hindus.[9] Count the seekers, or count the full members? It depends. In other cases, the national-level organizations may not represent a faith's entire U.S. community. For example, the 1992 *Statistical Abstract of the United States* listed only nineteen thousand Buddhists, an absurdly low number. Presumably, researchers mistook one or two Buddhist sects that were willing to report their memberships for the entire U.S. Buddhist population.[10]

These factors support the accuracy of Kosmin and Lachman's smaller figures. Yet other factors call them into question. Some critics have suggested that cultural and language barriers could have caused CUNY researchers to undercount non-Judaeo-Christians. Recent immigrants from India, Asia, or Africa may have been unfamiliar with opinion polls. Suspecting that pollsters were connected with the government or that data about individuals could be used in some threatening way, some might have claimed to be Christian in an attempt at protective coloration. In other cases, respondents may have answered incorrectly because their poor command of English led them to misunderstand survey questions. This is a problem Kosmin and Lachman themselves have acknowledged.[11]

Finally, we must admit that all studies—the older benchmarks that found larger non-Judaeo-Christian populations, as well as newer studies that report small ones—may reflect the biases and political agendas of their creators. In interviewing demographers I frequently heard the speculation that, until about 1990, figures were sometimes skewed to exaggerate the actual religious diversity of the nation. If there's little diversity, who needs demographers? As the figures rose, concern began to multiply about the implications of a multifaith society. Perhaps, my sources conjectured, it became popular to twist results the other way, in the direction of religious homogeneity, either to reassure WASPish sponsoring organizations or in hopes that underreporting diversity might defuse Christian backlash.

When the dust clears, we are left with the conclusion that there are no trustworthy figures for the New Outsider population. A safe guess might be that the United States is home to 500,000 to 750,000 Hindus, a similar number of Buddhists, and perhaps three to five million Muslims.

We should bring the same skepticism to the membership claims of the other non-Judaeo-Christian religious groups—some indigenous, others primarily immigrant—that fill out the New Outsider population. With that in mind, here is a snapshot of the smaller threads in the tapestry of religious America:

Baha'i: 1600 spiritual assemblies, 110,000 members (25–33 percent African Americans and Native Americans)

Confucianists: 100,000

Sikh Dharma: 300,000

Health, Happy, Holy Organization: 250,000

Jains: 50,000

Native American religions: 225,000

Wiccan: 10,000 to 100,000[12]

Some of these figures may be wildly wrong, but one can see that a demographic revolution is going on without resorting to statistics. Consider the increasingly visible penetration of medicine, engineering, and the sciences by professionals of Indian, Asian, and African descent. These are not only New Outsiders, but New Outsiders of status, wealth, and inevitably, growing social influence. This has two broad implications:

(1) Unlike Old Outsiders, New Outsiders expect majority culture to approach them from a platform of cognitive choice, not cultural imposition.

(2) Compared to the Old Outsiders, New Outsiders' conceptual and philosophical backgrounds have less in common with Christianity than those of Jews and infidels. Efforts to impose celebrations drawn from Christian roots will be recognized more quickly, will cause greater offense, and will spark harsher resistance than would the same impositions upon Old Outsider groups.

Whether members of the formerly dominant Christian ingroup like it or not, America has become a multifaith society, not merely multidenominational, as Christian Americans liked to pretend in the days when Jews and infidels were the only religious outgroups.[13] At U.S. President Bill Clinton's 1993 preinaugural service, Christian, Jewish, and Muslim clergy jointly performed the ceremonies. Passages from the Quran were read in Arabic, an inaugural first.[14] Evidence like this "suggests—no, proves —that the pluralism that we were talking about fifty years ago is now a reality."[15]

Multiculturalism and the New Outsiders

To deal fairly with America's demographic revolution, educators, and social scientists have adopted the concept of "multiculturalism." Multiculturalism is controversial because it asks America's dominant Christian ingroup to make concessions that hurt. The old ideal of assimilation was safer: "Leave them in the melting pot until they're just like us."

If you thought I was crazy to tackle Christmas, hang on. I will now attempt a short introduction to multiculturalism. Despite the abuses that have been committed in its name, multiculturalism offers us a blueprint for a society that encompasses true diversity, respects the differences between groups, and enables people of different backgrounds to share a political and social infrastructure without surrendering essential components of their chosen identities.

Multiculturalism opposes *ethnocentrism,* the belief that one's own ways represent the best or only way to live. Everybody has a culture; the first mistake of the ethnocentric is to imagine that their familiar web of beliefs and traditions is the natural one and that "people who engage in strange activities have a culture."[16] The second mistake is to imagine that intercultural collision is unusual. A survey of 171 countries showed that only

9 percent of them contained a single, homogeneous ethnic group. In the rest, intercultural encounter was the norm.[17]

The third mistake is to assume that when cultures clash, it is the outgroup, the subordinate or minority culture, that needs to adjust. That was the error behind assimilation. The ingroup has a culture too; it must join in the process of change. Because the ingroup culture commands a disproportionate share of society's resources, including the schools and the media, it should take the lead in responding to intercultural issues.

Multiculturalism: Anything but Easy

The multicultural ideal is audacious. Never before has a powerful ingroup proposed to meet outgroups halfway as a matter of policy. Yet like any new idea, multiculturalism can be implemented inappropriately, even abusively. On some American university campuses the rise of "political correctness" (PC) has challenged ordinary ideas of free inquiry and free expression. It is sad to see so many tenured leftists, who fought in their youths for freedom of expression, adopt a "kill the messenger" mentality in its place. Are we really so helpless before expressions of intolerance that we can only respond to bigots by hounding them out of the dorms? Have we lost confidence in our ability to win an argument with them? Is suppression the best, much less the only, response to an unpopular line of argument? PC hardliners have tragically failed to master the admittedly difficult task of showing tolerance even toward the intolerant.

Another unfortunate side-effect of PC culture, and one more directly relevant to the question of Christmas and the New Outsiders, deals with the mechanics of ethnic or religious identity. As pluralists, we want to defend the rights of outgroup members to express their differences. Yet we risk creating a tyranny of ancestry under which people are *compelled* to define themselves by accidents of gender, ethnicity, or preference.[18] Must women view their lives through the lens of feminism? Is a Muslim who opposes the *fatwa* against novelist Salman Rushdie inauthentic? Are Hispanics who feel attracted to Anglo culture traitors to their people? In other words, is ancestry destiny? As a secular humanist, I believe that insofar as possible, destiny should be something we *choose*.

Ancestry is not destiny. A true respect for diversity means respecting the right of individuals to accept or reject the cultures of their birth communities. It also means respecting the right of individuals to choose identities not originally their own. "Our cultures used to be almost hereditary, but now we choose them from a menu as various as the food court of a suburban shopping mall."[19] Cosmopolitanism and traditionalism are equally acceptable, equally culturally authentic, when they are the courses of individuals who have chosen them freely.

Islam, America, and the Multicultural Ideal

Now another quandary arises. What about outgroups whose authentic, voluntarily assumed traditions reinforce ethnocentricity? How can pluralists welcome newcomers whose cultures reject pluralism? As scholar of religions Martin Marty has observed, "the rest of the world never made the move to our style of rationality . . . Muslims didn't. Buddhists, Sikhs and Hindus didn't."[20]

Statistical quibbles aside, America's religious dialogue will soon be a four-way affair involving Christians, infidels, Jews, and Muslims. Other religions will participate too. But what will it imply to welcome Islam as a full partner in the discussion? More than a faith, Islam prescribes a political and social order. It provides a total blueprint for living in a way Christianity has not pretended to do since the Middle Ages. The West was chastened by the rationalism, skepticism, and relativism that followed from the Enlightenment. Sheikh Omar Abdel-Rahman, the exiled Egyptian religious leader allegedly associated with the assassination of Anwar Sadat and the 1993 bombing of the World Trade Center, expressed the concept in these words:

> In Christianity, you have a separation of church and state. . . . But Islam is very different: It covers every aspect of life—politics and economics, religion and social issues, science and knowledge. Therefore, it is not possible to differentiate between religion and politics.[21]

Rahman's politics may be radical, but his view of Islam is not. Can the multicultural paradigm make room for a tradition that explicitly denies pluralism? That is the challenge that we must face in attempting to bring conservative Muslim communities within the embrace of an open society:

> Multiculturalism and its moral liberal educational ethos are inherently unacceptable to Muslims who see the Quran as unrevisable and *shariah* law as providing complete moral guidance. For them there is "no room whatsoever for synthesizing the Quranic message with any non-Islamic practice or doctrine."[22]

In 1988 representatives of the Council for Democratic and Secular Humanism and other humanist groups attended a summit with high Vatican officials at Amsterdam's Royal Krasnapolsky Hotel. At that dialogue, French Cardinal Paul Poupard confided to Paul Kurtz his concerns that Muslims have never had a cultural experience parallel to the Reformation. That may seem an odd thing for a Catholic prelate to regret. "They've had no Bultmann to critically examine the Quran," Poupard told Kurtz, referring to Rudolf Bultmann, the mid-twentieth-century theologian who sought to "demythologize" Christianity. "And they are fanatical in their devotion."[23] Any misgiving that can drive a Catholic cardinal to wax nostalgic over Bultmann must be deep-seated indeed.

As a final bit of evidence, consider this cheery passage from Sura XXII of the Quran:

> As for the unbelievers, for them garments of fire shall be cut and there shall be poured over their heads boiling water whereby whatever is in their bowels and skins shall be dissolved and they will be punished with hooked iron rods.

There are equally intolerant passages in the Bible, yet some Christians have become authentic pluralists. But when we look at Muslim-Hindu conflicts in India and Pakistan, Iran's Islamic campaign against the Baha'i faith, the persecution of the Ahmadi sect by Muslim authorities in Pakistan, and the continuing death warrant upon Rushdie, we see cause for international concern. At this point, the collision of Western pluralism with Islamic fundamentalism raises more questions than it answers. I still dare to entertain the hope that the encounter can be managed without a retreat behind mutually fortified lines of battle. Clearly, difficult adjustments lie ahead for both sides.

Yet Islam is capable of compromise. In Britain, Muslim communities achieved cultural visibility decades ago. Muslim immigration rose immediately after World War II, when the notion of assimilation reigned unchallenged. Britain's Muslims behaved more like America's Old Outsiders. Compromising their heritage, they resignedly deformed their own traditions to make room for Christmas. They rationalized that Jesus was a prophet too, and patterned their Christmas observance after an Islamic *eid,* or festival day.

Just as Chanukah was originally a minor item on the Jewish calendar, the two authentic *eids* on the Islamic calendar were of modest significance. Yet today, middle class Muslims in London make quite an occasion of Christmas. They exchange gifts, share a festive (if alcohol-free) meal, and often trim Christmas trees.[24]

Armed with heightened expectations about diversity and fortified by fundamentalism, contemporary American Muslims seem unlikely to accommodate to Christmas like British Muslims of forty years ago. And Islam is not the only religious group in which militancy is growing. American Hindus, perhaps responding to rising fundamentalism among their co-religionists in India, are stepping away from eclecticism and preparing to defend their rights. Even New Outsiders whose faiths teach strict non-violence are finding the will to defend their traditions and world views in court. The "December dilemma" to which American Jews and infidels have long resigned themselves will take on very different meanings in the face of New Outsider opposition.

Christmas, Multiculturalism, and the First Amendment

The problem can be stated briefly. It is unlikely that New Outsider groups will long sit still for the bumpkin intrusiveness of Christmas American style. And their ability to resist—the moral legitimacy their protests will be perceived to carry, and their ability to marshal increasing economic, political, and cultural power with which to press their grievances—can only increase.

As we will see in the next chapter, rising sensitivity to the New Outsiders is already changing Christmas and Chanukah observances in public schools. The effects are spreading to other public places, and in time will ripple throughout society. Multiculturalism has already sparked the greatest advances in church-state separation since compulsory prayer and Bible reading were removed from public school classrooms in the sixties. Con-servatives are still stewing about that one. Recent initiatives in the name of diversity, some of which may force substantial changes in public ob-servance of Christmas, should bring conservatives close to apoplexy.

It is not that scrupulous secularization suddenly grew prudent. Rather, the rise of the New Outsiders is forcing us to recognize that some of our best-loved traditions had *always* presumed too much. They always smacked too much of Christianity. It is now incumbent upon mainstream America to let them go. We've learned to let black and white ride the same bus. We've learned to quit calling women "girls." We've even realized—many of us, anyway—that gays and lesbians are men and women, not moral monsters. It is time we learned how to get through a day of school, a city council meeting, or a Chamber of Commerce awards dinner without invoking a particular religion's god. It is past time we learned to survive December without expecting all Americans to join in celebrating the mythical birthday of one creed's Messiah.

Maybe our encounter with the New Outsiders will finally compel Americans to fulfill an obligation we have managed to avoid for more than two hundred years. Maybe we'll finally start living up to the First Amendment as its framers understood it. That would mean a complete divorce of the sacred and secular spheres in public life, something Americans have never managed before.

What would American life look like if that took place? All vestiges of religious symbolism, Christmas included, would finally be sundered from the purview of government. Religion would become a creature of the private sector alone, which seems quite capable of sustaining it. Where Christmas is concerned, even the private sector might back off were it to become evident that during November and December, New Outsiders would rather spend their growing wealth in retail settings unencumbered by Christian symbols.

But the fundamental and, in conscience, irresistible New Outsider demand will be that all religions be treated consistently. So if we are unprepared to end the favors that government grants to Christianity, we will have to extend them to all the world religions, and to infidelity as well. A moment's thought should show the laughable impracticality of *that*. Shall we close the Post Office for the whole month of Ramadan? Will Congress close its doors on Rosh Hoshanah and for *Diwali*, the five-day Hindu Festival of Light? Shall we shutter the banks in honor of the Baha'i Birthday of Bahaullah (November 12), *Baisaki*, the Sikh New Year (April 13), and for freethinkers, the birthday of Ingersoll (August 11)? Shall we print "In God, Yahweh, Allah, Vishnu, and To Whom It May Concern We Trust" on our currency? Shall officials be sworn in standing on ladders, their right hands raised while their left hands tremble atop teetering stacks of all the world's holy books? It seems more rational to treat all faiths with official, benign neglect, to harken back to the days when it went without saying that mail should be delivered on Sunday and that Congress should convene on Christmas Day.

Today Muslim and Hindu children in public schools are free to take their holy days off, but instruction continues without them. When they return, they must make up the work they miss. Jewish students who live in areas without large Jewish populations face the same hurdles. If we want to treat all religions equally, then public schools should also be open on Christmas Day. Let Christian children share the experience of bringing in notes from home and making up the work they miss. Rein in your reflexive response and answer honestly: What would be so bad about that? One thing the great teachers of all the world's religions have always agreed on is that it's not *supposed* to be easy to be devout.

*   *   *

Contemporary Christmas traditions that presume accommodation by non-Christian outgroups face inevitable reform. Christmas may not be singled out; in all likelihood, its observance will simply decay as New Outsider pressure forces a retreat of Christian symbolism in public life across a broad front. The opening shots of this conflict have already been fired: Twice in the first half of 1993, Muslim inmates led prison disturbances to demand greater freedom to practice their religion. At Cranston, Rhode Island, eight Muslim state prison inmates staged a hunger strike to protest a cost-cutting move that ended preparation of food in accord with Muslim dietary laws. In Lucasville, Ohio, Muslim anger helped to fuel a bloody riot and hostage standoff in which seven prisoners and one guard died.[25]

This is only the beginning. The process of adjusting to the New Outsiders is just starting. Let us hope it can be a peaceful one.

Even Watergate felon-turned-evangelist Charles Colson recognizes the change that is overtaking America: "[O]ur Judaeo-Christian heritage is no longer the foundation of our values. We have become a post-Christian society."[26]

Our challenge will be to build that post-Christian society in a multi-faith environment and to realize the promise of the multicultural ideal while avoiding its dangers. Individuals must not feel compelled by the majority to abandon their ethnicity. But individuals who choose to discard ethnicity altogether, or to choose the ways of a new group, must not be stigmatized, either by their community of origin or by well-meaning liberals inclined to lecture them about "abandoning their roots." If we do it right, majority and minority alike will realize that there is more to life than knowing what outgroup you belong to:

> Minorities in culturally diverse societies should not insist on unique rights as minorities. Rather, minorities should insist on their rights as human beings who have a legitimate role to play in an interdependent world.[27]

As for Christmas, I predict that it will eventually be abandoned as a *universal* public holiday. Multicultural forces will chip away at "public Christmas" until what is left no longer satisfies Christians. They may then seek to replace the holiday with a more narrowly sectarian, hence protected, observance. Either way, it seems unlikely that the Anglo-American Victorian experiment with "compulsory Christmas" will survive its bicentennial.

As we will see in the next chapter, a lot of wrangling lies ahead of us before that can occur.

Notes

1. William B. Williamson, "Is the U.S.A. a Christian Nation? Pluralism in the United States," *Free Inquiry* (Spring 1993): 33.

2. Beth Menge and Joshua Sherwin, "Muslims Celebrate Ramadan," Newark *Courier-News,* February 18, 1993.

3. Williamson, p. 32.

4. Ibid., p. 33.

5. Terry Muck, *Alien Gods on American Turf* (New York: Crossroad, 1991); Moorhead Kennedy, "We'll Have to Live with Islamic Fundamentalism," *Buffalo News,* March 21, 1993.

6. "Religions of the World," *Emerging Trends* (January 1993): 2–3.

7. "Where Are the Muslims in the United States?" *Free Inquiry* (Winter 1991–92): 15.

8. Barry Kosmin and Seymour Lachman, *National Survey of Religions Conducted by National Survey of Religious Identification* (New York: City University of New York, 1991).

9. Williamson, p. 34.

10. *Statistical Abstract of the United States 1992,* 112th ed. (Washington, D.C.: Bureau of the Census, Department of Commerce), Table No. 78. Though the Bureau of the Census publishes estimates of religious population volunteered by churches, the Census has not asked citizens to state their religious affiliation for decades on grounds of separation of church and state.

11. Vern L. Bullough, "Religion and the Polls," *Free Inquiry* (Summer 1991): 8.

12. All figures from William B. Williamson, *An Encyclopedia of Religions in the United States* (New York: Crossroad, 1992), except for Jains, furnished by the Federation of Jain Associations in North America.

13. Based on an observation by Brenda Almond, "Conflict or Compromise? The Dilemma for Religious and Moral Education," in James Lynch, Celia Modgil, and Sohan Modgil, eds., *Cultural Diversity in the Schools* (London: Falmer Press, 1992), p. 177.

14. Associated Press wire service story, January 20, 1993.

15. Williamson, p. 33.

16. Ricardo L. Garcia, "Cultural Diversity and Minority Rights: A Consummation Devoutly to be Demurred," anthologized in James Lynch et al., p. 106.

17. W. Connor, "A Nation Is a Nation, Is a State, Is an Ethnic Group, Is a . . ." *Ethnic and Racial Studies* 1, pp. 377–400, summarized in Garcia, "Cultural Diversity and Minority Rights," p. 104.

18. For a critique of multiculturalism from this perspective, see Arthur Schlesinger, Jr., *The Disuniting of America: Reflections on a Multicultural Society* (New York: W. W. Norton, 1992).

19. Neal Stephenson, "Blind Secularism," *New York Times,* April 23, 1993.

20. George W. Cornell, "Fundamentalism Storms Back: World is Being Buffeted by Religion-Linked Turmoil," *Washington Post,* April 24, 1993.

21. Mary Anne Weaver, "A Reporter at Large: On the Trail of the Skeikh," *The New Yorker* (April 12, 1993): 87.

22. Ian Vine, "Moral Diversity or Universal Values? The Problem of Moral Education Within Socially Segmented Societies," anthologized in James Lynch, et al., p. 182. Quotation within quotation from D. Hiro, *Islamic Fundamentalism* (London: Paladin Grafton Books, 1988).

23. Paul Kurtz, "The Church Under Siege: Reflections on the Vatican/ Humanist Dialogue," *Free Inquiry* (Winter 1988–89): 46.

24. Venetia Newall, "A Moslem Christmas Celebration in London," *Journal of American Folklore* (April–June 1989): 166–90.

25. *USA Today,* January 20, 1993; "Prison Rioters Demand Amnesty, Muslim Rights," *Newark Star-Ledger,* April 17, 1993.

26. Chuck Colson, "Can We Be Good Without God?" *Imprimis* (April 1993): 2.

27. Garcia, p. 119.

14

Confrontation in the Classroom

Who knows, maybe somewhere in the world Christmas *does* mean peace and goodwill. It hasn't meant that in American public schools for ten or fifteen years. Nor will the holiday be peaceful anytime soon for students, parents, teachers, principals, and school boards. Public schools have become a flash point in the Yuletide battle between traditionalists and multiculturalists.

Consider the conflict over religion and holiday observances in schools that shook Williamsville, New York, in 1992. In the issues it involved, in the identities of the principal players, and in the fallout it left behind, the Williamsville case is a preview of coming attractions for educators in other communities.

Williamsville was once a rural village ten miles east of Buffalo, New York. Suburban sprawl long ago overtook it. Today Williamsville is the crown jewel of Amherst, the region's fastest-growing "edge city." One engine of growth has been a mammoth State University of New York (SUNY) campus, established in the 1970s. SUNY/Buffalo's Amherst Campus is anything but pretty. Its repetitive, boxy structures strewn across scores of acres remind many of Brasilia, the sterile capital city Brazilian bureaucrats struggle to stay out of. Rumor has it that its mazelike outdoor walkways were redesigned after the campus riots of the 1960s so that authorities would always have a crossfire. The Amherst Campus was designed to be the largest single university campus in the western hemisphere. Though construction fell short of that goal, it is unquestionably the largest campus of the nation's largest state university system.

Ugly or not, a university that size attracts professionals: professors, physicists, engineers, physicians, and lawyers. Explosive suburban growth brought entrepreneurial companies, healthcare institutions, upscale housing, and with them more professionals. The Buffalo area usually trails demographic trends, but Amherst's growth created ethnic and religious diversity almost overnight. The village of Williamsville is now less than 40 percent Catholic, compared to a population in the surrounding area that is roughly two-thirds Catholic.[1] Informal surveys indicate that Williamsville is home to more than thirty religions. The more than ten thousand students of the Williamsville Central School District present the challenge of the New Outsiders in concentrated form. Diversity is high, but district managers have the resources, knowledge, and sophistication to respond to it, which is fortunate, for the stakes are also high. So many outgroup students are the children of influential professionals that a major infraction of their rights might have serious legal consequences.

When the trouble with Christmas landed on Williamsville, here is what happened.

On November 5, 1991, Williamsville Central School District Superintendent Harold E. Welker proposed to the Board of Education that an *ad hoc* citizens' committee on religion in schools be formed. Welker sought more than a Christmas policy. The *ad hoc* committee was charged to propose policy clarifications so that teachers could teach *about* religion with confidence, yet without offending members of religious outgroups. Welker sought to replace a patchwork of school-by-school practices with a uniform policy, and to address his own observations of growing diversity among students. In addition, the committee's work would address concerns that the schools shortchanged religious themes in teaching history and social studies, and would continue the district's response to some highly publicized anti-Semitic incidents a few years before.

The committee was formally empaneled in January 1992 with twenty-two members from varied backgrounds. Though none had been chosen to represent a specific religious group, the committee's members spanned a continuum of religious, ethnic, and cultural backgrounds.

Like other government bodies, school districts are forbidden by law to gather information about students' religious backgrounds. Third-party data on religious affiliation is famously unreliable, so Welker and the members of the committee acted on their personal judgments regarding Williamsville's diversity. Jacqueline Peters, Director of Communications for the Williamsville Central School District, said that the initiative bespoke "concern for *each* student and is not based on numbers."[2] According to Isha Francis, a parent who served on the *ad hoc* committee, this informality posed no problem:

> While it may be anecdotal, it's certainly easy enough to go around the school district and see in everyday life the make up of the Amherst/Williamsville community. Several temples and community centers have arisen over the last

years, funded and built by Hindus, Moslems, and Sikhs, among others. The Baha'i have a strong presence and you can find notice of Buddhist meetings in the area newspapers. The children from these diverse religious-cultural communities represent a significant presence in our schools.[3]

Over the next six months, the *ad hoc* committee reviewed existing cultural-sensitivity materials and examined religion policies already in effect in the district's various schools. The Williamsville Central School District had twice consulted Charles Haynes, a moderate church-state accommodationist who directs the First Liberty Institute at George Mason University in Fairfax, Virginia. As president of the National Council on Religion and Public Education, he led in drafting two timid religion-in-school guidelines, including one on school Christmas observances, that won the endorsements of organizations ranging from the National Education Association to the American Academy of Religion, the Christian Legal Society, the National Association of Evangelicals, and the Mormon Church.[4] Haynes recently developed a social studies curriculum in association with the conservative Williamsburg Charter Foundation.[5] One can hardly say that the district was being led astray by radicals.

In June 1992 the *ad hoc* committee drafted a proposed policy for submission to the school board. "An environment should be created and encouraged," reported the committeee, "where students of various ethnic backgrounds feel comfortable in sharing comments about their religious and cultural traditions. No student should be singled out to share or participate in such discussions solely on the basis of that student's identification with the cultural/religious heritage being addressed. A student's preference not to share or participate in such discussions should be honored and respected."

In similarly measured language, the committee proposed policies on issues including:

- *School activities related to religious holidays or themes.* "In . . . teaching about religious holidays or themes, special effort must be made to ensure that the activity is not devotional and that students of all faiths can join without feeling they are betraying their own beliefs. . . . [R]eligious plays or programs are inappropriate. . . . Organized holiday gift exchanges are inappropriate."

- *Religious symbols in the school.* "Temporary classroom use and/or display of religious symbols is permitted as a teaching resource or aid only . . . [A] display outside the classroom whose theme focuses on the religious holiday(s), tradition(s), or symbol(s) of any religion is not appropriate. . . ."

- *Religious music in school.* "Religious music should be appropriate for performance any time during the school year. Musical programs whose themes focus on religious holidays are not appropriate. . . . [R]equests for the student to not participate in singing or playing religious music will be respected."

- *District calendar scheduling regarding religious holidays.* ". . . [A]bsence from school for religious holiday observance is a legal absence. Out of respect for a student's observance of these holidays, teachers will be sensitive to the needs of the student by allowing them to make-up all new work, homework, and tests without penalty."

- *Dietary considerations regarding religious restrictions.* ". . . [T]he school lunch program will provide at least one vegetarian entree daily."

- *Curriculum and staff development regarding the teaching about religion.* Provides for continuing policy development, in-service education of teachers and other school personnel, and ongoing input by parents and guardians.

The proposed policy was innocuous enough. "So many of the things that were in the document were already being done," recalled Father Paul Nogaro, a member of the *ad hoc* committee. "It wasn't like we were proposing radical changes. We were in a sense solidifying what was already in effect."[6] But to Amherst's conservative weekly newspaper, the *Amherst Bee,* the committee's work seemed the calling card of the Antichrist. Terming it "a proposal to neutralize the effects of Christianity," the June 24, 1992, issue carried a sharply worded indictment of the policy by the paper's political columnist, an editorial lambasting it further, and a mail-in poll designed to generate unfavorable responses to the policy.[7]

"If a school district can be tut-tutted over religious music at holiday time or holiday gift exchanges," sniffed columnist Ray Herman, "one must wonder where we're headed. Does the sight of a Christmas tree in the hallway cause a child from a non-Christian home to blanch in sheer terror?"[8] If the writer cannot understand how Christian symbolism can anger or sometimes even terrorize some non-Christian students, we need hardly wonder where *he* is headed. Later in the column, Herman made his agenda transparent. Complaining about the provision requiring vegetarian meals, he quipped: "At the risk of seeming glib, if a tiny minority of parents feel oppressed by the cafeteria cuisine, why not pack a lunch for the kids! Or has the art of accommodation . . . gone out of style?"[9]

In an age when few still champion the melting pot, the call for minorities to practice "the art of accommodation" remains the last refuge of those attached to the tyranny of the majority.

The draft policy was turned over to a school board subcommittee for further development. The *Bee* attacked it once more during the summer, but the paper neither printed the text of the document nor summarized it fairly. Nor, say members of the *ad hoc* committee, did it attempt to interview committee members who had crafted it.

"I took great offense," said Williamsville teacher and committee chair Margaret Mendrykowski, "that the local newspaper made no attempt to talk to any one of us who'd been intimately involved" with drafting the policy.[10]

Calling the newspaper's conduct an "egregious error," Paul Nogaro complained: "They didn't even publish the document, but commented on the document without ever showing what the document said . . . no one had the document in hand."[11]

The board subcommittee continued to polish a draft policy based on the *ad hoc* committee's recommendations. Unfortunately, some of its most insightful suggestions, such as the ban on organized gift exchanges, were rejected.

Late in October, the crisis began. As crises often do, it started by accident. Just before the subcommittee was scheduled to present its redraft of the religion policy, Williamsville North High School principal Samuel H. Gang announced his decision to cancel the school's eighteenth annual holiday concert. In past years as many as four thousand elementary school students had been bused to Williamsville North for the December event. Financial concerns and growing awareness of cultural issues combined to doom it. "There have been objections over the past few years that the show was too religious in nature," Williamsville North Music Director Geoff Richter admitted.[12]

"I never attended it," said Margaret Mendrykowski of the concert, "but I heard about it several times and thought, 'Oh my gosh, I can't believe that's happening here in Williamsville.' My thoughts immediately turned to students to whom that time of year has been terrifically uncomfortable."[13]

If the North High cancellation represented a response to some of the same issues the *ad hoc* committee had addressed, it was nevertheless an independent reaction. Committee member Paul Nogaro termed it "an extraneous event—it had nothing to do with what we were doing."[14] Yet it ignited a firestorm of controversy that quickly swallowed up discussion of the policy itself. A Buffalo talk radio station built a week of inflammatory midday programming around the "Williamsville Christmas crisis." Criticism in the *Amherst Bee* intensified. On November 4, the paper called for the draft policy to be reworked. "Is it any wonder that outcry results when deeply embedded traditions are at risk?" the editorial demanded. It continued:

> The draft policy strangles itself on several points. For example, it first states that information about religious and cultural holidays and traditions focusing on how they are celebrated, their origins and histories should be part of instruction. But it then goes on to say that the means to teach about it, such as through plays, musical programs, and displays, are "inappropriate." How can that be when these things go hand-in-hand?[15]

The editorial muddied a distinction that members of the *ad hoc* committee had been careful to stress: the difference between *teaching about* religious holidays and devoting the power of school and state to their *celebration.* Elsewhere in the same issue, columnist Ray Herman asked:

> Will "musical programs whose themes focus on religious holidays" really cause some students to feel "they are betraying their own beliefs?" Or could it possibly be that students are more preoccupied with the next math test than plumbing the depths of theology and being psychologically scarred?[16]

If Mr. Herman were a lifelong atheist, his perplexity before the power of religious conviction might be comprehensible. To the best of my knowledge, Herman is a Christian and ought not to be so naive. I, for one, could tell him: When you're ten years old and religiously preoccupied, math tests pale before the *eternal* test you believe your life to be. Forced attendance at programs that promote observance of a faith not your own can engender a fear for your immortal soul that overwhelms everything else in your mind.

The school board tabled consideration of the policy until it could reconvene the *ad hoc* committee for further discussions. "I did not expect that there would be an overwhelming response," said physician Khalid Qazi, a member of the *ad hoc* committee.[17]

"The community didn't react to this at all," Isha Francis said of the controversy. "What happened was a very small number of people with a very clear, specific agenda reacted to it. Then certain media grabbed a hold of it, made it into a big thing—which it wasn't, even at that point— and created a firestorm."[18]

As Williamsville's stores and shops tugged on their holiday finery, the firestorm grew. Williamsville North rescheduled its holiday concert— now without a Christmas tree, Santa Claus, or any songs explicitly connected with Christmas—perhaps provoking more negative reaction than if the concert had stayed cancelled.

The inevitable Christian Right resistance group popped up: the Community Alliance to Restore Equality (CARE) began meeting in an Assemblies of God church. CARE was led by Williamsville parent Linda Falcone. Its founding was front page news in the *Amherst Bee*. "We are in an uproar," raged Falcone. ". . . I am sick of people having to tiptoe around the word Christian."[19]

"It was a very small group of people," said Isha Francis, "with a very narrow interest, and also a lot of frustration from some very unsuccessful politicking."[20] The area's Christian Right had been stunned six months before by its failure before the national media to close Buffalo's abortion clinics. Christian conservatives were reeling too from the election of Bill Clinton to the presidency. Area fundamentalists were hungry for a fight they thought they could win. Stridently, Falcone decried the religion policy as a conspiracy against Christians and an effort to strip Christmas from the schools. Moderates, largely unaware of First Amendment principles and the underlying multicultural issues, were perhaps too quick to sympathize with the distorted concerns she presented.

CARE announced that it would field candidates to unseat three school board members, including Board President Anne Rohrer, the next spring. The group attracted less welcome controversy when Falcone presented an anti-Semitic cartoon at a school board meeting. The cartoon showed a hook-nosed man hurling a hand grenade at a woman who was singing a Christmas carol. Above the man were written the names of four board members who were Jewish. Falcone later apologized, claiming she hadn't known what anti-Semitism was.[21]

Inevitably, the spirit of confrontation spilled into the schools themselves. Celebrating Christmas in arrogant ways became the accepted way for Williamsville students to rebel. At Williamsville North, home of the off-again, on-again holiday concert, seniors papered the cafeteria with Christmas and Chanukah decorations. Gamely, students Nickesh Pahade, a Jain, and Deepali Oberoi, a Hindu, asked if they could add symbols of their own holidays. They hung a sign saying "Happy *Diwali.*" They posted a banner that read "Celebrate all the holidays, not just Christmas." And they put up an *Om,* for Eastern religions the symbol of "the greatest of all mantras, or sacred formulas."

In minutes, some Christian students had ripped them all down, torn them up, and cast the pieces to the floor.[22] Those kids knew what "Christmas and Chanukah First" meant. They fully understood the intolerance that their stance demanded toward students outside the Judaeo-Christian mainstream.

By mid-December, the national media had focused on Williamsville. The school board announced that it would not attempt to reach a final decision on the religion policy before the following January. On January 5, 1993, conservative parent Jaime Cordero went before the school board in an attempt to derail the entire process. He charged that the *ad hoc* committee had conducted its meetings illegally. A motion to disband the committee and void its policy proposal failed in a 4–4 tie vote.

On January 12 members of the *ad hoc* committee appeared before the school board to defend their policy proposal. The discussion was interrupted when persons unknown pulled the fire alarm.

At a January 26 meeting of the school board, Superintendent Harold Welker ordered the religion policy returned to the committee for revision.

On January 27, the *Amherst Bee* presented its own proposed religion policy, which included such constitutionally dubious passages as

The use of religious symbols, of whatever form and derivation, such as a cross, menorah, crescent, Star of David, crèche, symbols of Native American religions or other symbols that are part of a religious holiday, are permitted. . . .[23]

On February 16 a revised draft of the religion policy was presented to the school board. The revision contained "softening" language but few real changes. An exemption had been added allowing students to wear religious jewelry and symbols on their persons or clothing. The draft was returned for further revision. The second revision, presented on February 24, included a number of cuts. The lightning-rod sentence "Musical programs whose themes focus on religious holidays are not appropriate" had been removed.

On Tuesday, March 2, Superintendent Howard E. Welker, 61, died unexpectedly of a heart attack while playing volleyball. The final vote on the religion policy, scheduled to take place hours later, was tabled—both in mourning and because of real confusion. If the policy had been approved, the next step would have been for Welker to lead in drafting the regulations required to implement it.

To their credit, no one from CARE—nor, so far as I can determine, any member of the clergy in the Williamsville area—claimed that Welker's death was a judgment from God.

After a week of introspection, the Williamsville School Board voted 6–3 to accept the revised religion policy on Tuesday, March 9. Despite the changes, members of the *ad hoc* committee I interviewed were satisfied with the outcome even if they were dismayed at what the process had become. "I personally wasn't that upset with the final document," said Paul Nogaro.[24]

Committee member Khalid Qazi summed it up in these terms:

It is still a positive step, because the recognition that many faiths, cultures, and groups were looking for—that has been recognized. . . . Students of different faiths and religions have been recognized to have special, separate needs. They were recognized before, to some extent. But [now] there is a uniform level of recognition that has been instilled to the staff at large. There is also a recognition in the public—and I'm talking about those who are responsible citizens, who want to be productive and positive and civic. So it has been a big positive step.

Was there everything that was put there in the beginning? Obviously, no. . . . But is there enough to make it worthwhile? I feel so.[25]

Whether the amended policy will result in regulations that adequately protect the rights of non-Christian students remains to be seen. Meanwhile, if the battle was over, the war continued. In May, Pat Robertson's pressure group, the Christian Coalition, circulated questionnaires to candidates running for three seats on the Williamsville School Board. Voter's guides based on questionnaire results were distributed in conservative churches to attract votes for conservative Christian opposition candidates.[26] If this constituted a takeover try by Christian Right activists with national connections, it failed. In a hard-fought election that attracted the highest voter turnout in twenty years, incumbents Anne Rohrer, Donald Henning, and Eugene Steinberg were returned to office. All had supported the religion policy.

What made the victory possible in the face of Christian Right muscle-flexing was a massive mobilization by Williamsville's New Outsiders. "People of minority religion and minority races came out strong today because they felt threatened," Steinberg told the media.[27]

The Lessons of Williamsville

The Williamsville controversy illustrates how hysterical rhetoric can escalate over trivial issues where Christmas is concerned. It is regrettable that the bans on gift exchanges and holiday-themed musical presentations were whittled away. Before long, I predict, they will be restored—perhaps after one of them causes the Williamsville Central School District to lose a costly lawsuit. The provision granting unlimited rights to display religious symbols on the person or on one's clothing will probably be scrapped after the same unintended consequence. (I'm waiting for the first student to show up wearing a swastika and defend it as a symbol of either Zoroastrianism or of Native American beliefs.)

Yet there really wasn't that much difference between the original *ad hoc* committee proposal and the painstakingly revised version that ultimately passed. Both began from the *assumption* that the former Christian hegemony over goings-on in school was a thing of the past. Neither was nearly as radical as the policies I expect to see lurching out of school districts in a few years' time.

Why are public schools so sensitive to controversies over religion in general, and Christmas observance in particular? All the concerns that prompt us to separate church from state are heightened in public schools. Parents deliver their children to schools for a most sensitive purpose, the shaping of their minds. Children have no choice about being there; parents who are not inclined toward home-schooling and do not care to pay for private education have little choice but to send them. Everything that raises our hackles when the government favors religion over irreligion—or when the government favors one religion over others—is maximized in the setting of the schools.

New Outsiders tend to interpret all the signs of Christmas, from crèches and carols to snowflakes and sleighs, equally as emblems of Christian dominance. That's why public schools are leading the culture toward a day when government resources will no longer be used to celebrate, or even to imply, *any* sectarian holiday, not even Christmas. The Maryland teacher's aide who took offense at a Christmas tree in an elementary school office, picked it up, and threw it in a parking lot a few years ago was behaving in a way that then seemed far out of step. I suspect that before too long, we'll consider that action "ahead of its time."

If current trends continue, I think that in thirty years American public schools will be totally Yule-free. Does this represent the imposition of a "religion of secular humanism" by the state? Hardly; it represents government finally learning what it means to keep a respectful silence. When the state behaves *as if* it were atheistic, it does not impose atheism. Rather, it maximizes the freedom of every creed to seek expression and development in private life, free from government's help and from its interference.

In the rest of this chapter I will sketch the development of public school policies on Christmas and the controversies they have raised. With the Williamsville incident in mind, we will see how school Christmas policies have changed since the bad old days of the Old Outsiders and why they're headed toward the arid spaces they will soon occupy.

Toward Yule-Free Schools

In the Old Outsider era, the "December dilemma" centered on the participation of Jewish children in pervasive Christmas observances. Despite years of Jewish activism and litigation, as the 1960s dawned public schools still catered to Christianity. Elaborate Christmas pageants often featured costumed reenactments of the Nativity story. Religious carols were sung and listened to without a second thought. Some schools made allowances for Jewish sensitivities, but as constitutional firebrand Leo Pfeffer made clear in 1967, "allowances" were not the solution:

> It is not a sufficient answer to say the Jewish child need not join in the singing or the pageant if he does not want to. It is unfair and unconscionable to place on the child the burden of isolating himself . . . to stand alone during the festivities and preparations for them—which in many schools occupy practically all the time in December.[28]

Nor was the answer to pump a "touch of Chanukah" into holiday programming. Attempts at this sometimes led to the ironic spectacle of Christian parents objecting to their children's involvement in Jewish observances! Also, interpreting Chanukah solely in relation to Christmas failed to acknowledge it as a holiday with a tradition of its own.

Today, full-blown Christmas pageants are almost unheard of in public schools. Even "secular Christmas" programs are falling out of favor. The two attitudinal shifts that made this possible began in the late 1970s. The first was a simple widening of focus. Educators acknowledged that Christmas observance in the schools offended not only Jews, but infidels as well. During the 1980s it became imperative to include New Outsiders in this calculus too.

> Christmas hymns in school assemblies may seem innocuous to most adults. But they are offensive and coercive to Jews, Muslims, Buddhists, atheists and others, and especially oppressive to the impressionable young.[29]

School policies that perpetuate inappropriate Christian dominance are not healthy for Christian children, either:

> The intensity of the Christmas curriculum in non-religiously affiliated schools and centers isolates children of minority faiths, *while contributing to the development of ethnocentrism in majority children.* [emphasis added][30]

This recognition of impropriety is a positive step. But it means little if schools intend to go on celebrating Christmas. Yet the National Council of Christians and Jews, the American Jewish Committee, and the American Jewish Congress still endorse and distribute the National Council on Religion and Public Education's "canonical" pamphlet on religious holidays in public schools, which says in part: "Does that mean that all seasonal activities must be banned from schools? Probably not, and in any event such an effort would be unrealistic."[31]

The second shift in attitudes, and the one that remains most controversial today, is the growing realization that it is not only realistic, but *necessary* to remove Christmas and Chanukah observances entirely from the public schools. Nothing less will suffice to safeguard the rights of children of diverse religious (and nonreligious) backgrounds.

That doesn't mean disregarding religion as a subject. One butchers American history by trying to discuss the Pilgrims without mentioning their Puritanism. What can be said about such colonial figures as Roger Williams and William Penn without summarizing the religious controversies of their times? But efforts to teach *about* religion in public schools raise problems of their own. Will teachers be objective enough to present the atrocities of the Crusades or the Inquisition? Will they assign readings from Paine's *Age of Reason?* Will they speak forthrightly about those sects that genuinely seem to have arisen out of a founder's mental illness or chicanery? Will students learn of St. Cyril ordering the murder of Hypatia, of the St. Bartholomew's Day Massacre, of the Crusaders who stopped on their way to the Holy Land to slay thousands of Jews? They are part of the human experience with religion too. What will teachers in Salt Lake City say about Joseph Smith and the origins of Mormonism? Objective history and Mormon doctrine disagree violently regarding Smith's past and his character. Which view will be presented? And how will teachers handle pupils like Christian creationists, whose religious views commit them to objectively erroneous ideas about the physical world?

Maybe religion really is too hot to handle. If so, the only way public schools can avoid the appearance of favoritism toward *anyone's* beliefs is to avoid the subject of religion altogether. If the teaching of history suffers for that, perhaps it is the price we pay for depending on government-run schools in a multicultural society. This is an issue on which people of reason and goodwill sharply disagree; I will not attempt to settle it here. Fortunately, I don't have to. Whether public schools are capable of teaching about religion or not, such traditions as holly on the blackboard, carols in chorus class, gift exchanges in homeroom, and Christmas trees in the school lobby do not teach about Christmas. They celebrate it, and are clearly improper.

Because of this second attitudinal shift, it has become increasingly common for public schools to scale back, "sanitize," or eliminate observances of Christmas and Chanukah. Educators and lawyers are way ahead of the rest of society on this point. That is one reason why their efforts to anticipate the trouble with Christmas often meet with intense popular resistance.[32]

Typically, as we saw in Williamsville, protests begin among conservative Christian parents who explicitly endorse school favoritism toward Christianity. As publicity snowballs, mainstream Christian parents are sucked into what becomes a torrent of outrage. In 1982 demonstrators shouted that members of the Medford Township, New Jersey, school board were "in league with the Devil" because they had drawn up a multicultural holiday policy. At least *that* didn't happen in Williamsville! Apparently, progress is possible.

Ironically, liberal clergy sometimes lead the fight for Yule-free, Chanukah-free schools. In 1989 an interfaith group asked the Bellingham, Washington, schools to discontinue all Christmas and Chanukah observances, right down to the singing of "Rudolph the Red-Nosed Reindeer" and "All I Want for Christmas Is My Two Front Teeth."

We have already visited Aurora, Colorado, where an elementary school sparked protest by banning "holiday trees." Denver's *Rocky Mountain News* ridiculed the decision, editorializing that a "decorated tree is not a religious symbol in any organized religion we know of." Surprisingly, the result was a flurry of reader mail that supported the school's decision:

> [S]how any child a photograph of an evergreen tree decorated from top to bottom with lights, ornaments, and bows, and ask them what it is. It's a safe bet that at least 99 percent would refer to it as a "Christmas tree." I would also wager a guess that the same number of children would also know its significance.
>
> The *News*'[s] implication that children need to be educated about these things does not have a leg to stand on. This culture is so overwhelmingly Christmas-conscious, that a little abstention from this religious holiday in our public schools would be, at the very least, refreshing.[33]

As in Williamsville, Christmas controversies often spark the formation of Christian counterpressure groups. This has also occurred on the national level. New Christian "negative ACLUs" lend legal muscle to parents, teachers, or employers under pressure to give up practices that show preference to Christianity. In 1992 the threat of legal action from Pat Robertson's American Center for Law and Justice (ACLJ) caused a Nevada school board to overrule an elementary school's ban on religious music at Christmas time. The Virginia-based Rutherford Institute put its weight behind the parents of Christy Fisher. The Austin, Texas, eighth-grader had been told by her principal that she must remove a reference to Christmas as "the day that Christians celebrate Christ's birth" from a poem she had composed before it could be published in the school paper. In this case, the Rutherford Institute was right. All Christy Fisher said was that Christmas is the day that Christians celebrate Christ's birth. That is a statement of fact, not of faith. To say that "some people believe thus-and-such" is not to endorse the proposition that their belief is true.

Progress—or Sterilization?

Some critics call stripping the schools of Christmas and Chanukah "sterilization." Others claim it actually violates religious freedom. Does it constitute hostility toward religion for government schools to put religion off limits? Not while there is a private sector in which religion can continue to hold sway, says sociologist Brenda Almond:

> [F]reedom of religion is one of the pillars on which a liberal society is built. And since a religion that is not transmitted to the next generation is a religion chopped off at its roots, a complete conception of freedom of religion must carry with it a right for people to bring up their *own* children in their religion. Religion, however, is embedded in wider cultural practices, and an education that stops with one's *own* children is only a partial fulfilment of a religious believer's aspirations. Nevertheless, if a society is itself politically and institutionally committed to no one religion, then this partial solution may be the best available, and *history has shown that religions can survive through family traditions even in the absence of wider social endorsement.* [final emphasis added][34]

Church-state separation attorney Ronald A. Lindsay puts Christian complaints of "sterilization" in proper perspective:

> What is going on here is whining: whining by individuals and groups who have been deprived of the *truly* privileged position *they* once enjoyed. For most of this country's history, theism, in particular Christianity, has enjoyed favor. Those who are thirty-five or older (somewhat younger if one grew up in the South) will have no trouble remembering the evidence of this privileged position. Organized prayers were a matter of routine in public schools. . . . Textbooks extolled the virtues of religion. The symbols of . . . Christmas and Easter were displayed on public property at public expense. . . .
>
> The courts have put an end to some, but certainly not all, of this collaboration between church and state. In doing so, the courts have upset many who assumed that this was the proper way of doing things, the American way of doing things, and who did not see anything coercive, let alone unconstitutional, about such practices. Not unnaturally, they have interpreted the courts' actions as an attack on religion, when in reality they were simply an attempt to put an end to the privileged position that religion enjoyed.[35]

Christmas in the Schools: Six Modest Proposals

Here, for what they're worth, are six proposals for future policies regarding religious symbolism, Christmas, and Chanukah in public schools. I view them less as recommendations than as predictions. If the trends described in this chapter continue, this is where the public schools are heading.

(1) *Public schools should not require, encourage, or abet activities that involve—or resemble—the observance of any religious holiday.* Students should be free to express their beliefs openly, and even to make reference to them in assignments. But statements of faith may render an otherwise exemplary student composition ineligible to be displayed on a bulletin board or published in a school newspaper, yearbook, or literary digest that consumes staff time or taxpayer funds.

(2) *Symbols of Christian, Jewish, or other religion's holiday observances must not be posted as decor by school personnel, or allowed to remain in place if posted as decor by students.* Since those symbols of Christmas which Christians consider "sacred" and those Christians consider "secular" are often indistinguishable to non-Christians, no symbols of the Christian winter holiday may be used as in-school decor. Trimming or display of a "holiday tree" and organized gift exchanges are prohibited, as are symbols of Chanukah, *Diwali,* or any other religious festivals during the times of year when their adherents traditionally observe them.

(3) *Holiday symbols, including religious symbols, may be presented for limited periods as aids to instruction about the observances in question.* If possible, such usages should be scheduled for times of the year other than when the holidays are traditionally observed. For example, teaching about Christmas in December may give an improper appearance of celebrating Christmas even if the timing was motivated purely by instructional considerations.

(4) *If teaching about religion is attempted, content and treatment must be fair, balanced, and objective.* In particular, both negative and positive aspects of religious experience and religious history must be included in class discussions.

(5) *Religious music pertaining to the holidays or rites of any faith may be played (as in playing a recording) as an adjunct to the teaching of music appreciation, or to teaching about the religion concerned.* Religious music, including music of secular origin that

has strong associations to religious practice, or whose lyrics imply statements of religious belief, may not be performed by students in any school-sponsored activity such as band, chorus, etc. Students may choose to perform such works if relevant for completion of an individual class assignment, but may not be required to perform such works in completing any school assignment.

(6) *Since schools cannot undertake to close in observance of all religious holidays, they will remain open on all religious holidays, including those of Christianity and Judaism, when such holidays fall on days when the school would otherwise be in session.* Schools should meet on Christmas, Good Friday, or Yom Kippur as they always have on the holy days of other world religions. Students may be excused for holy days or holidays appropriate to their religious background. Teachers should strive to avoid scheduling exams or other critical instructional events on any religion's holidays, but may do so if instructionally expedient. Students legally excused from school on holidays observed by their religion must be allowed to make up classwork or exams without prejudice, but may be required to visit the school building outside normal hours or to forgo a scheduled extracurricular activity in order to perform required make-up work.

Why Exclusion?

Obviously, these proposals go far beyond the modest religion policy adopted in Williamsville, New York. Their intent is frankly to exclude Christian and Jewish elements (as well as those of other world religions) from school-sponsored activities except when they are the objects of specific lessons about religion. But why exclusion, critics often ask? Why not *inclusion,* generally the preferred strategy of multiculturalists? The arguments should be familiar by now: First, there are simply too many religions. It is impractical for a school to favor them all as schools formerly favored Christianity and (sometimes) Judaism. Second, it is impossible to reconcile the contradictory doctrines that may be held—and defended with murderous certainty—by adherents of different faiths. Where government schools cannot enter a particular area of inquiry without trampling on *somebody's* faith, they must remove themselves from that area of inquiry. Third, the First Amendment demands that religious matters be handled differently, that is, more cautiously, from all others.

Ultimately, exclusion is the fairest policy. The inarguable demand of the New Outsiders will be for uniformity in the treatment of all faiths. Uniform *neglect* of all faiths is the only conceivable course for America's public schools.

Christians often respond violently to arguments of this sort. Writing with purse-lipped disapproval of the Williamsville religion policy, church-state accommodationist Richard John Neuhaus made the astounding claim that a multicultural society can only be tolerant if it gives first place to Christian ideals:

> The reason Christians are tolerant is not because this is a pluralistic society. This is a pluralistic society because most Christians are tolerant. And they are tolerant for Christian reasons.[36]

This view is common among defenders of the religio-political status quo. Not only is it breathtaking in its Christian ethnocentrism—and not only is it contrary to history, for Christians have often practiced intolerance—it is just plain wrong. If Christians are more tolerant today, the credit belongs to our secular society, which has taught them to balance the demands of Christianity against other imperatives in their lives.

In a multicultural, multireligious society, tolerance and mutual respect demand the secularization of public institutions and public spaces. To do that thoroughly, conscientiously, and *totally* will be a revolution in American life. The revolution is starting in public schools. Christmas as we have known it will almost certainly be among its casualties.

Down the road, the result of all this conflict will probably be a diminution in the intensity of the attention mainstream culture pays to Christmas, a move that should pay big dividends throughout American society.

Notes

1. Gerald Goldhaber, telephone interview, February 12, 1993.
2. Jacqueline Peters, "Response to Religion Questions," March 8, 1993.
3. Isha Francis, interview, May 6, 1993.
4. National Council on Religion and Public Education, "Religion in the Public School Curriculum: Questions and Answers" (Ames, Iowa: National Council on Religion and Public Education, 1987); "Religious Holidays in the Public Schools: Questions and Answers" (Ames, Iowa: National Council on Religion and Public Education, 1988).
5. Charles C. Haynes, *A Teacher's Guide to Study About Religion in the Public Schools* (Boston: Houghton-Mifflin, 1991), p. iv.
6. Paul Nogaro, interview, May 6, 1993.

7. Ray Herman, "Religion-in-School Debate Uses Children as Pawns," *Amherst Bee,* June 24, 1992.

8. Ibid.

9. Ibid.

10. Margaret Mendrykowski, interview, May 6, 1993.

11. Nogaro, interview.

12. Michele Darstein, "Cancelled: Holiday Concert," *Amherst Bee,* October 28, 1992.

13. Mendrykowski, interview.

14. Nogaro, interview.

15. "Rework Religion Policy for Fairness to All," *Amherst Bee,* November 4, 1992.

16. Ray Herman, "School Inappropriate Battleground for Religious Issue," *Amherst Bee,* November 4, 1992.

17. Khalid Qazi, interview, May 6, 1993.

18. Isha Francis, interview.

19. " 'Enough': C.A.R.E. Wants Religion Back in the Schools," *Amherst Bee,* November 11, 1992.

20. Francis, interview.

21. "Debate Over Religion Tests a Town's Faiths," *New York Times,* February 26, 1993.

22. Ibid.; Molly McCarthy, "Religion Policy Debate Also Divides Williamsville North Students," *Buffalo News,* February 28, 1993.

23. "Alternative from Community Alliance," *Amherst Bee,* January 27, 1993.

24. Nogaro, interview.

25. Qazi, interview.

26. "Vote Guide at Issue in Contest for School Seat: Christian Group Rates Candidates," *Buffalo News,* May 25, 1993.

27. "Williamsville Incumbents Returned to School Board," *Buffalo News,* June 10, 1993.

28. Leo Pfeffer, *Church, State, and Freedom* (Boston: Beacon Press, 1967), p. 490.

29. Steven G. Kellman, "Freethinkers Reject the Joy of Sects," *San Antonio Light,* December 9, 1992.

30. Steven A. Gelb, "Christmas Programming in Schools: Unintended Consequences," *Childhood Education* (October 1987): 11.

31. National Council on Religion and Public Education, "Religious Holidays in the Public Schools: Questions and Answers."

32. For a prescient summary of these issues that dates all the way back to 1976, see David L. Martin, "Strip the Halls of Boughs of Holly," *Learning* (December 1976): 29–30.

33. Letter to the editor, *Rocky Mountain News,* December 20, 1992.

34. Brenda Almond, "Conflict or Compromise? The Dilemma for Religious and Moral Education," anthologized in James Lynch, Celia Modgil, and Sohan

Modgil, eds., *Cultural Diversity and the Schools* (London: Falmer Press, 1992), p. 182.

35. Ronald O. Lindsay, "Neutrality Between Religion and Irreligion: Is It Required? Is It Possible?" *Free Inquiry* (Fall 1990): 19.

36. Richard John Neuhaus, "Starting Fights," *First Things: A Journal of Religion and Public Life* (April 1993): 58.

15

A Word to Infidels

In Cecil B. DeMille's silent epic *The Godless Girl* (1929), one scene concerns a meeting of a high school atheist group (imaginative guy, that DeMille). A new recruit is being inducted. He is required to stand before the group and swear an oath (to whom?) that he disbelieves in God and rejects the Bible.

Partway through the ceremony, the newcomer has a distressing thought. He asks whether being an atheist means that he will have to stop celebrating Christmas. Of course, the atheist students thunder. In that case, says the newcomer, I cannot join your group. I'm not willing to give up Christmas.

The atheist kids fall on the newcomer and beat him mercilessly.[1]

Aside from the violence, that is about what I expected when I gave up my religion. I simply assumed that becoming an atheist would mean giving up Christmas. During the years it took me to abandon my belief, I spent less time philosophizing about the existence of God than I did steeling myself emotionally for the tough life decisions—like bagging Christmas—that I thought a commitment to atheism would require.

If I knew then what I know now about America's infidels, I could have saved myself the trouble.

As associate editor of *Free Inquiry* and coeditor of *Secular Humanist Bulletin,* I've gotten to know atheists, agnostics, freethinkers, secular humanists, rationalists, and other infidels from all over the world. Some ignore the winter holiday. But an embarrassing majority keep Christmas or some analogous festival like the winter solstice.

It is too much trouble to defy the holiday altogether, these infidels tell me. Some argue that, though Christmas is admittedly shot through with superstitions, only the explicitly Christian elements are worth opposing. After all, it is fundamentalist Christians, not Druid priests, who

231

are electing creationists to school boards, banning textbooks, and bending the Constitution to their beliefs. So why waste energy trying to stamp out the pagan solstice? Yet if we infidels are committed to truth and critical thinking, how can we condemn *certain* superstitions and embrace others? Doing so seems counterproductive if we wish to be taken seriously as proponents of rational living.

American society is more tolerant than it was in the "bad old days." New Outsider pressures have heightened cultural sensitivity and broadened even long-established civil liberties. Today's infidels have more elbow room than those of a generation ago. In that spirit, I would like to offer:

Five Reasons to "Just Say No" to Yule

(1) *Christmas is not the birthday of anyone we know.* Begin with the obvious. If we infidels believe that Christianity is untrue, the alleged birth of Christ is not something we ought to celebrate. We shouldn't even get caught *appearing* to celebrate it.

(2) *Pre-Christian Christmas traditions are no less bogus than the Christian contributions.* Actually, we have seen that contemporary Christmas *has* almost no purely Christian components. But infidels can be too quick to embrace the fallacy that Christmas traditions with deep non-Christian roots are acceptable. Take mistletoe, for example. It is solidly pre-Christian, but still inappropriate for a humanistic holiday celebration. Infidels are not pagans who believe that evergreen boughs can repel evil spirits or influence fertility. Unbelievers should view the fruits of any superstition system, Christian or otherwise, with equal disfavor.

(3) *Contemporary Christmas traditions are bogus too.* Instead of embracing post-Christian holiday traditions just because they are not Christian, we should examine each one on its merits. Infidels who uncritically nudge their children into the Christmas maelstrom condemn them to spend one month a year indulging ways of thinking and a view of the world that they then spend the rest of the year discouraging. Why bother?

(4) *Infidels who keep Christmas or an analogue of it promote a myth of consensus in American culture that serves the fundamentalist agenda.* When infidels turn into "December Christians," keeping the shards of Christmas that suit them, they bolster Christian ideologues who claim that *everyone* celebrates Christmas. One of the

most powerful rhetorical weapons the Christian right possesses is the false idea that secularism, humanism, and infidelity are culturally marginal. We are probably America's largest single non-Christian outgroup, but that can be tough to prove when so many of us spend December in hiding.

(5) *Growing up different is hard, but growing up a hypocrite is harder.* Often infidels keep Christmas "for the children's sake." It's a lousy idea, for the same reason that two people who hate each other staying married for the sake of the children is a lousy idea. Why not raise our children Yule-free? True, they will never know the joys of Christmas with family and friends. They also miss out on all that loot and bear the stigma of being different. But look what else they miss: the fear of Santa Claus, the shopping frenzy, the immersion in superstitious thought and behavior, that corrosive acquisitiveness, and the disappointment when peace and goodwill fail to materialize. Yes, it is tough to grow up different. But infidels *are* different, and I question what we gain by teaching our children—much less allowing ourselves—to conceal rather than celebrate the things that make us unique.

If any Christian readers are still with me, please understand. I am not advocating that America's infidels rise up and take away *your* Christmas. That is your way, not ours. No, I believe that Christmas is fine—for Christians. Non-Christians should have the liberty of ignoring it. Equally important, we non-Christians should have the courtesy not to distort *your* observance, which has a deep and authentic meaning within your community of belief. We would do so with pleasure—if you'd let us.

The Solstice: A Workable Alternative?

Some infidels feel they get the best of both worlds by observing the winter solstice. Is the winter solstice a brilliant compromise? Does it let infidels join society's biggest party without betraying their beliefs?

I don't think so. What do we gain by ousting one outmoded, superstitious observance from our lives if we replace it with an even older superstition? I can't get excited just because the days are getting longer. What *does* excite me is that thanks to science and technology, most of us get through the winter painlessly. If infidels want a humanistic celebration, let's not celebrate the supine hope that spring will soon return, which amounts to obsessing on human impotence before the elements.

Instead, let us celebrate our human achievement in keeping the elements at bay. What images and rituals might be appropriate for such a celebration of mastery? The traditional festivals, including winter solstice, traded in human helplessness. I doubt they will have much to offer.

Infidels should hold out for something more creative and less corrupted by pre-Christian superstition than the winter solstice.

Do As I Say, Not As I Do

As members of an unpopular outgroup, we should consider the message we send the larger culture when we yield so easily to Christmas. In multicultural America outgroups get respect by highlighting their differences, not by hiding them. Accommodation earns minorities the status of doormats.

Ultimately, *any* festive observance at the end of the year, whether winter solstice or Chanukah, strikes mainstream Christians as acquiescence in the holiday as *they* perceive it. Our careful silences are drowned out when once we join in the common shout. More evidence for the "America is a Christian nation" gang! "Look," I can imagine Pat Buchanan saying as he spots a Christmas tree in another atheist's window, "Everyone's Judaeo-Christian at Christmas time."

We infidels have a stirring, even inspiring message. We tell of an undesigned, unintended, and unmanaged universe filled with possibility. We proclaim that this life is all we have, that the only meanings we can depend on are the ones we create for ourselves. We embody the ideals of life and love without religion. Yet who will listen to us if we appear as hypocrites because we cannot muster the will to forgo a holiday whose history and principles we would reject in any other setting?

I cannot think of a more graphic way for atheists, agnostics, freethinkers, and secular humanists to "out themselves" than for large numbers of us to live our beliefs openly, and unmistakably sit out the winter holidays.

Zero-Basing: Why Have Christmas At All?

One way to shake off the effects of past accommodation is what feminists call "getting outside the culture." It is an intellectual and emotional process of peeling away the assumptions, prejudices, and past accommodations that have accreted onto one's life. I call it "zero-basing," after the accounting principle of zero-based budgeting. In ordinary budgeting, you draw up each new year's budget by altering last year's; old decisions that informed that budget get validated without review. Zero-based budgeting solves this problem by starting from scratch. Nothing is carried forward; each line item starts from a base of zero and must justify its base allocation anew.

Try it. Imagine zero-basing your life. Regard the unthinkable and laugh. Uproot your deepest assumptions to see what's underneath. Conceive a method of inquiry that owes nothing to the old transcendental assumptions you have rejected. Feel free to try anything new, to reject the familiar, to follow inquiry where it leads. If you could go through the cafeteria line of life all over again, wholly unfettered, would you put Christmas on your tray?

"I'm not unfettered," comes the objection. "I have kids. I can't just chuck it all and say that they won't have a Christmas any more."

To which I can say only, Why not? Why not rescue their young minds from the burden of superstition and false expectations past Christmases have imposed? Why not spare the very young the whole dubious experience from the start?

One might worry that raising children Yule-free may create a "forbidden fruit" effect, priming them to adopt Christmas and the religion it symbolizes all the more ardently when teen rebellion sets in. If true, it is the only compelling argument against denying infidel children the holiday. Perhaps it was true decades ago, when an overwhelming majority of Americans kept Christmas in a distinctly Christian way. As New Outsiders grow in influence, we can expect traditional Christmas to seem less like the culture's default holiday. When infidel children can view Christmas as "something that some other people do," not as "something everybody but us gets to do," the lure of forbidden fruit will lose much of its sting.

There is another flaw in the forbidden fruit argument. By definition, infidels have chosen to give up much that makes other people comfortable—the idea of personal immortality, for example. If we try to spare our children everything that might lead them to envy religionists, sooner or later we will wind up restoring guardian angels, life after death, heaven and hell, and indulgences. At some point we have to stop squirming, accept our differentness, and admit it to our kids.

Holidays at All: A Bad Idea?

While we're zero-basing, let's move briefly beyond Christmas and ask a really broad question. If we were starting from scratch, might we opt to do without holidays altogether? Have we humans grown up so far, so fast that we no longer have need of festivals and the ritual and ceremony that go with them?

Our ancient holidays developed in a world of mystery and privation quite unlike the world most of us inhabit today. Consider the revolution that science, technology, and a naturalistic world view have wrought. Today, at least in the First World, most humans live to die of old age. Most children live to become adults. There is usually enough to eat. Many diseases are curable. Small families are sufficient to ensure that society goes on. Men and women can view the phenomena of nature with understanding and respect, instead of with superstition and uncomprehending fear. Even when a natural disaster is unavoidable, there is often advance warning. Aid comes quickly, and the victims can confront their experience fortified by their understandings of the physical processes involved. Moderns whose homes are destroyed by a storm, earthquake, or tornado are still homeless, but at least they are not simultaneously homeless and mystified as to what hostile spirit has done this to them.

We should never underestimate the progress this represents. It is utterly unprecedented. It overthrows all the pessimistic assumptions about life that guided hundreds of thousands of years of biological and social evolution. Life is far from perfect, but the terms on which it is lived have changed more in the last two hundred years than in all the rest of human history. I suspect that they have changed so drastically that the whole idea of a holiday—that is, a special day set aside from the humdrum grind of life for the enjoyment of socially approved excess—no longer serves real social or emotional needs.

Sprees of gluttony made sense whenever possible in cultures attuned to privation. Do they make sense in a culture of plenty? Or is the very idea of a holiday irrelevant when so many of us live lives of agreeable consumption day in and day out?

When we confront the modern world of purpose and possibility, we cannot know for certain what is right. But we can know that almost without exception, our instinctive assumptions, our received social forms, our musty rituals and ancient traditions are *wrong*. They developed in response to and were superbly attuned to a world of mystery and limited expectations that no longer exists. Consequently, whatever may be the appropriate social and cultural response to the conditions of modern life, it is far more likely to be an innovation yet unthought of than to be any hand-me-down of our past.

If the ancient holidays met our ancestors' needs, then it is quite unlikely that they will meet ours. Have human beings progressed so far in their control over nature and in their understanding of their thought processes that they can get by with fewer illusions, fewer rituals? Have we grasped enough of life's true meaning—or of what the physical universe offers us in place of "meaning" as our grandparents understood it—that we can dispense with a few of our communal security blankets? Dare we attempt at least the occasional unblinking glimpse into the existential abyss on whose edges we all make our lives? If even holidays will cease to matter, what hope is there for Christmas?

Yet can humans really live without all these happy irrationalities? Don't they scratch psychological itches that burn deep inside us? Don't we need all those little lies to insulate us from the sterile truth that the universe doesn't give a damn for us? If we confront *that* truth too directly, mustn't we go mad?

I have heard that argument advanced by thoughtful humanists who believe that people are not yet ready to cast away their myths. Of course, I hear the same argument from religionists defending the "necessity" of believing in life after death, in eternal justice, in faith healing, or in the power of tea leaves to foretell the future.

Self-awareness, reason, language, science, and technology have given human beings the power to change their world faster than biological evolution can keep up with. It is up to us to update our natures, to remake ourselves in the image of the world we are creating as we go. Why us? There is no one else. Why not wait for nature? It is too slow. If we try to limit intellectual evolution to biology's pace, our ingenuity will surely kill us.

A Holiday Fit for an Infidel

Enough zero-basing. What if holidays, as such, are all right after all? What if the trouble with Christmas concerns Christmas alone? Then infidels might take up some new holiday after they cast off Christmas. It need not be a winter holiday; it needn't involve pine trees and wrapping paper. If we could start over, what might we expect from a humane and positive festival?

A humane holiday should be global and universal, equally relevant to all humans, regardless of their cultural heritage or where they live. A 1989 declaration by the International Humanist and Ethical Union (IHEU), an international coalition of national humanist associations, captured the right tone:

> Although we must recognize our obligations and responsibilities to the local communities, states, and nations of which we are citizens, we also need to develop a new sense of identity with the planetary society of the future.[2]

If we're starting from scratch, we should insist on a holiday that works for everyone on earth at the same time. Christmas doesn't qualify; it is too bundled up with harvests and solstices and the coming of winter. At this level Christmas makes sense only in temperate zones with one harvest per growing season. Worse, Christmas works in only one temperate zone at a time. When the days get longer in the Northern Hemisphere, they get shorter in the South.[3] No, we want a holiday that can make intuitive sense anywhere on the planet. Come to think of it, people may one day live on Mars or on planets that orbit other suns. Maybe we should really plan ahead, and rule out any holiday concept that depends on cosmological accidents unique to a single planet or star.

A humane holiday should reflect human concerns and achievements, not merely mute events in the natural world. Humans are not only shaped by the world, they shape it. Christmas in its agricultural and astronomical aspects simply echoes astronomy. It lacks inherent human purpose and meaning. Of course, the winter solstice does the same. A proper holiday should celebrate people, not coincidences in the sky.

A humane holiday should honor human aspirations and capacities. Using intellect and ingenuity, humans largely tamed winter. The greater our mastery over it, the more regressive it seems to keep a holiday that celebrates its midpoint, as though we were still huddled in caves counting the days till the earth might turn green again.

This is an ambitious list of characteristics. I meant it as a tool for choosing. If a holiday cannot be found—or invented—that meets all of its requirements, this infidel would prefer to do without holidays at all.

The Answer to Christmas

After all we've seen of the the trouble with Christmas, what is the answer? For infidels, the most appropriate answer is "Ho ho ho? Thanks, I'll pass."

More atheists, freethinkers, and secular humanists need to treat Christmas as "just another day." Skip the feasts. Sit out the exchange of gifts. Put in a normal day's work if you can. Infidelity is hard for believers to take seriously when its advocates so visibly cashier their principles rather than pass up an excuse to eat, drink, and be merry.

A respectful but uncompromising denial of Christmas is consistent with most infidels' convictions about religion and rationality. What most of us do instead is not. Living without religion, without ritual, and without superstition may seem more attractive to members of other communities when we carry *ourselves* consistently and look comfortable doing it.

Some infidels find my approach overzealous. They think it carries too high an emotional cost. Or they think it's too much work. They dismiss it as one more case of throwing out the babe with the bathwater. Yet many of us—certainly those of us who gave up Christianity to become infidels—threw out the Babe long ago. The mystery is, Why are we so reluctant to part with the bathwater?

Notes

1. Synopsized by silent movie buff Ranjit Sandhu, based on his viewing of a rare print held by the George Eastman Museum, Rochester, New York.

2. "A Declaration of Interdependence: A New Global Ethics," in Paul Kurtz, Levi Fragell, and Rob Tielman, eds., *Building a World Community: Humanism in the Twenty-First Century* (Buffalo, N.Y.: Prometheus Books, 1989), p. 357.

3. In this respect it is interesting to recall that when Christmas moved below the equator in the past—for instance, when British prisoners and colonists brought it to Australia—it continued to be celebrated on December 25 even though it fell in midsummer. Victorian England gave rise to a whole genre of illustrations showing how Australians celebrated Christmas, the point of which was to show how profusely those Aussies could sweat. Human nature being what it is, maintaining Christmas as a universal holiday would just degenerate into a nasty kind of "Northern Hemisphere chauvinism," blindly imposing what is basically a temperate zone harvest festival on people for whose calendars it is ludicrously irrelevant. There's a word for this form of chauvinism, I am told: *boreohomo-hemispherocentricity*. It is associated with the belief, engendered by reading too many maps, that north really *is* up. Of course, as humanist Greg Erwin once pointed out, where north and south are concerned "there is no up." To counteract this tendency we must return to Australia, where one can buy a copy of "McArthur's Universal Corrective Map of the World," a world map with south at the top. No one who hopes to be hemispherically correct should be without one. You don't realize how profoundly cartographic convention has distorted your, pardon the expression, view of the world until you look at this upside-down map and try to figure out why your sense of propriety feels so outraged. See Denis Wood, "The Power of Maps," *Scientific American* (May 1993): 93.

Epilogue

Don't Worry, Be Merry!

As we end our encounter with Christmas, I have good news and bad news. The bad news first: Christmas has to change. Irreclaimably rooted in the religious and cultural homogeneity of Anglo Victorian culture, it is far too limited to be the principal, universal holiday of a multicultural society much longer.

Now the good news: Christmas *can* change. Our vague feeling that it has been with us forever is part of the holiday's artifice; the Victorians built in false nostalgia from the start. Contemporary Christmas is less than 150 years old. It was concocted through processes we understand well. It has not passed through all that many hands. The principal inventors were five Dead White Anglophone Males and a Queen, the DWAMQs: Washington Irving, Charles Dickens, Clement C. Moore, Thomas Nast, Francis Church, and the indefatigable Queen Victoria. A few others have put their mark upon the holiday: Haddon Sundblom refined the image of Santa for those unforgettable Coca-Cola ads. Robert May gave us Rudolph the Red-Nosed Reindeer, whether we wanted him or not. "Dr. Seuss" perfected Scrooge's potential for villainy in the figure of the Grinch. As Philip Roth reminds us in *Operation Shylock,* Irving Berlin revenged world Jewry upon Christendom by composing "Easter Parade" and "White Christmas," converting the two most sacred days on the Christian calendar into, respectively, a fashion show and a holiday about snow. Finally, we should not forget whoever it was that forgot to renew the copyright on *It's a Wonderful Life.*[1]

As for Christmas, what a few specific men and women helped to invent a century and a half ago, other men and women can reinvent today. The DWAMQs never understood how they were reshaping their society; we will. With luck, we will benefit from having a clearer idea of what we are doing.

In an increasingly multicultural society, trying to hang a universal holiday on the latticework of a Christian feast no longer makes sense. As the centers of power, wealth, innovation, and culture shift south, toward parts of our country where winter means little, the idea of a midwinter festival makes even less sense. As our culture forges stronger links with tropical nations and with countries in the Southern Hemisphere, where winter comes in June, a "universal" winter festival makes no sense at all.

As the New Outsiders push America closer to being the open society it was always meant to be, we non-Christians may have to find new and more authentic ways to express our yearnings for peace and goodwill, or we may choose to contemplate more realistic goals. Either way, Christmas will lose its utility for us.

The trouble with Christmas is that it's stretched way too tight. In time, the swelling will go down. So here's to a future in which Christmas is as popular as, say, playing softball or reading romance novels, but no more. Here's to a future in which you can find a parking spot at any shopping mall on December 23. Here's to a future in which non-Christian children will not feel like freaks for one month out of twelve. Here's to a future in which the socially conscious will condemn "Yule-ism" just as they do racism or sexism, instead of practicing it. Here's to a future in which on December 25 there is something else to do.

Haltingly, the process has begun. In 1992 Tele-Communications Inc. (TCI), the nation's largest cable TV operator, mailed a memo to customers of its digital music service *warning them what channels would have Christmas music and when it would start.* I was gratified to see that of the thirty channels of CD-quality music the service provides, fewer than a dozen would carry Christmas music at all. Not that Scrooge owns TCI; *you* try to program continuous Christmas favorites for a twenty-four hour, no-announcer-breaks reggae channel! For the first time since 1984, I didn't have to take increasing refuge in my disc and tape collection as December wore on. On Christmas night I listened to chamber music and jazz, unsullied by so much as a jingle bell. Whether TCI intended it or not, that little memo captured everything I'm pushing for in a future Yule-optional society. Those who want to immerse themselves in Christmas know where to tune and when; those who want to avoid Christmas know which channels to lock out on their remote. This country is big enough for both!

Christmas is not inherently bad. It's like a smelly, bad-tempered dog that wouldn't bother me if only he stayed in *your* yard. Who knows, once Christmas is cut down to size, it could make a great little sectarian holiday for Christians again. What the Outsiders, Old and New, will replace it with will depend on how much the idea of a midwinter festival still resonates in our climate-controlled lives.

I'd like to close with a few notes of reassurance. First, to the merchants and economists who will rush forward to warn that without Christmas spending, America will collapse: Relax! It is not as though every society that made it off the barter system has centered its economy on an annual festival of excess. Christmas was barely a bump on the financial horizon when Charles Dickens sat down to write of Cratchit and Scrooge. Like the holiday itself, the economic centrality of Christmas is recent. It too can be reversed.

Anyway, even if I am right, the downsizing of Christmas will be gradual. There will be plenty of time to adjust. Since Christmas blimped up, the global economy has managed to absorb the automobile, the telephone, powered flight, wireless transmission, antibiotics, the Bomb, and several violent redraftings of the map of the world. It will survive the de-blimping of Christmas.

To committed and nominal Christians: You can relax too. No one's going to take your Christmas away—as if anyone could. But the realization may grow in you that Christmas is *yours*. It's not everybody's; it should lose nothing of its value for Christians if not everyone observes it by their sides. In an America that respects Christian and non-Christian alike, where people who sit out Christmas need not feel out of place, it may actually be easier to observe a satisfying and "spiritually" relevant Christmas within Christian and Christian-inclined communities. Christmas may become more of what conventional Christians want it to be if they invest less energy in trying to haul everyone else aboard their bandwagon.

Who knows, Christian Americans may find they enjoy being released from the responsibility of being society's unofficial recreation directors for one month each year.

Now comes the lone exception to all this friendly reassurance: Santa Claus. There's no way to put this gently. The jolly old elf is bad news. Even if you are a serious Christian who keeps Christmas as an authentic sectarian feast, the Santa myth has nothing productive to offer you.

Over the centuries, oral culture amassed a great deal of wisdom about raising children. If Bruno Bettelheim is right, much of that wisdom found its way into authentic myths, fairy tales, and fables. The same cannot be said about the Santa Claus myth, which burst upon the scene in nearly final form during one of the most deeply repressed and neurotic periods in Western history. The Santa myth is one of the most effective means ever devised for intimidating children, eroding their self-esteem, twisting their behavior, warping their values, and slowing their development of critical thinking skills.

No matter how you feel about the rest of Christmas, do your kids a favor. Brick up your chimney—Santa Claus must go!

The trouble with Christmas? It's just started its diet and it's grumpy as hell. But don't worry. Be merry! That is, if you feel like it.

Happy Newton's Birthday to all—and to all a good night.

Note

1. *It's a Wonderful Life* lost money in theaters. Only recently has it eclipsed *Miracle on Thirty-Fourth Street* and *White Christmas* as Everyone's Favorite Christmas Movie. The credit goes to penny-pinching local television stations. Because its copyright was not renewed, *It's a Wonderful Life* entered the public domain prematurely. Local TV stations could air it cheaply, so they did—over and over and over, like a pile driver. Since Americans are conditioned to think that any old movie with supernatural overtones that they have seen too many times to count is *The Wizard of Oz,* it should be perfectly clear why *It's a Wonderful Life* is now a classic.